Praise for Michelle Bowden's system for outstanding presenting

'I can say that I have personally never seen my team members this excited or engaged about a training course before. A big thank you from me, I can feel your passion for this development from the feedback from my colleagues.'

Darren Hanna,
Group Head of Data Intelligence & Analytics Group, Westpac

'Loved every minute of the presentation skills workshop—it was magnificent. Best course I've attended in my long career and it will leave a lasting impression for me professionally and in life. We were challenged to be great at engaging and persuading our customers in meetings, presentations, virtually and live. Michelle is a one in a million person—engaging, fun, prepared, motivating and inspirational. 6/5!'

Dean Puhalovich,
Principal Solution Engineer, Salesforce

'I've worked with Michelle for many decades to take my presentation skills to the next level. Over the years Michelle's approach has become second nature. I now use her Persuasion Blueprint coupled with her delivery and engagement techniques to ensure that I express myself with influence in any situation from the tearoom to the boardroom. Her formulas are highly recommended.'

Pauline Blight-Johnston,
CEO, Genworth

'I loved everything about Michelle's 3-phase system. It made me step out of my comfort zone and extend myself. I gained many practical tips and pointers from Michelle, her book and her masterclass that are essential for everyday activities, communication, and of course presenting. In fact, over the years I have been compelled to immerse my team in Michelle's formulas so they could all achieve communication success. Thanks a million!'

Candice Fitzgerald,
Head  *ons – Regions, Boehringer-Ingelham*

'Your masterclass has made a big difference to our business Michelle. We are engaging so much better with our clients now. Your winning formulas have ensured we are securing more work for the future.'

Joe Fusca,
Managing Direction, Graphite Projects

'I have learnt so much from Michelle and her first edition of *How to Present*. I used to get super nervous before presenting. Michelle has given me the confidence to design and script my presentation to include storytelling and audience motivation. Still, the biggest takeaway for me was learning to speak confidently. It is a work in progress, but I love that I have a toolbox that ensures I can continue to grow and develop.'

Samantha Middleton,
Head of Marketing and Communication,
Nelnet International

'Everyone needs Michelle's wonderful models and formulas for presenting and public speaking. My academic and admin teams and I have been working with Michelle for years to shape compelling presentations that achieve excellent results. Her approach is practical, memorable and will build incredible confidence for you—no matter your current presentation skills level.'

Professor Evonne Miller,
Director, QUT Design Lab,
Queensland University of Technology

'I will cherish Michelle's persuasive presentation skills training for life! Michelle is a wonderful coach. She is very perceptive, an expert in her area and very engaging! I loved Michelle's ability to build rapport with our group, keep us honest and really help us laser sharpen our focus on what we are communicating about and how we go about it. For someone like me, whose native language is not English, Michelle's framework and tips are so beneficial and eye opening!! Keep doing what you do best Michelle!'

Mahalakshmi (Maha) Rajagopalan,
Program Management Office Manager, Device Technologies

'I was terrified of public speaking and for 20 years did everything I could to avoid it. 3 weeks after attending Michelle's training I presented to 200 people with excellent results and now I'm actually looking forward to the next opportunity - completely unbelievable! I highly recommend this book and Michelle's masterclass to you if you are nervous when speaking in public.'

Amie Roberts,
Professional Life Coach

'Honestly I don't think today's training via zoom could have gone better! You were outstanding! There is always a slight chance that people won't be as engaged virtually as they would in a live environment. Well you talk the talk Michelle. Your ability to captivate on zoom is as good as any live presentation. I couldn't be more pleased and the feedback from our extensive network has been tremendous.'

Gajan Sundaram,
Director of Network Partnerships, Proloan

'During the lockdown (due to COVID-19) Michelle ran a series of fantastic Executive Masterclasses on Persuasive Presenting for C-level Executives via Zoom for my clients who are CFOs and Finance Directors. Each and every time she captivated the audience from the start. Attendees loved it and got a lot out of it. She really hit the mark with the content and audience described Michelle as, 'great, awesome, passionate, fantastic, worth listening to, informative, relevant, engaging and compelling!'. They were very impressed with the amount of practical information they could implement immediately. Michelle is definitely someone worth listening to in an area that is so important. She's mastered the transition from live events to virtual presenting.'

Simon Tobin,
Director, Tobin McClintock

how to
PRESENT

Revised Second Edition

how to PRESENT

Revised Second Edition

The ultimate guide to presenting live and online

MICHELLE BOWDEN

WILEY

First published in 2023 by John Wiley & Sons Australia, Ltd

Level 1, 155 Cremorne St, Richmond Vic 3121

Typeset in Merriweather 9.5pt/14.5pt

ISBN: 978-1-119-91235-4

 A catalogue record for this book is available from the National Library of Australia

Cover design by Wiley
Author photo: Tim Pascoe

Disclaimer
The material in this publication is of the nature of general comment only, and does not represent professional advice. It is not intended to provide specific guidance for particular circumstances and it should not be relied on as the basis for any decision to take action or not take action on any matter which it covers. Readers should obtain professional advice where appropriate, before making any such decision. To the maximum extent permitted by law, the author and publisher disclaim all responsibility and liability to any person, arising directly or indirectly from any person taking or not taking action based on the information in this publication.

I dedicate this book to my beautiful, strong, headstrong, clever, funny and confident daughters, Holly, Madi and Annabelle.

My wish for you is that you continue to be happy, healthy and assertive women who achieve your potential through courageous communication.

And to you, Ian, for without you there would be no book!

CONTENTS

FOREWORD

At two times in your life, you are totally alone: just before you die and just before you give a speech or presentation.

You have to admit, those moments before you're called to the front of the room or up on stage to address a crowd can be absolutely frightening.

Yet it doesn't have to be this way.

It seems hard to believe, but some people not only are not scared of presenting, but actually delight in it.

There are people who don't 'um' and 'ah' their way clumsily through a presentation. These people deliver their point eloquently and effortlessly. And there are people who mesmerise with their words.

And here's the crucial point: these folks weren't born superb orators. They didn't pop out of the womb with a microphone and some opening gags. They learned to speak brilliantly, step by step.

And so can you.

It's certainly a skill worth mastering. Those who can present well often earn more, get promoted faster and get their way more often. In our fast-moving world, it's usually those who can package their thoughts beautifully who get all the rewards.

So it seems you have two choices. Either hide your light under the proverbial bushel, or take the oratorical bull by the horns and learn this speaking game once and for all.

Choose the latter and your challenge becomes simple: finding an awesome teacher. Why is that so simple? Because you're already holding one in your hands.

Michelle Bowden's book is a masterwork of the field. She knows not only everything there is to know about presenting eruditely, entertainingly and potently, but also how to teach her gems of knowledge in a way that's fun and that stays with you when you communicate in life.

So if you've ever yearned to wow them in the aisles and have them hang on your every word, congratulations — you've found the book that can help you do just that.

Learn its priceless lessons, and you'll soon be giving speeches that leave others speechless.

Siimon Reynolds
Entrepreneur, author and professional speaker

ABOUT THE AUTHOR

Michelle Bowden is an authority on persuasive presenting in business. Michelle's name is such a synonym in corporate Australia for presentation skills that people don't say, 'I'm going to persuasive presentation skills training', they say, 'I'm going to Michelle Bowden!'

She is the bestselling, internationally published author of:

- *How to Persuade: The skills you need to get what you want* (Wiley)

- *Don't Picture Me Naked*

- Exceptional Presentation Design

- *STOP! Your PowerPoint is killing me!*

- Confident Speaking Vocals

- *How to Present: Presentation Skills Tips from the Masters*

Michelle is also:

- multimillion-dollar pitch and capital-raising coach to executives across industry

- editor of *How to Present* magazine and producer of Michelle Bowden TV

- creator of the Persuasion Smart Profile®, a psychological assessment tool that reports on your persuasive strengths and weaknesses in business

- Certified Speaking Professional, the highest designation for speakers in the world; Michelle's keynote presentations educate her audiences on the theory and practice of persuasive communication at work and at home.

Michelle has delivered her two-day Persuasive Presentation Skills Masterclass more than 950 times for over 12 000 people over the past two decades.

Style and approach

Michelle conducts public, in-house and virtual persuasive presentation skills masterclasses for employees from all levels, across all industries. She is renowned for achieving results through learning and laughter. She is an expert, generous and passionate adult educator with the highest standards in relation to behavioural change. Her keynotes, workshops and courses are based on the idea that interaction, high energy and fun, combined with proven theory, create results for your business. Michelle's passion is to see people performing at their best. It's time you worked with Michelle so you can present well, speak up and influence people!

THANK YOU!

I was surrounded by strong, powerful and inspiring adults from a young age, and each of these people encouraged me to stand up and achieve my potential. My confidence-boosting parents were always pushing me forwards, helping me believe I could do anything. Both my parents have a strong belief that there's no point doing anything unless you're going to strive to do it properly. And this value has definitely rubbed off on me! Now, as a presentation and influencing skills expert, I am continually exposed to amazing, courageous, inspiring people who are my friends, colleagues and role models. How lucky am I? I can't believe I get to hang out with such motivated people.

This book is a reflection of many of the things all of you have taught me, and through this book we all continue to inspire others to step up and shine their light on others so they strive to be their best. Thank you for your inspiration.

To all my wonderful clients (some of whom appear in the case studies or testimonials in this book, sometimes with names changed) — you are the ones who continue to light my fire. You challenge me and help me to step up as I help you to be the best you can be. I wish you all the power, courage and success in the world.

A heartfelt thank you to my wonderful mum for proofreading my initial manuscript back in 2009 for me. I love you, Mum.

Thank you Syann Williams, voice coach extraordinaire, for all your support and teaching. Syann is a master at helping people uncover their most confident, authentic and charismatic voice.

A special mention to Lucy Raymond from Wiley, who saw the potential of my first book, believed in me and knew *How to Present* would be a bestseller from the start. And three cheers to the whole Wiley team who helped me to rewrite an already great book that will now continue to help people to stand up and be heard in their lives — even online! I love you all! Entrepreneur Siimon Reynolds, thank you for writing your brilliant foreword in this book. I am so grateful.

And last but most definitely not least, thank you Warwick Merry, CSP CVP, for taking me by the hand (even when I was kicking and screaming) and showing me that virtual presenting doesn't have to be stressful. You showed me that clients sometimes prefer virtual over live presenting, and that virtual training and speaking can, in fact, be a wonderful experience for all involved. Your tips are peppered generously through this new edition. You are a lifesaver and an excellent person!

INTRODUCTION
WELCOME TO THIS BOOK

Have you ever wondered why some people seem to fast-track it to senior levels in business, even when there are other more experienced or expert candidates? Or have you noticed that when it comes to the best jobs, some people seem to have it all?

How come in meetings, a select few have the ability to say exactly what they mean with such confidence, clarity and influence, even when they are under pressure? How do they do that? Do they have some sort of magic or secret?

No doubt you've experienced the opposite, too. Have you ever sat in a business meeting — either online or in person — where it seemed the person talking was just raving on and on about nothing very interesting? Did it seem to you that they might as well have been saying 'blah, blah, blah'? Did you wish you were somewhere else?

Or what about your own skills? Have you ever run a meeting where you could see the people in your audience glazing over or switching their cameras off as you were talking, making you feel frustrated or inadequate? And did you wish you were somewhere else then too?

The more successful executives and senior people I meet, the more I realise that, regardless of their intelligence and business acumen, these successful people know how to present their ideas in an influential, compelling way. They know how to showcase their professional expertise. They know how to structure their thoughts and connect with people, and they say what they want to say in a way that resonates with their audience. Whether presenting online or in person, they inspire and compel their audiences to take action!

As a presentation skills expert, I have had the opportunity to work with many thousands of people. My experiences have taught me that most people are completely unaware of the hundreds of little tips, techniques and secrets that can combine to create an exceptional influencer who achieves exciting results. I have observed that once people know what to do to influence their audience and actually do it, they automatically increase their success at work and at home.

TIP

Michelle says,

'Anyone can be an exceptional presenter!'

I've witnessed people's self-esteem and confidence develop exponentially, as they achieve results they never thought possible in their conference or board presentations. I know many people who now close more deals and are more successful in job interviews.

And that's why I wrote this comprehensive book. My wish for you, whether you are already an effective presenter or not, and whether you mainly present online or in person, is that you read this book and use it often to guide and inspire yourself in order to achieve better results for you, your organisation and your audience.

Unlike other presentation skills books, this one is written with a step-by-step approach for businesspeople who are striving to present their ideas with confidence, clarity and influence. It is my life-changing, award-nominated, two-day Persuasive Presentation Skills Masterclass in a book. To decide which of the plethora of information to include for you, I have used the questions my clients have asked me over the years as we learned together in my mentoring or training sessions. To my knowledge, there is nothing like it on offer, where people in business are introduced to a simple, profoundly practical, step-by-step approach to standing up at work and presenting their ideas.

I approach presenting from a completely practical and readily applicable perspective, based on many decades of experience as a presentation skills trainer, mentor, speaker and author. I have a passion for seeing people perform better than they thought possible, and I'm so excited about this opportunity to share my expertise and experience with you. My intention is to simplify the skill of presenting and teach you what you need to do, one step at a time, so you can speak up and be awesome!

Success in business excites me. So many strong, competent businesspeople have so much to offer in the workplace. This book will not only open your eyes to the possibilities, it will also give you the tips, techniques and secrets to ensure it happens for you!

And invaluable techniques are in the following chapters. Why are they invaluable? Because they address all of the very common mistakes that presenters can make — and I outline my top 10 of these mistakes in the next section.

Top 10 business presentation mistakes

Here are the top 10 things that presenters make the mistake of *not* doing:

1. *Realise that it's not about them and it is all about their audience:* Most presenters are too focused on themselves.

2. *Remember 'I am in control':* Many presenters don't realise they must be in complete control of themselves, their message and their environment if they are to maximise the likelihood of behaviour change in their audience.

3. *Analyse their audience before writing the script:* In fact, many presenters don't think at all about who will be in their audience and how that might change the way they should deliver their messages.

4. *Rehearse:* Sadly, most presenters run from one meeting to another, making very little time to even think through what they are going to say, let alone rehearse it out loud to check how it's going to sound.

5. *Warm up:* If you've ever tripped over your words, you will know how much it can fluster you and make you nervous. Tripping over your words also reduces your credibility.

6. *Connect with their audience:* They make PowerPoint their presentation and read it to their audience. 'Death by PowerPoint' includes relying too heavily on information-packed slides that no-one can read, an approach that does not work.

7. *Use their body to support their message:* For example, they place their hands over their crotch in what is known as the fig leaf, crotch clutch or reluctant nudist posture — gestures that detract from the overall message.

8. *Really look at their audience between slides:* Audiences know when you are there for them rather than for yourself, and indirect or fake eye contact will result in a lack of connection and engagement with your audience.

9. *Pause:* They use filler words like 'um', 'ah, 'and so' instead of pausing. These mannerisms can make you look uncomfortable and will detract from the power of your message.

10. *Call their audience to action and close the presentation with strength:* When a presenter fails to state their desired outcome, the audience will likely simply go back to work and change nothing.

Let's make sure this isn't you — the rest of this book is about showing you how!

How to get the best value from this book

I recommend you read through the chapters of this book and do the activities where possible. Then, when you have a more formal presentation coming up at work, whether online or in person, you can go through the steps one at a time, ensuring that your message is well crafted and that you maximise the likelihood of achieving your objectives.

Remember, it doesn't matter how good your message is if no-one is listening. And it doesn't matter how intelligent, creative or hard working you are if no-one is listening. So let's make sure your audience listens to you when you speak!

CHAPTER 1

Persuasive presenting at a glance

Every important presentation should be planned. The good news is that the more practised and accomplished you are at crafting your message, the more efficient and effective you will become.

Exceptional presenting has only three phases:

1. Analysis — where you work out what you'd like to achieve and, importantly, what your audience needs from you. This is where you ascertain the current state of your audience as well as your own desired state for them.

2. Design — where you put your presentation together, making sure that you shift your audience from their current state to your desired state.

3. Delivery — where you communicate the message to your audience so that they are compelled to take action.

This three-phase approach is results oriented. Ultimately, it will help inspire you to:

1. step up and really be heard by the people around you

2. structure your message so it's clear and compelling

3. deliver your message with excellence (no matter how dull you think your subject is!), so that your audience responds positively.

I have watched and then given feedback to many thousands of people over the last few decades. I've helped thousands of people write winning scripts and I'm so passionate about this subject that I've immersed myself in the work of other theorists and subject matter experts. I want to enable anyone with a desire to learn how to present to quickly grasp both the fundamental and advanced skills required to become a brilliant presenter.

TIP

Michelle says,

'It doesn't matter how intelligent, creative or hard working you are if no-one is listening when you speak up.'

Looking at the research

My 2010 survey of more than 800 respondents from the business world shows that audience members are pretty tough when it comes to whether or not they will listen in a presentation. Conservatively, they give presenters fewer than 5 minutes to prove themselves before they switch off. Most people said they give a presenter less than 2 minutes to prove themselves before they switch off and think about something else. This means you don't have much time at all to connect with your audience, capture their attention and make a positive impression. It's critical you start strong. (Chapter 5 will show you how to do this.)

When asked about workplace presenters they had seen face to face:

- 50 per cent of respondents thought presenters were a bit boring.

- Only 52 per cent of respondents thought that presenters delivered their presentation so that audience members could relate to their message.

- Only 38 per cent of respondents thought the presenters understood their needs as an audience member.

- Only 40 per cent of respondents found the presenters to be engaging.

- And, sadly, only 28 per cent of respondents said that they were moved to action after the most recent presentation they attended.

Death by PowerPoint isn't working!

When asked in the same survey about slide presentations they had seen in the last 12 months:

- 70 per cent of respondents said that workplace presenters generally relied heavily on PowerPoint slides. This limited their ability to connect with the audience and make their subject matter engaging and memorable.

- 55 per cent of respondents said that, in general, presenters read from their PowerPoint slides — at which time the audience members mostly chose to switch off and think about something else.

It's clear from this research that business audiences are asking for a new and better approach to presenting that doesn't involve death by PowerPoint.

We know we need development

When asked in the same survey about presentations they deliver at work:

- More than 60 per cent of respondents admit to using their slides to help them remember what to say.

- Nearly 60 per cent of respondents admit to being frequently nervous before giving presentations, which reduced their ability to connect with their audience.

- Only 37 per cent of respondents feel that they are engaging, persuasive presenters.

- 75 per cent of respondents believe that they would receive more respect for their knowledge and expertise if they were better public speakers.

And my work in the years since my 2010 survey has only confirmed these findings. My most recent survey conducted in 2022 asked businesspeople about their common practice in online meetings. This survey found:

- 97 per cent of respondents admitted to sharing their screen in online meetings and never selecting 'stop share' to bring the view back to all the faces on the screen. It was like watching a TV show for the audience — one slide after the next.

- 93 per cent of respondents felt disconnected in their online meetings (whether they were the presenter or the audience member).

- 86 per cent of respondents felt increased tiredness or 'zoom fatigue' after a day of online meetings as compared with their memory of attending meeting after meeting of 'live' interactions prior to COVID-19.

Virtual platforms aren't (always) the answer

I feel strongly that just because we can use virtual platforms, doesn't necessarily mean we should! Email, phone and, increasingly, good old-fashioned 'live' meetings are alternative options.

And even though we have the technological capability to share our screen (and render our face the size of a postage stamp to take the pressure off our public speaking), that doesn't necessarily mean we should! After all, it's close to impossible to create a connection, build rapport and persuade someone when you can't really see their face.

What to do about 'Zoom fatigue'

And, yes, it's not in your imagination! 'Zoom fatigue' is real. Since the global pandemic of COVID-19, researchers far and wide have begun studying and reporting on this phenomenon that causes us to be more tired in a video call than during a face-to-face live meeting.

Video calls force us to focus more intently on the conversation in order to absorb the point, require the audience and presenter to both stare directly at a screen for too long without any visual or mental break, and cause cognitive overload (and confusion) when audio and visual cues are out of sync due to dodgy internet connections.

Zoom fatigue was investigated by psychologist Jeff Hancock and his team from Stanford University. They interviewed 10 322 respondents and released their findings in 2021. One in seven women reported feeling 'very' to 'extremely' fatigued after Zoom calls, compared to around one in 20 men. Some experts suggest this is due to what is known as 'mirror anxiety' — that is, women are more likely than men to look at themselves on the screen rather than at the other audience members or straight into the camera. The researchers concluded that it is important to maximise the benefits of virtual meetings while simultaneously reducing any psychological costs.

Suggested 'fixes' to the problem of virtual meeting exhaustion are:

- video-free meetings — just sound, no camera
- guidelines regarding the length of meetings
- rules about breaks between meetings
- standards outlining how frequently people meet online.

What does all this mean?

All this research into presenting — both face to face and online — means that, 13 years after the first edition of this bestselling book was published, we are still going to too many boring presentations (live or online), where the presenter is not enjoying themselves and the audience is enjoying themselves even less! In some cases, these interactions are causing people to feel fatigue and experience burnout.

Making a conscious decision to take your communication seriously is, therefore, critical. Please know that anyone can be an exceptional presenter. It doesn't matter whether you are presenting live or virtually — you can 'wow' your audience, you can engage them and compel them to action and, yes, you can have them remembering you for years to come no matter how dry or technical your subject matter. You can enthuse and delight people if you put your mind to it! It's just a matter of knowing what to do and actually doing it.

Let's be clear on what presenting means

I believe presenting is any form of communication with another person (including virtually, face to face, over the phone, by email or through the internet). Presenting can be one to one, or with small and large groups. I believe we present both formally and informally. In short, most people in business present every day of their lives — over and over again.

Presenting is about connecting with people through the words you choose to say and the way you choose to say them. When you present, you show people who you are and how you can help them. It's an opportunity to step up and be noticed for what you can offer. Presenting provides a unique opportunity for you to showcase your professional expertise and accelerate your career.

Many people think of presentation skills as the techniques that help you to have a confident voice and good posture, or that help you design your slides. I believe that presenting is not just about an ability to speak clearly with precise articulation and beautiful posture, and it's definitely not about your slides! Of course, presenting does include these things — and it is much, much more.

> **TIP**
>
> **Michelle says,**
>
> 'Presenting is about connecting with your audience through the use of a clever structure and masterful delivery.'

Many people confess that their standard approach to presenting is to spend most of their time on their visual aids or slide presentation, and then just hope that they can wing the rest. At best, the slides end up restricting the presenter's ability to connect with their audience; at worst, this approach forces the presenter to simply read out their slides to their audience. I'm sure you'd agree that neither of these options is very good for your audience.

Successful, confident, engaging presenters think deeply about their audience, and they are sure about what they are trying to achieve. In short — they do the work! They respect their audience and they master their craft.

If you want to be a confident, influential, impressive presenter, understanding your audience — before you even think about designing what you're going to present — is critical. If you take some time to think about what the current state of your audience is and then work out what you would like to achieve, you'll be much more likely to begin your presentation in a confident frame of mind. You'll also maximise the likelihood of changing your audience's behaviour — which is usually why we present, isn't it? Regardless of whether you wish to sway opinion, introduce controversial ideas or change long-standing policies or redundant methods, understanding your audience will help you feel so much more confident. Chapter 2 gives you the specifics on how to do this.

Successful presenting is also about staying true to yourself. In the business world, many people spend a lot of their time trying to please or impress others. If you find yourself doing this as you're presenting, you may lose a sense of yourself. You may become confused about who you really are, and the result is that the audience can then find it difficult to connect with you. Thank goodness the world is made up of all types of people. And I know that whoever you are, whatever your style, you are gorgeous!

Instead of trying to be someone you are not, just know you are fantastic — and be as good as you can at being you! In other words, focus on your strengths and on being the best you that you can be. That's the key to ongoing confidence, rapport and authenticity as a presenter.

TIP

Michelle says,

'It's important that you are as authentic as possible.'

Remember, exceptional presenting has only three phases:

1. Analysis
2. Design
3. Delivery

All you need to do is go through these three phases step by step and you will influence your audience to change their behaviour. It's really that simple! And remember the wise words of author and international speaker Marianne Williamson, who said, 'Our deepest fear is not that we are inadequate. Our deepest fear is that we are powerful beyond measure ... We ask ourselves, Who am I to be brilliant ...? Actually, who are you *not* to be?'

Guiding principles for presenting

Through my research and work, I've developed the following guiding principles, which should be your presentation mantra every day you go to work. Your guiding principles are:

- It's not about me. It's all about the audience!

- I respect my audience, prepare in advance and strive to master my craft.

- I understand that structure is essential for both me and my audience.

- I will always use proven formulas for structuring my communication, so everyone wins!

- I am confident and interesting and I will strive to be as good at being my authentic self as possible.

- It doesn't matter how good my message is if no-one is listening! I will do what I can to help them listen.

- Presenting is a lot more than a nice voice, good body language and some slides.

- Presenting is about connecting with people through the words I choose to say and the way I choose to say them. I will choose carefully!

Nerves and presenting

Of course, this wouldn't be a presentation skills book if I didn't address what many surveys say is the greatest fear in the world — the fear of public speaking! Let's talk about that right now.

Most people feel very anxious before important presentations. For many people, this anxiety can extend to informal team meetings or presentations to colleagues, even if such events occur regularly.

If you are one of the many people who feels nervous before a presentation, you will probably know that this nervousness can present itself in a variety of forms. Symptoms can be as mild as sweaty palms, a dry mouth, blushing or a thumping heartbeat, or can be more severe — through to physical illnesses such as the shakes, vomiting or diarrhoea (to name just a few!). No wonder public speaking is considered to be up there with some of the greatest fears in the world! These awful symptoms can significantly reduce the amount of enjoyment you derive from communicating at a high level with others.

Well, it's time for some good news. Presenting can be fun! In fact, I believe presenting should be fun. Managing nerves is mostly to do with your approach, regardless of whether you are presenting at work or in a conference environment.

Moving from 'fight or flight' to eustress

In 1915, the concept of fight or flight was developed by Dr Walter Cannon to describe an animal's response to threat. Essentially, you can think of this theory like this: when you are faced with stress (presenting is very stressful for many people) you have two choices:

- *Fight it:* In other words, you can soldier on and push through your discomfort to beat the feeling. If you choose to fight, you can make the most of the opportunities that emerge and step up and be heard so people know what you are capable of.

- *Run away:* That is, you could choose to flee, avoid presenting, and delegate the job to a colleague. If you flee, you will avoid the stress and conflict, but you will also pass up the chance to showcase your professional expertise. No-one will know what you actually think or feel about the subject, and you may find yourself being passed over for future opportunities.

This understanding of fight or flight from Dr Cannon can be coupled with a concept described by Dr Hans Selye, who discovered and documented the fact that as humans we experience two main kinds of stress: distress and eustress.

Distress is the bad, or negative, kind of stress that weakens and disables you; eustress, on the other hand, is a positive, or good, stress that enables you and makes you powerful. The main way to turn your distress into eustress is to use the power of your mind and your self-talk to reframe in your mind that you are a strong and confident presenter, and you will do a great job when you present.

Another way to make your stress positive is to try really hard to keep reminding yourself that the presentation is not about you: it's all about the audience. If you can focus your attention on how your audience is feeling and what they need to hear from you, your nerves will immediately begin to dissipate. This is because you have less space in your brain for analysing your own consciousness. In other words, if you are more focused on your audience, you will be less preoccupied with yourself.

You can use a number of excellent techniques to reduce your nerves and increase your enjoyment when presenting — and they don't include imagining your audience naked! What a laugh! I've been told stories time and time again from presenters who were told by their manager to imagine their audience naked, and they either froze on the stage or felt more nervous than ever.

> **TIP**
>
> **Michelle says,**
>
> 'Imagining your audience naked will not work, so please don't do it!'

You will manage public speaking nerves if you understand your audience (chapter 2), prepare thoroughly (chapters 3 to 8), rehearse (chapter 9), warm up your mind, voice and body (chapters 9 and 10), and connect with your audience by 'extending the self' (chapter 11) or projecting into the camera (chapter 20).

If nerves really are a problem for you, taking steps to eliminate your limiting beliefs, being yourself, and actively seeking positive feedback (chapter 18) is also important.

Let me tempt you towards increasing confidence by briefly touching on some of these elements before examining the nerves dilemma in more detail through the course of this book.

Common mistakes people make in attempting to reduce their nerves

The two common mistakes people make in an attempt to reduce their nerves are:

1. They make themselves too dependent on slides.

2. They avoid presenting altogether and delegate to someone else.

Let's explore this in more detail.

SLIDES ARE NOT THE PRESENTATION

Some people cope with the pressure of presenting by making their slides the focus of their presentation. They simply read from, or heavily rely on, their slides. This is not ideal if you are trying to persuade an audience. For some help on how to design your presentation so that you don't need to rely on your slides, read chapters 4 and 5.

AVOIDANCE IS NOT THE ANSWER

Other people cope with the pressure of presenting by doing their best to avoid presenting altogether! One wonderful client of mine had avoided presenting for 24 years of his career. He had even quit jobs to avoid presenting. In a program I ran recently, a participant aged 24 told me that both his parents had spent their entire careers quitting jobs to avoid presenting. He was on my program to ensure that he wouldn't repeat the negative, vicious and very contagious cycle he observed as a child.

Jenny's story

Jenny attended my Persuasive Presentation Skills Masterclass in 2017. In her introduction to the group, she explained she hated public speaking. She was frequently so nervous she could barely breathe. She admitted to us that she hadn't even been sure she would be able to walk through the front door of the venue where my masterclass was being held, much less sit in the actual training room. And then Jenny paused. It felt like quite some time passed. We all waited respectfully for what she was about to say next.

Jenny took a big breath and then she explained, 'I'm just so sick of everyone else being promoted ahead of me, taking credit for my ideas, and essentially "stealing" opportunities from under my feet because I am too scared to speak up and own my work, my ideas and my achievements.'

Wow! Powerful stuff, hey? And yes to Jenny! Don't let someone else take credit for your work because you didn't know the presenting formulas to follow. Learn the formulas, express yourself and be rewarded for your efforts. Life is too short to give everyone else a leg up first!

Thank goodness you have this book. Please keep reading!

Top tips for developing more confidence when presenting

No single thing, magic formula or short cut is a panacea for a lack of confidence when presenting. If you feel you are lacking in confidence, consider a change of approach. Begin by writing a slogan in big letters:

IT'S NOT ABOUT ME. IT'S ALL ABOUT THE AUDIENCE!

And then try the following tips:

- Analyse your audience.
- Structure your message.
- Rehearse until you can't get it wrong.
- Breathe deeply using your diaphragm.
- Relax your muscles.
- Focus fully on the audience.
- Use the power of your mind.
- Get feedback.

The following sections (and chapters in this book) provide further help in each of these areas.

ANALYSE YOUR AUDIENCE

Spending some time analysing both the current and desired state of your audience is critical. This way you will better understand what your audience needs to hear in your presentation, and you will also be much clearer about what you need to achieve from the presentation. This step is so important because without it you will be creating slides or just winging your presentation with no clear purpose. When you sense during the presentation that you're going nowhere fast because you're unclear about what you need to say and the best way to say it, you may well feel even more nervous!

> **TIP**
>
> **Michelle says,**
>
> 'Remember the good old saying: perfect preparation prevents poor performance.'

STRUCTURE YOUR MESSAGE

If you have a nice, tight, well-crafted message, and you have designed it with a model that allows you to remember the information without relying on notes, then of course you'll feel more confident.

REHEARSE UNTIL YOU CAN'T GET IT WRONG

Yes, I know that's bad news! I don't know anyone who loves rehearsing — and I'm connected with most of the top speakers in the world! It's a fact that great speakers rehearse until they can't get it wrong. For more information on how to rehearse quickly and efficiently, see chapter 9.

BREATHE DEEPLY USING YOUR DIAPHRAGM

Breathing is something we take for granted. We think and breathe all the time. Unfortunately, one of the most common pieces of feedback that I give to clients in presentation skills training and coaching is to breathe! Although diaphragmatic breathing (chapter 10) does take some practice, it will provide you with many benefits:

- You will feel calmer.
- Your voice will be more powerful.

- You will retain your clarity of thought, because when you breathe deeply your heart pumps oxygen around your body and to your brain more efficiently.

RELAX YOUR MUSCLES

Releasing the tension in your body and simply relaxing is something that takes lots of practice. Just think about all those millions of people around the globe who engage in some kind of meditation, yoga or massage to try to wind down. You may not have the time or the money to go off for a massage the hour before every presentation you deliver. So what can you do to help yourself? Try to ascertain where you hold your tension. Perhaps it is in your shoulders, neck or face. Some people even hold tension in the buttocks. Once you have isolated your problem area, try tensing and relaxing the muscles associated with that area. Do this just before you present — you will be amazed at the difference. Chapter 11 provides some detailed exercises for you.

FOCUS FULLY ON THE AUDIENCE

You may agree that when you are nervous, your focus is on the symptoms that indicate nervousness. In other words, you become aware of your thumping heartbeat, the butterflies in your stomach and an increased body temperature. And often the more you focus on the symptoms, the worse they get — and you feel even more nervous!

A secret called 'extending the self' can help you to stop being so self-focused. The idea behind extending the self is that if you can find a way to fully focus on your audience, you won't be aware of feeling the various nervous symptoms, and that means you won't feel nervous.

Chapter 11 elaborates on this important technique for you.

USE THE POWER OF YOUR MIND

Many of the best presenters use the power of positive thinking before they present. They imagine themselves as successful, confident, engaging speakers and are often delighted with the results. You should not, of course, let this technique change you into something that you are not. Rather, it should help to bring out an inherent quality that you believe you are not yet displaying. Chapter 9 explores mind power in more detail and includes some fascinating examples.

GET FEEDBACK

Many people focus a lot on their negative points and their nervousness, rather than on their positive attributes. Setting up a system at work where you can give feedback and receive it from people you respect, and who are sensitive to your needs, is a great way of finding out what you are doing well. This can boost your confidence tenfold (For more information on this, see chapter 18.)

TIP

Michelle says,

'Believe in yourself. You can do it!'

After decades of experience, I really believe that most people are more nervous than they need to be, simply because they have no idea what they are supposed to do to manage their nerves.

Today is the day to get ready to transform yourself from a nervous presenter into a confident, engaging presenter who achieves results. Use the tips, tools and techniques in this book to dramatically reduce your nerves and make presenting an enjoyable experience for yourself, no matter the circumstances you find yourself in!

And even if you are not a typically nervous or anxious presenter, many insights in this book can still help you connect with your audience and persuade them to accept (even love) your ideas so you get more of what you want. How exciting — let's go!

CHAPTER 2

Working out what you want to achieve from your presentation

You will probably agree that many business presentations are held simply to inform the audience about status — that is, to update them about what's happening with the team, the project or the business. If you have ever been to one of these information sessions, you will know how deadly boring sitting in an audience being informed can be! The reason it's boring is because updates are often general in their nature. They can feel unnecessary because they aren't specifically related to you and what you do at work. While it's nice to know what's going on, depending on the way the presenter explains their point, the information doesn't always seem that relevant to you.

When you are the presenter, while some of the people in your audience like to be informed, probably a whole lot of other people are really hoping that you will help, interest, motivate, empower and even inspire them with your presentation. As inspirational author William Arthur Ward said, 'The mediocre teacher tells. The good teacher explains. The superior teacher demonstrates. The great teacher inspires.'

When you make a presentation, how much time do you spend thinking about the different types of people in your audience? What is your current approach to presenting?

Think about your answers to the following questions:

- Before designing your presentations, do you spend some time thinking about your audience and their expectations of you? Or are you more likely to focus on what you want to say?

- When you present in business, is it possible that people in your audience sometimes leave the meeting feeling confused about the point of your presentation?

- Do you know how to prepare for a presentation so that you influence your audience to do what you want?

TIP

Michelle says,

'Preparing thoroughly before you design your presentation is essential.'

Thorough preparation before you even start to design your slides or presentation script is the secret to making successful presentations — whether online or face to face. Think about what you would like to achieve and how you're going to serve your audience before you work out what you're going to say and design your slides.

Preparing for a presentation with a five-step analysis

You can use a simple and quick process to prepare thoroughly — which I call the five-step analysis. These five steps help you work out what you would like to achieve, what the audience needs from you and the shift you'll need to achieve for everyone to be happy.

The five steps are as follows:

1. Identify your topic.

2. Decide on your goal.

3. Create your purpose.

4. Determine your leading statement.

5. Analyse your audience.

The following sections take you through the five steps.

Step 1: Identify your topic

The first thing you need to do is work out what your topic is. Your topic is the content area on which you will speak. It's the broad subject; for example, climate change. Keeping your topic broad is important — at this stage, your topic is so extensive in its nature you could speak for days on the subject if you wanted to.

Let's look at some examples.

EXAMPLE 1

If you work in the pharmaceutical industry and want to run a session on good clinical practice (GCP), your topic is 'good clinical practice'.

EXAMPLE 2

If you work in human resources and want to present on ways to improve engagement in your business, your topic is 'engagement'. You can see that the topic is big and broad in nature rather than specific.

EXAMPLE 3

If you work in data analytics and are presenting on the importance of root cause analysis, your topic is 'root cause analysis'.

EXAMPLE 4

If you are presenting on the importance of improving your team's customer service, your topic is 'customer service'.

EXAMPLE 5

If you are presenting on the importance of selling more of a specific product you offer (let's call it 'product x'), your topic would be the name of the product. The topic would be 'product x'.

Simple isn't it? It takes approximately three seconds to come up with your topic. And the good news is now you've started!

You may have noticed that the topic often sounds a bit boring. And that's not a bad thing! In my decades of teaching presentation skills, I've met thousands of people who tell me they procrastinate when it comes to putting their presentation together. Seriously — they address every other task in their in-tray or on their to-do list rather just sitting down and writing that presentation! Can you relate to that?

Identifying your topic is just meant to get you started on your presentation creation. Keeping it broad and simple prevents you from procrastinating or using the excuse that you can't yet think of an exciting name for your presentation so you can't start at all! You can write the exciting name later — for now, just identify your topic.

TIP

Michelle says,

'Identifying your topic in Step 1 of the five-step analysis prevents you from procrastinating!'

Step 2: Decide on your goal

The second step of your analysis is to decide on your goal. A goal explains what you want to achieve with your presentation. In other words, it's what you want your audience to do once the presentation is over. The goal is completely focused on you and what you want, and is your egocentric perspective on your presentation. Having a clear goal ensures that your presentation is more targeted and achievement focused than if you were to simply talk on the topic.

Importantly, your goal is never just to update, educate or inform. Although, yes, you are definitely going to update, educate and inform, the goal is always to *convince*. Therefore, a goal generally begins with the words 'To convince' — for example, 'To convince my audience that our organisation should play a role in reducing greenhouse gases.'

Let's look at some possible goals, using the same examples from the previous section.

EXAMPLE 1

For the GCP example:

If your topic is 'good clinical practice (GCP)', your goal might be, 'To convince the medical investigators to comply with GCP'.

EXAMPLE 2

For the engagement example:

If your topic is 'engagement', your goal might be, 'To convince my team to take steps to make this workplace a fantastic place to come to every day'.

EXAMPLE 3

For the root cause analysis example:

If your topic is 'root cause analysis', your goal might be, 'To convince the audience to complete a root cause analysis for every problem they encounter'.

EXAMPLE 4

For the customer service example:

If your topic is 'customer service', your goal might be, 'To convince my team that they have to improve their customer service'.

EXAMPLE 5

For the sales example:

If your topic is the product ('product *x*'), your goal might be, 'To convince the team that they must sell more of product *x* than our old or previous offering'.

Step 3: Create your purpose

The third step in your analysis is to come up with your purpose. Your purpose is what I call the 'sexy title' of your presentation, and it goes in two places:

- Firstly, your purpose appears on the invitation to the meeting (including the conference agenda and calendar invite).

- Secondly, your purpose appears on your first slide — if you are using slides. Don't put your broad (and likely boring) topic on your first slide.

Remember that your topic is meant to be a bit dry or boring. After all, it's just the topic about which you will speak. Now that you're in the flow, you can think of a more interesting name for this presentation. It should be something that engages your audience and has them sitting up on the edge of their seat, thinking, *Oh great! I'm so glad I'm here!*

TIP

Michelle says,

'You don't want to put your topic on your first slide — that will have everyone running for the hills!'

You can likely see that the previous step of setting your goal is presenter-focused. That is, it communicates what you, the presenter, want to achieve from your presentation. Now you need to flip your objective, and move it away from being presenter-focused and toward being audience-focused. This will set you on the right path to ensuring that you truly engage with your audience before you even speak.

The way to work out your purpose is to ask yourself, 'What is my goal?' (Step 2) and then turn your goal into an audience-focused statement. Another way to create your purpose is to ask yourself, 'What does this audience want from me?' Where possible (and without overpromising!) call your purpose that. Let's look at an example.

Bernard's story

Bernard works in finance in a large corporation. Every month, Bernard has to present to all staff at a meeting called the 'Business intelligence update'. Can you just imagine how enthusiastic the team leaders in Bernard's business are to attend a meeting with this title?! What a dreadful name for a meeting!

After doing some work with me, Bernard decided to call his meeting something different. He thought deeply about what his audience wants from this particular meeting. In truth, usually a lot of data needs to be discussed each month, and it is often confusing and difficult for the team leaders to sort through this data and use it to make good decisions.

Once Bernard realised this was the case for his audience he came up with the perfect name. (Drum roll...) He called it 'Clarity in a sea of data!' Perfect! And, yes, Bernard told me that people turned up to his meeting more open-minded and interested to be there.

Handy tip: Sometimes in your company, standard meetings will have a name that can't be changed. For example the 'Quarterly business review' (QBR). If this is the case, use the standard meeting title that everyone knows, and put your purpose as a byline underneath the standard title.

Using the quarterly business review example your purpose could be 'Quarterly business review: What should our focus be next quarter?'

Using the example from Bernard's presentation in the case study, your purpose would be, 'Business intelligence update: Clarity in a sea of data!'

When it comes to creating a purpose, if you're struggling in your busy life to think creatively, you might find it easier if you use the words, 'Why we should', 'How we could', 'The benefits of' (or any other iteration of this concept).

Let's use the same examples to outline how you can implement this step of determining your purpose.

EXAMPLE 1

Using the 'good clinical practice' topic, your purpose could be any of the following:

- 'Why GCP is critical to the success of our trial.'
- 'How we can ensure compliance in our practice.'
- 'How the proposed changes will affect you in your department.'

EXAMPLE 2

For the 'engagement' topic, your purpose could be:

- 'We can make our company a great place to work!'
- 'Making Company x an employer of choice.'
- 'Your role in making this the best workplace in Australia!'

EXAMPLE 3

For the 'root cause analysis' topic, your purpose might be:

- 'Analyse. Diagnose. Fix: Understanding why incidents happen.'
- 'How determining root causes can make your work more efficient.'
- 'Setting yourself apart! Be the person who can get to the root of a problem quickly and fix it permanently.'

EXAMPLE 4

For the 'customer service' example, your purpose might be any of the following:

- 'The benefits for our customers when we deliver excellent customer service.'

- 'How to ensure we exceed customer expectations.'

- 'Exciting changes to help us improve our service!'

EXAMPLE 5

And if you are speaking about product x to an internal audience, your purpose could be any of the following:

- 'Product x will improve our sales figures for the year.'

- 'Product x — the key to achieving our targets.'

- 'How to demonstrate product x.'

To recap, your purpose is the audience-focused version of your goal. It is your goal (which is presenter-focused) stated from your audience's perspective. In other words, it is written in a way that would make sense to and interest your audience. It can start with the words 'Why we should', 'How we could' or 'The benefits of' (or similar variations) but it doesn't have to — if you can think of something more fascinating, go for it!

Step 4: Determine your leading statement

At Step 4 of your analysis, you work out your leading statement.

A leading statement:

- is your key message — it's the thing you really want your audience to believe about this matter

- is often contentious in nature — meaning that the audience is likely to want to argue or disagree with you about this statement

- must be reasonable.

Let's look at some possibilities for how your goal and purpose can guide your leading statement, again using the same examples from the preceding sections.

EXAMPLE 1

For the 'good clinical practice' example:

- Your topic is GCP.

- Your goal might be, 'To convince the medical investigators to comply with GCP'.

- Your purpose could be, 'Why GCP is critical to the success of our trial'.

- Your leading statement might be, 'Strictly adhering to GCP is critical to the success of our trial'.

EXAMPLE 2

The 'engagement' example:

- Your topic is engagement.

- Your goal might be, 'To convince my team to take steps to make this workplace a fantastic place to come to every day'.

- Your purpose could be, 'We can make our company a great place to work!'

- Your leading statement might be, 'With some simple, fun initiatives we can make our company a great place to work'.

EXAMPLE 3

The 'root cause analysis' example:

- Your topic is root cause analysis.

- Your goal might be, 'To convince the audience to complete a root cause analysis for every problem they encounter'.

- Your purpose could be, 'Analyse. Diagnose. Fix: Understanding why incidents happen'.

- Your leading statement might be, 'Every problem has a root cause, and it's our job to find it'.

EXAMPLE 4

The 'customer service' example:

- Your topic is customer service.

- Your goal might be, 'To convince my team that they have to improve their customer service'.

- Your purpose could be, 'Exciting changes to help us improve our service!'

- Your leading statement might be, 'We can exceed our customers' expectations'.

EXAMPLE 5

For the 'sales in product x' example:

- Your topic is product x.

- Your goal could be, 'To convince the team that they should sell more of product x than our old offering'.

- Your purpose could be, 'Product x will improve our sales figures for the year'.

- Your leading statement might be, 'Product x is the key to achieving your bonus this year'.

Table 2.1 (overleaf) outlines how each of these elements comes together.

TIP

Michelle says,

'Use steps 1–4 to think through exactly what you need to achieve in your presentation.'

Table 2.1 Pulling together your topic, goal, purpose and leading statement

Example 1: GCP	• *Topic:* GCP.
	• *Goal:* To convince the medical investigators to comply with GCP.
	• *Purpose:* Why GCP is critical to the success of our trial.
	• *Leading statement:* Strictly adhering to GCP is critical to the success of our trial.
Example 2: Engagement:	• *Topic:* Engagement.
	• *Goal:* To convince my team to take steps to make this workplace a fantastic place to come to every day.
	• *Purpose:* We can make our company a great place to work!
	• *Leading statement:* With some simple, fun initiatives we can make our company a great place to work.
Example 3: Root cause analysis:	• *Topic:* Root cause analysis.
	• *Goal:* To convince the audience to complete a root cause analysis for every problem they encounter.
	• *Purpose:* Analyse. Diagnose. Fix: Understanding why incidents happen.
	• *Leading statement:* Every problem has a root cause, and it's our job to find it.
Example 4: Customer Service	• *Topic:* Customer service.
	• *Goal:* To convince my team that they have to improve their customer service.
	• *Purpose:* Exciting changes to help us improve our service!
	• *Leading statement:* We can exceed our customers' expectations.
Example 5: Sales in product x	• *Topic:* Product x.
	• *Goal:* To convince the team that they should sell more of product x than our old offering.
	• *Purpose:* Product x will improve our sales figures for the year.
	• *Leading statement:* Product x is the key to achieving your bonus this year.

Step 5: Analyse your audience

Step 5 of the five-step analysis is where you analyse your audience and, given your topic, goal, purpose and leading statement, start to determine the specifics of your intentions. This is the time to think about how your audience's thoughts and emotions need to be shifted so you achieve your objectives.

Paul's story

Paul is a customer service representative who is part of the Staff Representative Committee (SRC) in his company. The SRC is a body of staff-elected members who represent the views of their teammates at monthly meetings, and advocate for change to improve the workplace. As an SRC member, Paul has to deliver a number of presentations in a variety of forums. Paul also presents at the monthly induction program for new starters.

When Paul was first asked to present at the monthly induction program, he designed some slides to outline what the SRC was. Over the first few months of presenting his slides, Paul found his audience was not interested in his presentation and he felt that his presentation didn't encourage any of the new starters to join or get involved with the SRC. His fears were realised when he received feedback on the evaluation forms saying he was 'boring'. Oh dear!

Paul realised that he was presenting with a topic (the SRC) in mind rather than a goal and a purpose. After learning about the five-step analysis process, Paul changed his approach and here's what he came up with:

- His topic was the SRC.

- His goal was, 'To convince the new starters to get involved with their local SRC'.

- There were so many purposes he could choose to use. After some careful consideration, Paul decided his purpose should

(continued)

be, 'How you can improve your work environment and meet new people by getting involved with your SRC'.

- His leading statement was, 'The SRC helps ensure Company X is a great place to work — and we need YOU!'

Once he had identified his goal and purpose, Paul changed his slides and started to present his message with his purpose at the front of his mind. He found that he was much more engaging and the audience seemed more interested in his presentation. They could feel he was presenting for them, not for himself. Audience members would actively seek him out in the tea breaks to congratulate him on his presentation and also ask him questions about how they might get involved. This, in turn, boosted Paul's confidence as a presenter tenfold.

Paul discovered what persuasive presenters already know: when you present with a clear goal and purpose in mind, you are more likely to achieve the outcome you desire.

As you know, audiences are made up of a variety of different people with different ideas, attitudes and approaches to tasks and challenges. They attend your presentation with all sorts of things going on in their minds, along with other distractions and agendas — many of which are *not* related to your presentation! At Step 5 of the five-step analysis, you need to step into your audience's shoes and decipher what they are thinking about you and your message, so you can shift them to your way of thinking.

In this busy life we lead, finding the time to reflect on your audience can seem difficult. However, if you do it, you will find that the rest of your preparation is quick and easy.

Handy tip: When you think deeply about who will be in your audience, what they might be expecting from you and what you are trying to achieve, you will be ideally placed to affect a change in their attitudes and behaviour.

I suggest you aim to take your audience members on a journey: one that transports them from their current mindset to your desired mindset. This approach will work much better than simply expecting your audience to adopt your views, interpret information or reach conclusions in the same way as you.

To help you analyse your audience's current and your desired state more deeply, and shift your audience from their current mindset, use the Think/Feel/Do model shown in figure 2.1.

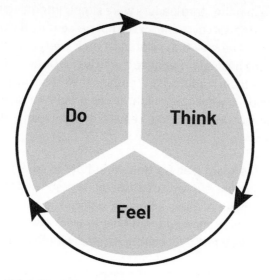

Figure 2.1 The Think/Feel/Do model

Jen's story

Jen is a senior manager in a huge Australian corporation. Every year her organisation conducts an engagement survey. Ironically, the employees in her company are reluctant to engage with an engagement survey! Jen implemented a number of prizes and awards for people as incentives to complete the survey. Despite these prizes and rewards, much scepticism remained about the value of an engagement survey.

(continued)

Once the survey results were collated each year, a slide presentation was created in head office and disseminated in the form of a presenter's pack to all the team leaders in the company, so they could explain the results of the survey to their team members.

Jen reflected on the results of the engagement surveys over the past few years and wondered why it was that little improvement had been seen in the engagement scores.

She realised that the team leaders were simply informing the team of the results of the surveys. They were not presenting the information to their teams in a way that related to their everyday issues at the coalface of the business. Because it was just an information session or update, the team leaders didn't engage their team members in any discussion about what they might do as a team to improve things in the workplace in light of the results, so they might all feel more engaged at work.

Jen had all the team leaders trained in how to explain the results of the engagement survey. Importantly, she showed them how to analyse the needs of their audience before the presentation was delivered. She also showed them how to work out what they were trying to achieve when they communicated with their team.

This simple strategy meant that the team leaders were able to engage their team members in meaningful discussions about potential improvements to the workplace. The discussions were audience-focused and completely tailored to the everyday issues, challenges and successes of the audience members. The team members listened and participated actively in the discussions. They made some plans for improvement and then engaged with their own plans.

In the following year, the engagement scores improved by 25 per cent and staff turnover in the business dropped.

Can you see how Jen's story relates to you as a presenter?

Every time you present (online or in person), you should aim for your audience to think, feel and do something. After all, you want them to understand concepts or information; you want them to feel one or many different emotions; and you want them to do something, even if it's just to continue to support you. You want to influence them.

TIP

Michelle says,

'Causing a behavioural change in your audience is the mark of an excellent presenter.'

And the good news is that facilitating behavioural change is quite an easy process — as long as you are clear on exactly where you are shifting your audience both 'from' and 'to'.

ANALYSING THE CURRENT STATE OF YOUR AUDIENCE

In order to influence your audience, you should first show them that you understand them and their current circumstances. People like to be understood. So what are your audience members thinking, feeling and doing now? This is their 'current state'. Your role as the presenter is to shift the audience's behaviour from their current state to your desired state. What you are doing is changing their attitudes and behaviour.

To analyse your audience's current state, spend some time thinking about the answers to the following questions:

- *What is my audience thinking about me, my message and my department or company?* For example, if you're trying to convince people to use root cause analysis more often, they may think of you as the rule enforcer and hence pretty boring. They may also think that they already conduct root cause analysis, and want to add some insights to your meeting from their own experience. They may think the action you're suggesting is too hard and not worth it, or they might not know how to make it work. They may think that your team is hard to deal with, and perhaps even slow to deliver.

- *What is my audience feeling about me, my message and my department or company?* Again using the root cause analysis example, your audience members may feel confronted by you and your team, they may feel threatened by your suggestion, or embarrassed that they haven't thought of this themselves. They may even feel annoyed by your team and frustrated at how slow you are to change what's not working. They may feel excited because this is the missing step in their practice.

- *What is my audience doing?* What will the atmosphere or vibe of the meeting be like before you present? Perhaps your audience will be sitting politely in the meeting room waiting for you to begin. They might be chatting among themselves. If it's a virtual meeting, perhaps their cameras are off and you're not even sure they are there! Or maybe they have logged on and are greeting each other enthusiastically.

The current state analysis is so important because it helps you to be realistic about what to expect when you walk (or log) in to your meeting or presentation.

ANALYSING THE DESIRED STATE OF YOUR AUDIENCE

The desired state is much more exciting because this is where you can aim high and achieve some excellent outcomes! Plan your desired state by asking yourself:

- *What do I want the audience to think about me, my message and my department or company?* Again using the root cause analysis example, you may want the audience to think that you are passionate, inspiring and relatable. You may want them to think that your message is important, can be implemented quickly and simply, and that it makes things easier overall. You may want your audience to think your team is expert, trustworthy and gets things done.

- *What do I want the audience to feel about me, my message and my department or company?* For the same root cause analysis example, you may want your audience members to feel inspired, motivated and empowered by you. You may want them to feel excited by your message. And you always want your audience to feel compelled to take the action you require — that is, conduct a root cause analysis. In addition, you may want your audience to feel supported and empowered by, and trust for, your team.

- *What do I want them to do once I have finished talking?* Using the root cause analysis example, you want them to conduct root cause analysis for all future issues.

TIP

Michelle says,

'You always want your audience members to feel compelled to take the action you require.'

DECIDING WHETHER EVERY PRESENTATION NEEDS A 'FEEL' AND A 'DO'

People often suggest to me that what the audience *thinks* about the presentation message is surely the most important concern of a presenter — especially if they are professionals in research and development, legal, engineering, analytics, finance or accounting, for instance, and they care about the detail.

Certainly, the think aspect of your presentation is important — and it's also true that if your presentation doesn't address the feel and do (because you believe that you really only need to inform your audience), then you should save everyone the effort of attending your presentation. Just send the presentation facts to them as an email and they can read it on the train.

More than likely, though, if you only focus on the think part of the Think/Feel/Do model, you are missing the opportunity to get some sort of emotional response and a subsequent action or result from your presentation.

Remember the saying from Carl W Buehner (often misattributed to writer and civil rights activist Maya Angelou), 'They may forget what you said — but they will never forget how you made them feel.' Take the opportunity to evoke emotion in your audience, no matter how dry or technical your subject matter.

When it comes to the 'do' in your presentation, maybe you could be asking your audience for their continued support, to endorse you at the appropriate times, to talk with others about what you are doing, to come to you when they have questions, or to update you on their activities if they relate to your project.

TIP

Michelle says,

'Every presentation should include a "do"!'

Yes, I recommend you try to find the 'do' in your presentations and ensure you remember to call your audience to action. I explain in chapter 5 how you can achieve this cleverly.

Understanding your audience is the first phase in the creation of any presentation. If you apply the Think/Feel/Do model before designing your presentation, you will be way ahead of the pack. How exciting!

DETERMINING HOW LONG THE THINK/FEEL/DO ANALYSIS WILL TAKE

Provided that you are presenting to people you have had some exposure to at work, you will find this technique likely takes you only about 5 minutes.

If you are presenting to a group of people who are completely unknown to you, the process might take longer. The thing to remember is that if you take the time to get to know your audience, you will feel much more confident when you are delivering your presentation and you will also be more likely to cause your audience to shift their attitudes and behaviour.

COMPLETING THE FIVE-STEP ANALYSIS IN A GROUP

If you are co-presenting with someone, make sure that you're both (not just one of you) fully up to date with the five-step analysis prior to meeting the client or audience. Every person presenting needs to be clear about the topic, the goal, the purpose, the leading statement and the Think/Feel/Do you are striving for.

If you are part of a pitch team or a group presentation, completing the five-step analysis as a group is a wonderful idea. In this way, everyone is on the same page regarding what you are all there to achieve.

When I work with big pitch or BID teams, this is what we do. Everyone is part of the analysis. No-one is left behind, and the client sees a collaborative group of people with a cohesive, consistent and, therefore, trustworthy message. Brilliant! For more information on how to pitch and persuade, check out my other book: *How to Persuade: The skills you need to get what you want* (also published by Wiley).

Kate's story

Kate is a professional, well-spoken senior manager in a research and development organisation. She came to me to see if she could work out a way of reducing her disabling nervousness when she addressed different teams and departments in her organisation. As a secondary objective, she was keen to be able to increase the take-up of her message.

I asked Kate to outline her process for designing a presentation. As is often the case with people I meet, she explained that she typically designed a number of different slides that outlined what she wanted from the audience and then worked out what to say about the slides. It became increasingly obvious that she didn't typically spend any time understanding what her *audience* wanted from the presentation.

(continued)

What we know is that people are more likely to change their behaviour if they have rapport with the presenter. And building rapport is difficult for the presenter if they don't understand their audience.

We went through the Think/Feel/Do technique for analysing the audience. Kate now uses this technique often and believes she achieves agreement more quickly and easily. She also feels her nerves are better managed in senior management presentations, because she is prepared and knows what she's about to walk into!

Thinking through the Think/Feel/Do model helps you understand where the audience is and where you want them to be. Once you have completed this critical phase of your preparation, you are in a perfect place to design the actual presentation that shifts your audience from their current to your desired state.

TRY THIS

1. Think of a presentation you have to deliver soon. It could be an informal presentation to just one other person, an online meeting you have to run, or it could be a more formal presentation to a huge audience. It's up to you to choose the scenario that is most relevant to you.

2. Go through the process of working out your topic, goal, purpose and leading statement. You can use the template provided in my website if you prefer — just go to www.michellebowden .com.au/howtopresent.

3. Take yourself through the analysis of your audience's current state as described in this chapter (Think/Feel/Do). Write your responses from the outlined sections or into the relevant parts of the template.

4. Take yourself through the analysis of your desired state as described in this chapter (Think/Feel/Do) and write your responses down or into the relevant parts of the template.

5. Reflect on the difference between the audience's current state and your desired state. Does a small or big difference exist between the responses in the current and desired state? Do you have to shift them a long way?

6. Is the list of goals or objectives you have set for your presentation achievable?

7. What benefits do you feel you would derive from completing such a thorough analysis of your audience before beginning the design phase of your presentation?

TOP TIPS
for the analysis phase of your presentation

- The five-step analysis process will fast-track the design of an effective, impressive presentation.

- Start your preparation by working out your topic. Your topic is the content area on which you will speak and is broad in nature.

- Once you have your topic, work out your goal. A goal is a statement of what you want to achieve and is completely focused on you and what you want. Goals generally begin with the words, 'to convince' (or a similar variation).

- From the goal, you next flip your presentation so it is audience-focused. What does this audience want from you? What can you call this presentation so that before you even speak, people see your first slide and want to be there?

(continued)

- Your leading statement is your key message. It's the thing you really want your audience to believe about this matter.

- Your audience will be thinking, feeling and doing something at the start of your presentation. This is their current state.

- Often when you present, you want your audience to move to thinking, feeling and doing something else. This is your desired state.

- Your role is to shift the audience from their current to your desired state.

- The Think/Feel/Do model is a valuable audience analysis tool for the preparation stage of your presentation.

- If you take the time to get to know your audience, you will feel much more confident in your delivery of your presentation.

Phase 2: Design

Write your presentation

CHAPTER 3

Structure your message

Congratulations on completing your presentation pre-work using the five-step analysis in chapter 2. If engaging and/or persuading your audience is important to you, it's a good idea to capitalise on the time you have already taken to understand your audience better by converting your five-step analysis notes into a presentation that addresses the needs of all your audience members so you can achieve maximum results. This chapter outlines how to structure your message so your point is clear and interesting for your audience.

Let me ask you: how do you normally go about structuring a presentation? In the past, have you designed your presentations by going to PowerPoint and either collating existing slides or creating a few new ones and then working out what to say about them? Or perhaps you have used the 'introduction, aim, credentials, body one, body two, body three, summary, conclusion' model, which is commonly taught in schools and universities. Or maybe you used one of a variety of mind-mapping techniques available, such as the fishbone. Do any of these methods sound familiar?

These approaches tend to be presenter-focused models, and tend to be content driven.

If you are keen to impress and even persuade your audience in your presentation, what you need is an audience-focused model that addresses the different needs and expectations of all the different people in your audience.

You see, individuals take in information differently, learn differently and form opinions differently. As a result, individual members of your audience will be silently preoccupied by different agendas and expectations they have of you. These agendas and expectations lead them to formulate certain unspoken questions that they are expecting you to address in your presentation.

When it comes to structuring your presentation, I recommend you use a learning styles model that helps you tailor your message to the unspoken questions your audience members are asking. This applies to virtual and face-to-face presentations, and will guarantee that you will achieve more buy-in because you're catering to the diverse needs of your audience — rather than creating a presentation that is too focused on your needs.

Aaron's story

Aaron is a wonderful client of mine who, before meeting me, had avoided presenting for 20 years of his career. Yes, that's right: 20 years! He had even quit jobs to avoid presenting. When he came to me, Aaron worked as a counsellor for a major corporation. His role was to support clients by giving both advice and care over the phone. He was fantastic at his job. He had received countless letters of support from his clients and their families and was much loved. He was also very successful in increasing sales for the organisation through his commitment and drive.

Much to his horror, Aaron was asked by his manager to begin a series of presentations across the country to the people who referred his counselling service to their clients. His role would be to explain what he did and to convince the referrers to continue to work with him by referring their clients to him as often as possible.

Well, you can just imagine what he did! He told me that he could either quit his job or go to the GP to get a prescription for beta blockers! (Beta blockers reduce the effect of excitement and physical exertion on the heart, reduce the dilation of blood vessels, and also reduce tremor and breakdown of glycogen.) Neither of these choices, in my opinion, was the ideal solution.

I think it's amazing how, once you learn what you need to know about exceptional presenting, it becomes not that nerve-racking after all. Don't get me wrong: after five two-hour coaching sessions and lots of rehearsing, Aaron was still what most people would call nervous, but he was also very excited and he knew he was ready for anything.

Aaron knew he would do well with his presentations because he had put in a lot of planning and rehearsal, and he had crafted his script with his audience in mind. He knew he was going to convince the audience to send lots of clients his way. And just as he suspected, after avoiding presenting for 20 years, he totally nailed his first presentation. Many people came to Aaron at the end and commented on how impressed they were. They said things like, 'You were the best presenter at this event'. What an outcome!

It's critical that you realise that talented presenters are made, not born! Successful influencers and presenters respect their audience, structure their message for their audience, and rehearse and master their craft. They do the work!

What Aaron realised is that a fundamental technique for influencing others and for reducing your own nerves is to structure your message to meet the needs of your audience. This increases the chance they will do what you are asking them to do, which is wonderful for your own confidence levels.

TIP

Michelle says,

'Talented presenters are made, not born! They respect their audience, structure their message for their audience, and rehearse and master their craft. They do the work!'

If you have a clear, well-structured, audience-focused message that convinces your audience, and you have designed it with a model that allows you to remember the information without relying on notes, then of course you will feel more confident — just like Aaron.

Handy tip: It's important to structure your message in a way that meets the needs of all the people in your audience, not just the people with the same learning or listening style as you!

An audience-focused model

The model that I suggest you use when structuring your presentations was developed by Dr Bernice McCarthy, a world-leading researcher, academic and educationalist. Dr McCarthy drew on the various theories of adult learning proposed by psychologists and theorists throughout the ages, such as Carl Jung, Jean Piaget, Kurt Lewin and David Kolb. She is passionate about both the diversity of learning styles and the various needs of the different learners in one classroom. In other words, she feels strongly that not all learners should be presented to in the same way. She created an instructional system that addresses the intrinsic needs of all audience types.

Dr McCarthy called her model the 4MAT System (see figure 3.1). This system recognises that individuals need to have four key questions answered. In some cases, the questions are explicit and known by the audience members and the presenter. In other cases, the questions are more virtual in nature and, therefore, not yet conscious for either the presenter or the audience members.

In most cases, by virtue of their personality and preferred learning style, audience members will be more likely to ask one of these four questions. In order to be convinced by your argument, each audience member will need to have their primary question answered. This is not to say that they will not be interested in the other questions too. In order to capture the hearts and minds of all audience members, you will need to be sure that your presentation answers all four questions in a given order.

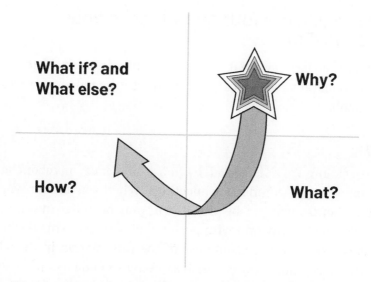

Figure 3.1 The 4MAT System for structuring your presentation

Adapted from Bernice McCarthy's 4MAT model (from *4MAT in Action: creative lesson plans for teaching to learning styles with right/left mode techniques,* by Bernice McCarthy and Susan Leflar, 1990, About Learning Inc.)

The model highlights the four key questions to address in your presentation:

1. *Why?* The audience member has a need to clarify the context and rationale.

2. *What?* The audience member has a need to identify the detail in what is to be learnt.

3. *How?* The audience member has a need to explore how to use and apply what is learned.

4. *What if?* and *What else?* The audience member needs to know the alternatives for the new information so they can modify, adapt and create new contexts. They also need to know what will happen if they do and don't take the action you have suggested.

How to use the four questions in your presentation

Let's take a look at what you can include in each of the 4MAT System quadrants so you can be sure to use the model as effectively as possible.

WHY?

The question *Why?* is asked by most audience members at the beginning of presentations or meetings. When you answer *Why?* for your audience, you are helping them gain personal meaning and connect new information with personal experience. This helps your audience establish the usefulness of the information in their lives. You are addressing questions such as, 'Why should I listen?', 'What's in it for me?' and 'Why is this relevant to me in my life?'

TIP

Michelle says,

'When you answer the *Why?* question early in your presentation, you will engage people and they will be more motivated and inspired to listen to the rest of your message.'

WHAT?

The question *What?* is answered next to deepen your audience members' understanding of concepts and processes. This is where you deliver the facts, figures, data, information, research and statistics in your presentation. It's also where you must remember to explain your credibility and the evidence that supports your information. You would answer questions at this point for your audience such as, 'What is the subject matter we are discussing?', 'What do I know about this?', 'What analysis or research has been conducted to come to this conclusion?' and 'What are the facts of the matter?'

I think you will agree that this is the most commonly answered question in most business presentations.

HOW?

After you have answered *What?* you next need to answer the question *How?* This is where you explain the steps and the application of the content you have covered in the *What?* section of your presentation. In this section you can facilitate concrete, experiential learning activities where your audience can get in and try it. You would specifically answer such questions as, 'How does it work?', 'How do I install it?', 'How will I implement it?', 'How will I use it?', 'How can I apply it?' and 'How will we make this happen?'

WHAT IF? AND WHAT ELSE?

The questions *What if?* and *What else?* are the final questions you should answer in your presentations. This is where you add your extra thoughts and information. At this point, you tie up all the loose ends and remind your audience about your key messages. You also give the audience a chance to explore some of their questions in a question–and–answer session, and then close with a bang. Take the opportunity in this section to look for possibilities outside the square by answering questions such as, 'What if we did it this way instead?', 'What else can we do to maximise the return on investment?', 'What if XYZ happens — what will we do?', 'What if we don't do this at all?' and 'What if we do give it a try?'

McCarthy wisely said, 'All real change involves major uncertainty, and we cannot deny the questioning time to others simply because we have already answered the questions for ourselves'.

TIP

Michelle says,

'The presenter who can move effortlessly through the various questions in the 4MAT System is the presenter who will elegantly address the needs of their entire audience and be more likely to achieve results.'

Sticking to the order of the 4MAT System

Some people ask me whether the four questions of the 4MAT System need to be always addressed in the same order. The simple answer is yes. You should answer the questions in the order presented here:

1. *Why?*

2. *What?*

3. *How?*

4. *What if?* and *What else?*

Once you start using this model, it quickly becomes common sense. You cover the *Why?* first because answering the *Why?* question will motivate your audience, so they are fully engaged by you and your message.

You cover the *What?* next because the audience needs to hear your facts and information. *What?* comes before *How?* because your audience can't apply the information if they don't know what it is! In other words, your audience needs to understand *What?* you are talking about — the history and facts and statistics behind your content — before they can apply the information in a meaningful way.

You cover the *How?* after you cover the *What?* because your audience is now motivated to listen, and they understand what you are talking about — the context of your message. They are now ready to think with you about the implications of your message and how to apply, use or implement your information.

Finally, you cover the *What if?* and *What else?* so you show your audience that you have all the bases covered. You also recap your main messages because, interestingly, we know that for most audiences, by the time they hear the summary, they've forgotten the beginning. Sad but true! So you should always tie things up for them, summarise, call them to action, answer their questions, point out the pros and cons of the message, and close with strength.

The benefits of structuring presentations using this audience-focused model are as follows:

- You think about the needs of your audience.

- You're much more thorough and don't just cover the part of the message you find interesting — which, unfortunately, is what most people do.

- You don't assume the audience wants to be there — the model helps you assume you have some work to do to shift them, which is a realistic approach to your business presentations.

- The model is simple — you have only four questions to answer.

- It feels like common sense when you learn it, so it is logical and easy to remember and use.

Using the 4MAT System in your life

The 4MAT System has so many applications in your life. These include:

- Formal presentations — to groups of any size, online or face to face.

- To set up meetings — for example, 'This is why we are here; this is what we are going to cover; this is how we're going to do it; and here are the consequences of sticking or not sticking to our rules.'

- Impromptu presentations — for example, you are in a meeting and someone asks you a question and you had no idea you were going to be called upon to discuss this subject. Can you relate to that scenario? Have you ever been in a team meeting where someone asked you a question and you bumbled your way through the answer only to curse yourself afterwards for messing up the opportunity? Once you have the 4MAT System locked in, working through the four questions in your response becomes almost unconscious.

TIP

Michelle says,

'You can use the 4MAT System to answer unexpected questions or deliver an impromptu response.'

Remember to apply the following motto from chapter 1 to any presentation: It's not about me. It's all about the audience!

TRY THIS

1. Think of a communication or presentation you have coming up in the next few weeks.

2. Practise delivering your message addressing all of the *Why?*, *What?*, *How?*, and *What if?* and *What else?* questions in the correct order.

3. Notice how thorough this type of presentation is for your audience.

4. What do you see as the benefits of using this model for structuring your messages?

TOP TIPS
for structuring your message

- Make sure you use an audience-focused rather than a presenter-focused model for structuring your presentations.

- Use the four questions that form the basis of Dr Bernice McCarthy's 4MAT System when structuring your message.

- The questions in the 4MAT System are *Why?*, *What?*, *How?*, and *What if?* or *What else?*

- When you use these questions to structure your presentation, you will find your message is more thorough and you will be more likely to address the needs of all your audience members and achieve your presentation objectives.

CHAPTER 4

Design your presentation

Now that you have analysed your audience and have understood the 4MAT System for structuring your message, it's time to design or write your presentation. As the Chinese philosopher Confucius said, 'Success depends upon previous preparation, and without such preparation there is sure to be failure'.

Please be careful not to misunderstand what is meant by 'design' in this book. The design phase of a presentation is commonly misunderstood to be the creation of slides. In fact, while the design phase does include the creation of some slides, the essential component of the design phase is nothing to do with your slides. Design is where you work out what you are actually going to say when you present. It's the creation of what many people might call your script.

TIP

Michelle says,

'Designing your presentation has very little to do with the slides you are creating; it's all about carefully selecting the right words to say to influence your audience to change their thinking and behaviour.'

How much do you actually enjoy preparing what you're going to say? When it comes to designing your presentation:

- Do you procrastinate? Do you find yourself unearthing every other possible job, no matter how small and insignificant, before sitting down to design your presentation script?

- Do you find the design phase of presenting unenjoyable, arduous and the least fun part of preparing your presentation?

If either of those sounds true for you, you will likely be thrilled to know that a really simple design technique can help you to:

- find a logical flow to your presentation

- include all the information you need, in the right places, without gaps

- uncover creative ways to present your message so that you stand out.

Guess what? Using this technique means you won't need to read from your notes — you won't even have to look at your slides to remember what to say next!

Sounds too good to be true, doesn't it?

Storyboarding: a magical design technique

The magical technique for designing your presentation is called storyboarding. This technique was first used by Walt Disney as early as the 1930s and is now used extensively around the world by filmmakers and creative people in business to plan out or brainstorm an outline for a script, a book, a campaign, anything at all — even a presentation.

Disney's model uses three hats — you know, hats like you wear on your head. The three hats are called the Dreamer (where you brainstorm your ideas), the Realist (where you allocate your ideas to the correct part of the 4MAT System, see chapter 3) and the Critic (where you make some judgements about what you'll keep, what you will reject and the order in which you will make your points).

You do have to figuratively 'wear' each hat at different points in the design process, but don't worry — you don't have to go out and buy three hats! Simply follow the process outlined in this chapter and experience how easy, thorough and effective it is.

Storyboarding is easy and quick, and best of all you can use the storyboarding concept with the 4MAT System discussed in the chapter 3.

The storyboarding process

Figure 4.1 shows the process for creating a storyboard at a glance, and how this connects with the four questions of the 4MAT System.

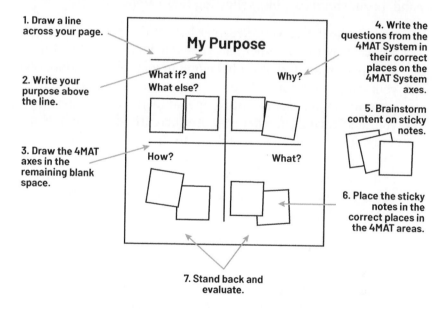

Figure 4.1 Constructing a storyboard

Expanding on this, here is the storyboarding process in more detail. First, set yourself up:

1. Take a large piece of flipchart paper and some chunky felt-tipped pens.

2. Stick the top edge of the paper on a wall slightly above your eye line, so you are looking up at the paper.

3. Draw a line across the top of the page about 10 centimetres from the top.

4. Write the purpose of your presentation (which you worked out in phase 1 of this book) at the top of the paper, above the line at the top of your paper. This is to help you stay focused when you are wearing the Dreamer hat and brainstorming ideas for this presentation.

5. Draw the four questions from the 4MAT System using cross-like axes that take up most of the paper (refer to chapter 3).

6. Write the questions: *Why?, What?, How?, What if?* and *What else?* in the correct places on the 4MAT System.

Second, begin storyboarding, following these steps.

1. *Brainstorm:* Put on your Dreamer hat for this phase. When you are wearing the Dreamer hat, your role is to come up with any content at all that could belong in your presentation. Give yourself permission to be as creative as possible. Remember, your aim is to come up with some fantastic ways of moving your audience from what they are currently thinking, feeling and doing to what you would like to them to think, feel and do. Some of your ideas will no doubt be wild and impractical, and that's okay at this stage. Just get everything you know about this matter out of your head and on to the sticky notes — clear your mind.

2. *Summarise:* Each time you think of an idea, summarise the idea into one keyword.

3. *Write it down:* Write the word down on a sticky note in BIG writing that's really easy to read. Be sure you aim for keywords rather than an essay on each sticky note!

4. *Stick it:* Once you have written the keyword onto a sticky note, put the sticky note above the line at the top of your page. Of course, sticky notes help you to speed up the storyboarding

process. (It's quite alright to stick the sticky notes over the top of each other at this stage.)

5. *Allocate:* Once you have finished with your Dreamer hat, take it off (metaphorically, that is!) and replace it with the Realist hat. Remember, the Realist hat is where you allocate the sticky notes. So at this stage of the process, you simply take each sticky note and put it into the correct part of the 4MAT System. In other words, put the *Why?* points into the *Why?* section, and so on.

6. *Analyse:* Once you have allocated all your sticky notes, take off the Realist hat (again, metaphorically speaking) and put on the Critic hat. Remember, the Critic hat is where you make some judgements about what you'll keep and what you will discard. At this stage of the process, you should critically analyse your content. How many ideas have you put in each quadrant? Have you favoured one quadrant over others? Do you need to put your Dreamer hat back on and think of other ideas for one or more quadrants that currently look a bit empty?

7. *Cull:* Take away duplications or any ideas that, on second thought, don't look like they belong in this particular presentation. Also consider how presentable your more creative ideas are. Were any of your ideas too radical for your audience? If anything doesn't seem to work in your presentation, now you're having a good look at it, throw those sticky notes away so they are not on your storyboard anymore.

8. *Add:* See if you can think of any extra information or new ideas that you'd like to add into this particular presentation and pop them down on new sticky notes and put them in the correct section on the storyboard.

9. *Organise:* Put the sticky notes into a pattern (any pattern) within their quadrant. You might like to put them in horizontal lines, vertical lines, diagonal lines or circles, whatever works for you.

Michelle says,

'The only rule with the pattern on your storyboard is that it must make sense to you, because this is how you will best remember your points under each quadrant in the 4MAT System.'

Congratulations! It's time to take off your Critic hat and present!

Whether you realise it or not, you are well on the way to being able to present — online and offline — without notes! You see, your choice of pattern will actually help you to remember your points. Amazing! Magic! And by not referring to your notes you will be more believable and engaging, and better connected with the people in your audience.

Michelle says,

'At all costs, you want at least to try to present without referring to your notes. This is because every time you look at your notes, you're sending a message to your audience that you don't know your content, which in turn reduces your credibility and overall effectiveness.'

Taking advantage of the storyboarding benefits

Storyboarding offers many benefits, including the following:

- *It's a memory tool:* The writing, sticking and re-sticking of the sticky notes helps embed your key messages in your memory.

- *It's quick:* You just start work on your presentation without that dreadful procrastination — seriously, you have no more excuses!

- *It's comprehensive:* Storyboarding ensures you address all the important areas for everyone in your audience, not just the people who listen and learn the way you do.

- *It's freeing:* Just get those ideas out of your head so you can bring order to the chaos in your mind.

- *It's interesting and engaging:* You can deliver your presentation without looking down at your notes. This means you can have eye contact with your audience, which is great for building rapport.

- *It's confidence building:* When you know you have put in the right amount of work to get the message to a professional and effective stage, and you know that it meets the needs of your entire audience, how could you be anything other than confident? You will be able to stand up there and deliver your message with the confidence that preparation gives you.

- *It's flexible:* Have you ever found that people interrupt you while you are presenting and this makes you go horribly off track? Well, using storyboarding means that you will know your messages well enough to stop when you are interrupted, address the matter that has been raised, and then go straight back to where you were up to in your message. Fantastic!

Michael's story

Michael called me in to work with him on a very important pitch to the executive in his business. He was requesting a dramatic increase in budget for his department.

Michael had spent many long days working in PowerPoint to structure his message. His concern was that the message still didn't flow effectively from an audience perspective. He had noticed that it was even difficult for him to remember which parts of the message he should deliver before others; consequently, he felt that he would appear disorganised as he presented the content. He could tell deep down that he wasn't going to get the buy-in he needed.

(continued)

I explained to Michael that PowerPoint is not the best place to start when designing a presentation. Seeing all your information and structuring your points logically is difficult to do straight into your slides. And, most importantly, designing this way tends to be presenter-focused and will likely diminish your ability to influence your audience to shift their thinking or behaviour.

I convinced Michael that he should abandon the presentation he had spent so much time working on. Instead of wasting one more second on a design that wasn't working, we storyboarded his presentation.

Michael brainstormed his key points above the line on his large piece of flipchart paper. Then he assigned each sticky note to the appropriate 4MAT System quadrant, added some new ideas, took away some ideas that he could now see didn't belong, and placed the remaining sticky notes in a pattern. Guess what happened? His new, revised and compelling presentation was completely designed in 15 minutes!

Next, Michael followed my Persuasion Blueprint (covered in detail in chapter 5), so that he increased the chance of persuading his audience to say 'yes' to his request.

And what was the result? Michael was awarded the budget he requested. He was relieved and overjoyed, and I was thrilled for him too!

Storyboarding works — I suggest you give it a go!

TRY THIS

1. Collect some flipchart paper, some chunky, felt-tipped pens, some reusable adhesive (for sticking the paper to the wall) and sticky notes.

2. Follow the steps in this chapter to storyboard your own presentation.

3. Remember to have a purpose, not a topic. For example: 'Why trek in Borneo?', 'Why exercise?', 'Why travel?' or 'How to get fit'.

4. Make sure you use the three hats of storyboarding: the Dreamer, Realist and Critic.

5. Why not have a go at giving the presentation without looking at your notes?

6. Know that if you believe in yourself, storyboarding will really work!

7. When you finish, don't turn around and look for what you missed — that's not the spirit! Turn around and be proud about what you remembered and exclaim with gusto: 'I am an exceptional presenter!'

My experience is that when people learn the 4MAT System for structuring their message, they think it's great! In fact, after learning this model, many of my clients go home and teach it to their children for school presentations because it's so easy to use. And I really believe it is an effective guide. It is a practical, theoretically rigorous, audience-focused model. The main thing that's tricky about this model is that, when you first learn it, knowing what sort of thing to say for each of the four questions can still sometimes be difficult. This is what chapter 5 is designed to help you do.

TOP TIPS
for designing your presentation

- Storyboarding is a tool used in conjunction with the 4MAT System for designing your presentation in a short amount of time.

- Storyboarding ensures that you capture all your critical ideas quickly and succinctly, and stops procrastination.

- Storyboarding is also a memory tool, reducing your need for notes and allowing you to connect with your audience.

- Using sticky notes when you storyboard helps you to speed up the process and to remember your key points.

CHAPTER 5

Script your presentation

In 2006, after much research and development, I developed a model that helps you move from your series of one-word points on your storyboard to a fully developed, detailed and scripted presentation that will shift your audience from their current to your desired state. I call it the Persuasion Blueprint.

My Persuasion Blueprint combines all of the key elements of a persuasive presentation, and helps you know exactly when to say the things you want to say — and say them with precision, accuracy and linguistic mastery. Specifically, my Persuasion Blueprint will help you achieve the following:

- build deep rapport with your audience

- stimulate your audience to listen actively

- manage audience conflict or objections

- influence your audience to think, feel and do what you have planned

- ensure that you answer the questions audience members are asking (both unspoken and spoken), regardless of their personality

- feel confident that you have prepared thoroughly and can deliver expertly for any audience.

Here is the Persuasion Blueprint in brief:

- *Step 0:* Hook your audience's attention.

- *Step 1:* Build rapport with your audience.

- *Step 2:* Assert your perspective using a leading statement.

- *Step 3:* Motivate your audience to pay attention.

- *Step 4:* Proactively manage audience objections.

- *Step 5:* Control and relax your audience.

- *Step 6:* Deliver the facts, figures and data.

- *Step 7:* Explain the steps for implementing your ideas.

- *Step 8:* Provide any other information.

- *Step 9:* Summarise your three key points.

- *Step 10:* Call your audience to action.

- *Step 11:* Manage questions and answers.

- *Step 12:* Highlight negative and positive consequences.

- *Step 13:* Close with a sizzle!

The following sections go through each of these steps in more detail — and they can be applied to all presentations, whether online or face to face. You might like to think of a presentation you have coming up that you could use as a working example as I go through the various steps. At the end of each step, you can stop and write out the relevant content for your specific working example.

Step 0: Hook your audience's attention

In your experience, how do most people start meetings and presentations? I often hear people launch straight into the introductions and rules. For example, they say, 'Welcome everyone, my name is *x* and today we are going to talk about *x*.'

Oh dear. This is not a great opening! If your audience was uninterested or bored before they arrived, they'll certainly stay that way with a beginning like that! Audiences are used to dreadful, clumsy and unsophisticated openings to meetings and presentations. That's why it's so refreshing for an audience when you deliver your opening with confidence and charisma. Well, how do you do that?

Exceptional presenters don't launch straight into their presentation and they most definitely don't introduce themselves first. They recognise the need to hook their audience's attention and captivate them. Therefore, a better way to begin your meeting or presentation (even your email) is with an icebreaker that hooks your audience's attention and has them sitting up excited for more! (Note that this is Step 0 because, in some situations, this step is not always necessary. It's a great option for you to consider if needed.)

What is an icebreaker?

An icebreaker can be an interesting fact, figure or statistic that you deliver in your first 30 seconds to help your audience lean in and take notice of what you have to say. It's called the 'icebreaker' because its job is to break the ice.

Icebreakers don't have to be positive, and they don't have to build rapport. They can be about something that is either fascinating or shocking. As long as the icebreaker wakes people up and has them on the edge of their chairs, it's doing its job brilliantly.

The steps for delivering an icebreaker are as follows:

1. Hook the audience with an interesting fact, figure or statistic.

2. Introduce yourself and welcome them to the meeting or presentation.

3. Link your icebreaker to your content. Be sure to let your audience know what you are there to talk about or what they will achieve from listening to your presentation.

Here are some of the best icebreakers I have heard over the years:

- It's not the cards you are dealt. It's the way you play them. My name is x. Let's talk about how to live your best life.

- One in six people in Australia claim they are bullied. My name is x. Let's really understand the impact of our cultural footprint on our organisation.

- Our sales team creates conversations. Our marketing team creates awareness. And our branding team creates an impression. Or put another way — sales is asking someone out on a date, and marketing and branding is a large part of why they say 'yes'! I'm excited to discuss our marketing priorities for 2022 with you. Today let's agree our branding and marketing priorities, and plan what each of us needs to do to make selling our products easier.

- Did you know that if we got all the sweet biscuits that we manufacture in one year and laid them end to end, they would stretch from here in Sydney, Australia, to New York City? That's a lot of biscuits. Welcome everyone! Today let's talk about the manufacture of our sweet biscuit range.

Delivering an effective icebreaker

The following tips will help you use icebreakers effectively:

- Icebreakers are delivered before you introduce yourself.

- They must link to the content of your presentation.

- Use the word 'let's' after your introduction rather than 'I want to talk to you about...' *Let's* is a lovely inclusive word that pulls your audience in.

- Icebreakers must be delivered in a conversational way, or you will look like you have been reading a presentation skills book!

- Ideally, you mention the subject of your icebreaker in the body of your presentation and again in your close to provide continuity.

- Repeat key numbers in your icebreaker. For example, 'Between Company X and five of our major competitors, over 34 000 liquor products are sold. Yes, 34 thousand! This includes over 8000 products our competitors sell that we don't. Welcome to this Ranging Library workshop. Let's dive into how using this new tool can help keep track of our competition and improve our own range!'

- Stack three, six or nine statistics for impact. For example, check out this great example from my client Meegan (numbers have been changed):

84 per cent of teachers in the last x months considered leaving the teaching profession. 30 to 50 per cent of teachers leave within the first x years of teaching. 75 per cent of teachers are stressed because of their work. This is a profession in distress!

60 per cent of primary school children in rural or remote Australian government schools miss at least x months of school per year. Children from very remote areas are x times more likely than those from major cities to be subject to a substantiated child protection report. These are the children in our schools.

My name is Meegan. Let's talk about why we must ensure teachers are trauma informed so we prevent our precious students falling through the cracks.

TIP

Michelle says,

'Icebreakers can be a very effective way to begin a presentation. Why not use a slide while you deliver your icebreaker? Include a gorgeous image on the slide and ensure it bleeds right to the edges of the screen. This will visually reinforce the icebreaker you are using.'

Handy tip: Icebreakers are an excellent way to begin any conversation with anyone. Do what you can to include them as often as possible so you embed the delivery of icebreakers as your new impressive skill.

TRY THIS

1. Think of an icebreaker you could deliver in your next presentation.

2. Write it down and rehearse how you will say it a few times so you sound natural, authentic and conversational.

3. Plan and rehearse the link from your icebreaker to your content, so that your presentation opening is as smooth as possible.

4. Design a beautiful slide with an image that bleeds right to the edges of your screen to reinforce your words.

Step 1: Build rapport with your audience

Once you have hooked your audience's attention, it's time to build rapport with them so they feel connected and open to your ideas. How do you do that?

Exceptional presenters recognise the need to build rapport with their audience as a priority.

TIP

Michelle says,

'The purpose of your presentation opening is to achieve 100 per cent inclusion. That means every single person in your entire audience is in agreement with you from your first word!'

What is rapport?

Rapport is your connection or relationship with your audience. You may have noticed that it is easiest to build rapport with people who are just like you. That's why you look like your friends! (And it's also why you look like your pet! Ha ha!) And you may also be painfully aware that it is often difficult to build rapport with people you don't like or people who are not like you.

When drafting the opening statements of your presentation, remember that you're not only presenting to people who are exactly like you. In fact, you're commonly presenting to people who are nothing like you. So while you will naturally build rapport with audience members who are like you, what are you going to do about all those other people?

When you begin your presentation, your aim should be to achieve 100 per cent inclusion. That means you are trying to achieve a 100 per cent success rate at getting your audience to agree with your opening statements so that they are then open-minded to the rest of your message. Wouldn't that be awesome? Sounds too good to be true, doesn't it?

TIP

Michelle says,

'Use inclusive statements that build rapport with your audience to begin your presentation.'

Building rapport

In order to achieve a high level of inclusion from the outset of your presentation, the best way to begin is to use what I refer to as inclusive statements.

Inclusive statements are statements that your audience members will understand, relate to and agree with. The two types of inclusive statements are universals and truisms.

Universals are statements that everyone will understand and relate to. For example:

- Many people would like to be more successful.

- Most of us would like to have more money to spend on things we enjoy.

- Many of us would like to be loved in our lives.

On the other hand, truisms are statements that are true just for the particular audience that you are presenting to at the time, in this particular forum. For example, if you are speaking to a group of entrepreneurs in a motivational seminar you might say:

- Many of you are awesome at setting and achieving your goals.

- While you are already successful in your current endeavours, many of you are here today because you are searching for the key that will inspire and empower you to further greatness.

- Many of you are excited about the opportunity to unlock your full potential.

In other words, a universal statement is common to all people across all industries and environments. A truism is true just for the people you are presenting to at the time and, therefore, is more audience-focused. For that reason, truisms are more likely to be industry-, profession- or organisation-specific.

As you can see from the examples, inclusive statements can be used very effectively to show empathy for your audience members and their situation. These statements build rapport with your audience because they reflect your audience's attitudes back to them. Every time you make a statement that your audience members can relate to, they nod to themselves and think, *Yes, this person understands what I think about this matter. They know what it's like to be me.* This is what we call rapport.

Making sure audience members agree with you

A personality filter known as the matcher/mismatcher filter helps explain why some people seem more able to agree with your ideas than others. It's an important filter to understand when your aim is to build rapport with everyone in your audience.

Matchers are people who look for what is the same about what you have said. For example, you say, 'What a beautiful day today!' and a matcher will reply with, 'Yes, I can't wait to go for a walk after work' or 'Yes, it is so sunny'.

On the other hand, mismatchers naturally notice risk and difference in what you are saying. Using the same example, if you said 'What a beautiful day today!', they may say, 'It was better yesterday' or 'It may rain later'.

Being a matcher or a mismatcher isn't a good or bad thing. You can't fail a personality test! It's just a scale to help you understand why some people seem more agreeable on the surface than others.

We know most audiences will generally contain several (if not many) mismatchers. That means we need to be clever with our words when we use universals and truisms to retain that 100 per cent inclusion.

The way to maintain your inclusion with all audience members is to avoid saying absolutes such as 'all', 'never', 'everyone', shouldn't', 'can't' or 'won't'.

Instead, you can add a few clever little words to your inclusive statements to ensure that the people with a tendency to be the devil's advocate cannot disagree easily with your statements. These words include 'most', 'some', 'several', 'various', 'many', 'few', 'others', and 'or not'. (You'll notice my earlier examples of inclusive statements use such words.) Indeed, many other similar words will achieve the same outcome for you.

Let me give you an example. If you said to your audience, 'You've all seen an excellent movie in the past week', some people could likely disagree with the statement. If they disagree with your statement, you haven't been successful (yet) in gaining their agreement on anything that you have said so far.

If, on the other hand, you said, 'Whether you've seen an excellent movie in the past week *or not...*' or '*Many* of you will have seen an excellent movie in the past week', or even '*Several* of you have seen an excellent movie in the past week', then you would create or maintain the 100 per cent inclusion that you desire.

Here's another example. If you said, 'You'll all agree with the need for a carbon tax', some audience members would be able to disagree with you because of the use of the absolute 'all', which makes this statement exclusive, not 100 per cent inclusive. Now, what about this as an alternative: 'Regardless of whether you agree with the need for a carbon tax or not, you will agree that we should consider carefully the long-term impact of climate change for Australia'.

Writing inclusive statements

There are many inclusive statements you could choose to say at the start of your presentation. The trick is to come up with the best choices! No pressure! It is certainly very important that you write the best possible inclusive statements to begin your presentation.

I have observed people using this technique incorrectly and they end up demonstrating that they have spent little time thinking about the needs of their audience. Perhaps you know what I mean?

The most obvious example I can think of is when corporate trainers welcome their participants back after a morning tea break and make a comment about the morning tea as their opening statement for the next training subject, 'Weren't they lovely fluffy scones, everyone?' While this is actually a truism (because all audience members likely did see or even eat those fluffy scones), this kind of statement can be perceived as a bit superficial. It's the kind of statement that someone makes when they can't think of anything else to say. It is more effective to talk with participants in the break and then open with a statement at the start of the next training subject that relates to those conversations and the content the audience is about to learn. For example, 'I had some good conversations with some of you in the break and I now understand that some of you would like to spend more time discussing examples of inclusive statements'.

Do you remember that in the five-step analysis process (refer to chapter 2), you wrote down your leading statement? You may recall that this is your key message, is often contentious and must be reasonable. The best way to come up with the perfect inclusive statements is to first write down your leading statement, and then work backwards. Ask yourself, 'If this is my leading statement, what universals and/or truisms could I say that would link together, make sense together and lead the audience to believing my leading statement?'

TIP

Michelle says,

'It's critical you are completely audience-focused when writing your opening.'

Working out what your audience already knows to be true

Make sure you get right into your audience's shoes and come up with the best, most insightful and inclusive opening statements that you can, so that you truly reflect what they care about (in relation to this matter) and, therefore, maximise your rapport with them. When you are writing your inclusive statements, ask yourself the following critical question:

'What does my audience know to be true?'

Once you have a few answers, make sure that they all link to your subject, and flow naturally and seamlessly from one statement to the next.

Here are some potential opening statements:

- If I were going to present to a group of financial planners, I might say, 'You would be aware of the turbulence in the financial markets at present. Some of you may have found that client concerns have increased markedly following the recent performance of the international sharemarket and the subsequent negative media coverage. Many of you would be speaking with clients who want to withdraw their funds from share-based investments.'

- If I were presenting to a group of customer service representatives, I would reflect what they know to be true with the following: 'Many of us have been on the receiving end of poor customer service, and we know that it often means we won't go back to that service provider if we can help it. Many of us would expect that the customer service division of [Company X] strives to provide excellent service.'

Can you spot the inclusive statements in each of these examples?

Deciding on the number of inclusive statements

The number of inclusive statements you should use depends on the current level of rapport you have with your audience. Perhaps you know your audience well or you are in the same profession or organisation as your audience, and you are in agreement about the content of your presentation. In this case, you will probably need fewer inclusive statements than if you were an outsider. On the other hand, perhaps your level of rapport is low, and/or your audience members don't agree with you at all. If you know from your five-step analysis (in chapter 2) that they are not thinking, feeling or doing anything you desire, you will need more inclusive statements.

I provide a simple formula for you to follow in table 5.1.

Table 5.1 Formula for building rapport with your audience

Level of rapport	Number of inclusive statements
If rapport is non-existent	You need at least three inclusive statements.
If rapport is okay	You need at least two inclusive statements.
Even if rapport is excellent	You need at least one inclusive statement.

In other words, the number of inclusive statements you need is directly related to your existing level of rapport. When I am opening my two-day Persuasive Presentation Skills Masterclass (on which this book is based), I start with 15 inclusive statements! Yes, 15! Now, I am lovely. And each participant in my masterclass is also lovely. But at the start of the two-day immersive experience, we don't know that about each other. We are not yet in rapport. That's why I choose to use 15 inclusive statements that will ensure that I have undeniable rapport before I start covering any content.

1. Write down your inclusive statements for an upcoming presentation.

2. Rehearse how you will say them a few times so they sound as natural, authentic and conversational as possible.

Other ways to build rapport

You can also build rapport with your audience members by being as similar to your audience as possible. This is also known as 'pacing' your audience and is what many salespeople call 'matching and mirroring'. Matching and mirroring is where you ensure that your voice, body language, eye contact and dress (to name just a few things) are similar to the voice, body language, eye contact and dress of your audience. In this way, the audience feels you are like them, and it's true that we like people who are like us. Pacing builds rapport with our audience. Remember, though, that pacing, or matching or mirroring, is not the same as mimicking your audience. Mimicking often involves a degree of sarcasm and will, therefore, generally break rapport.

TIP

Michelle says,

'It's important that you don't pace your audience in an obvious way or you will look like you are using a technique on your audience and that will break rapport.'

You can match and mirror many aspects so you seem similar to the members of your audience. These aspects include your audience members' eye contact, body language, vocal variety, language (including slang and jargon), breathing, energy, dress, interests and attitudes. As speaker and TV host Kirsty Spraggon says, 'Find the part of them that matches with a part of you and you'll be sure to create a meaningful relationship'.

TRY THIS

1. Some people find pacing easier to do than others. Think about the next time you have to present and make a list of all the ways you could pace (or be like) your audience.

2. Be sure you put all the necessary steps into action so you can pace effectively from the very minute you are in front of your audience.

Step 2: Assert your perspective using a leading statement

After building rapport with your audience in the opening statements by using inclusive statements that reflect what they already know to be true, you are in the perfect position to introduce your key leading statement. This is your main idea, view, opinion, proposal or argument, which by definition will be more contentious. As entrepreneur, author and motivational speaker Jim Rohn wisely said, 'Asking is the beginning of receiving'.

As outlined in the five-step analysis (refer to chapter 2) the defining characteristics of a leading statement are as follows:

- It is your key message and the thing you really want your audience to believe.

- It is contentious in nature — meaning the audience may well disagree with you.

- It must be reasonable. Thinking up a leading statement your audience will never agree with is pointless. If it is so contentious it's ridiculous then better not to waste your time with that. Make sure your leading statement is something the audience could eventually (after some very powerful inclusive statements) agree to.

If you have completed your five-step analysis (discussed in detail in chapter 2), you will have already written your leading statement.

Using your leading statement with your inclusive statements for a powerful opening

Imagine you are walking in your neighbourhood. As you are walking along, you see your friend jogging up ahead. Let's say for the purpose of this example that you want to catch up with your friend. What would you have to do? Yes, that's right — you'd have to start jogging towards them, wouldn't you? But let's just say that you don't like jogging much! So you catch up to them and, after jogging with them for a while, you slow down and start to walk. What do you think your friend would be most likely to do? Yes, I think so too: they would probably slow down and walk with you. This is what we call 'pacing and leading'.

Pacing is when you jog with your friend, at their speed or pace — you are as like them as possible. In the context of your presentation, it's where you match and mirror their voice, body language, eye contact and dress. And it's when you deliver your inclusive statements that reflect what they already know to be true.

Leading is when you slowed down and your friend changed to your pace. In the context of your presentation, leading is where you deliver your leading statement, or the key message that you must have your audience believe.

In other words, when it comes to the opening of your presentation, you pace your audience's attitudes through the use of inclusive statements and then you lead the audience by stating the thing you want them to believe (your leading statement).

TIP

Michelle says,

'You don't have permission to lead your audience until you have first paced them.'

You pace and lead in the opening of your presentation by first making some inclusive statements that reflect to your audience what they already know to be true. These inclusive statements must link together and make sense one after the other, and should lead the audience to believe your leading statement. Once you have said your inclusive statements and you have built some strong rapport, you then say your leading statement.

COMBINING INCLUSIVE STATEMENTS WITH A LEADING STATEMENT

Here is an example for you.

> Many of us have been on the receiving end of poor customer service, and we know that it often means we won't go back to that service provider if we can help it. Many of us would expect that the customer service division of [Company X] strives to provide excellent service. Customer care at [Company X] is committed to exceeding our customers' expectations in a variety of ways and, as a result, we have as little as 10 per cent customer churn each year.

You can see in this example that the three inclusive statements make it easier to accept the leading statement about commitment and customer churn rates. Without the inclusive statements before the leading statement, you could appear too direct or confrontational. You don't have permission to lead or influence your audience until you have built rapport using inclusive statements.

AVOIDING MANIPULATION

Perhaps you're wondering whether structuring your opening in this way is manipulative. The difference between persuasion and manipulation is in your intentions. If you are coercing someone to believe or do something that is not in their best interest and is just for you, then, unfortunately, that sounds like manipulation to me! You will probably have to use either an aggressive or passive approach with your audience. And you'll probably feel a bit guilty too!

If, on the other hand, you are completely focused on meeting the needs of your stakeholder or audience and provide an element of freedom in their decision-making process, that is not manipulation. That is persuasion. Persuasion is the assertive approach to influence. You cannot be simultaneously manipulative and persuasive.

For more information on how to persuade, check out my book *How to Persuade: The skills you need to get what you want* (Wiley).

TIP

Michelle says,

'You cannot be simultaneously manipulative and persuasive.'

Pacing and leading is the oldest influencing technique around. Have you ever stopped to think that you cannot *not* influence? It's true, isn't it? We are constantly influencing others — sometimes knowingly, other times unknowingly. I suggest that, when it comes to presenting, you would be better to influence others with care and concern and attention to your audience's needs in a premeditated way, and with the utmost care for your audience members, than to try not to influence them and accidentally do something unethical, such as suggesting something inappropriate or offending the audience in some way.

Negotiators use pacing and leading all the time. In fact, you can probably see that the need to build rapport by pacing and leading the audience to your way of thinking doesn't just exist at the start of a presentation. Clever communicators pace and lead all the time, in the opening, middle and close of a conversation, in order to influence the other party.

Remember that you don't have permission to lead an audience unless you have first paced them. In other words, you can't ask for anything unless you have established rapport. (Well, you can ask but without rapport they will probably say 'no' to you!) It's my experience that you can get anything you want if you can get your head around how to use this fabulous communication technique called pacing and leading.

Pacing and leading is a most exciting technique! Without this technique, you will struggle to build strong rapport and you won't maximise your ability to lead your audience to agree with your leading statement or your key message. I recommend pacing and leading as a strategy for opening your presentations.

TRY THIS

1. Go to the presentation you are working on as you read through this book. Ensure that your inclusive statements from Step 1 of the Persuasion Blueprint link powerfully to your leading statement at Step 2 of the Persuasion Blueprint.

2. Check that your inclusive statements in Step 1 and your leading statement in Step 2 are not a repetition of your icebreaker. Icebreakers and pacing and leading are two separate techniques. The icebreaker hooks the audience's attention and the pacing and leading builds rapport and influences the audience to believe your key message. Make the most of what each technique can do for a powerful opening to your presentation.

3. Ensure the combination of Steps 1 and 2 builds strong rapport with your audience.

Step 3: Motivate your audience to pay attention

Have you ever stopped to think about how many meetings you attend in a day at work (face to face and virtual) from which you derive very little value? How many meetings do you think you attend simply because you should, only to find that when you arrive all you can think about is all the other work that is piling up while you're in the meeting? When you feel like that, it's clear that you don't know the benefits of attending the meeting and you will probably struggle to be attentive and emotionally connected. The presenter might as well be saying, 'blah, blah, blah', because you find it so hard to pay attention.

We know that most audience members turn up to meetings and presentations thinking they are going to be a complete waste of time. I surveyed around 800 past participants from my Persuasive Presentation Skills Masterclass and they said that, on average, 72 per cent of the meetings they attended were either completely unrelated to their roles, or at least unhelpful to them achieving their goals. Wow! No wonder our colleagues are typically passive when they sit in our meetings.

Presenters commonly think that the motivation to listen and then to act or to follow their recommendations is obvious, and does not need to be stated overtly. Presenters also commonly think that people are motivated by the same things. This is definitely not the case!

Your audience members will (consciously or even subconsciously) be looking for their WIIFM? That is, 'What's in it for me?' You have not earned the full attention of your audience until you answer this question for them.

Given that we know it's quite possible that many of the people in your audience are not that keen to be there, it makes sense that it's your role as the presenter to motivate everyone to want to listen to you. When you understand what motivates people, motivating your audience to sit up and pay attention to your message is actually very easy.

When you are preparing your presentation, keep reminding yourself that you are not designing it for yourself: you are designing it for your audience. It is not about you — it's all about your audience. Work out what motivates them and promise it — and then deliver! Do you know how to have your audience sitting on the edge of their chairs wanting to hear more from you?

TIP

Michelle says,

'Work out what motivates your audience and promise it—and then deliver!'

Understanding what motivates people

We know that your audience members are motivated to act in one of two ways. They are either motivated to move away from pain, risk or discomfort (sometimes referred to as the 'stick'), or they are motivated to move towards the positive and the rewards (sometimes referred to as the 'carrot').

To help you understand how this motivation preference works, let me tell you about Simon and Annie.

Simon's story and Annie's story

Simon exercises regularly at 5.30 am every morning. Some mornings he wakes up with the alarm and thinks, 'Oh no, I am just too tired to get up this morning!' The thing that makes him get out of bed is that he believes the early hours of the morning are the best part of the day and he loves being out there hitting the pavement, having a run.

He knows he will feel good, look good and have more energy throughout the day if he exercises first thing. So, despite his initial lack of interest in getting out of bed, he does get up and he does exercise. Simon has a move *towards* preference.

Annie, on the other hand, has a move *away* preference. She exercises at 5.30 am nearly every morning too! When Annie's alarm goes off, she also often feels like she is too tired to get up. She really wants to press the snooze button and roll over and go back to sleep. The thing that motivates Annie to get up is that she knows that if she doesn't, she will put on weight, feel sluggish throughout the day and feel guilty for not exercising. In other words, the thing that motivates Annie to get up and exercise is her desire to move away from negative results and guilt.

Either way, both Simon and Annie are motivated to exercise.

Here's another example. Imagine you are driving in your car and you come to an area where you know a speed camera is located. What would you do? Yes, you'd probably slow down immediately (even if you were not speeding!). In that moment in your car when you slow down, you are probably motivated to move away from future pain (an accident, a monetary fine or a loss of points on your driver's licence). Your motivation in that scenario is move away.

The alternative is that you slow down because seeing the speed camera reminds you that you are keen to drive safely — you like the idea of keeping yourself and your passengers safe. In this example, your motivation is move towards.

Did you notice with these examples that Simon and Annie still both exercise and, if you were in your car, you would still probably slow down? Your motivational preference doesn't determine whether you act, only your motivation for acting.

Your preference to move towards reward or away from pain is a personality filter. It's important to remember that personality filters are not good or bad, positive or negative. Your preference is your preference and good for you! Just be pleased you now have further self-awareness about what does and does not motivate you, and make sure you remember that not everyone is motivated by the same things as you.

MOTIVATING YOUR AUDIENCE TO LISTEN REGARDLESS OF THEIR PREFERENCES

When you want to motivate your audience, use a language pattern that motivates both the move towards and move away people in your audience.

Include the following words in your WIIFM statement:

- reduce — for the move away preference
- maintain — to capture the people in the middle
- improve — for the move towards preference.

This language pattern will help you to motivate all people.

Here is an example:

> Let's work together to reduce errors and inconsistencies in our data, maintain our customer approach and achieve our KPIs for the quarter.

This 'reduce, maintain, improve' language pattern answers the 'WIIFM?' question.

Handy tip: Sticking with the pattern order I have recommended here is a good idea while you are getting used to using it. I recommend that you start with the thing that you are reducing and finish with what you're improving to take advantage of a phenomenon in speaking called the 'law of primacy and recency'. This law suggests that people will remember both the first and last thing you say, with a particular focus on the last thing they hear. You want the most positive sounding part of your WIIFM statement at the end.

Remember also that many organisational cultures focus on the positives, so even though the *reduce* is a positive, it uses a word that implies it is negative and so people may think you are being pessimistic. If you finish on the *improve*, people will really hear your positive intentions.

By the way, you don't have to have a *maintain* in your WIIFM statement if you can't think of a good one. You can leave that section out if nothing sensible is coming to your mind.

ALTERNATIVE WORDS FOR DELIVERING THE WIIFM

You are very welcome to choose from a whole host of alternative words to reduce, maintain and improve. Some suggestions are provided in table 5.2.

Table 5.2 Alternative words for your WIIFM statement

Reduce	Maintain	Improve
Decrease	Uphold	Progress
Lessen	Preserve	Develop
Diminish	Keep	Expand
Cut	Continue	Increase
Trim down	Keep up	Advance
Condense	Sustain	Boost
Shrink	Retain	Amplify
Ease	Carry on	Encourage
Lower	Persevere	Spread
Cut down	Protect	Further
Abate	Support	Heighten

CHOOSING NOT TO USE THE WIIFM STATEMENT

If you decide not to use the WIIFM statement, and so don't include what your audience will reduce, maintain and improve, you will probably continue to motivate the people who are similar to you — because you'll continue to motivate your audience according to your own preference.

So if you have a move towards preference, you will continue to tell your audience what they will gain from doing what you want — but the move away people will remain unmoved! If you have a move away preference, you will continue to tell your audience what they will avoid by doing what you want — and the people with a move towards focus will remain unmoved!

Overall, it is a good idea to use the WIIFM language pattern in your presentations.

TRY THIS

1. Write your WIIFM statement for your working example, remembering this goes after your leading statement at Step 3 of the Persuasion Blueprint.

2. Make sure that you include at least a move away and a move towards, so that your WIIFM is motivating all types of people in your audience, not just the people like you. Otherwise, you will naturally use the pattern that matches your own preference!

Step 4: Proactively manage audience objections

Excellent work! You have now written your icebreaker, your inclusive statements, your leading statement and your WIIFM (Steps 0 to 3 of the Persuasion Blueprint). Now it's time to manage any audience objections.

When you completed your five-step analysis (chapter 2) you might remember that you had the chance to ask yourself, 'What is my audience thinking, feeling and doing before they arrive?' It's at this stage of the five-step analysis phase that any unspoken but often quite serious objections to you, to your content and to your team and company will be made obvious to you. The process you go through in applying the Think/Feel/Do model (chapter 2) should enable you to anticipate most objections in advance. Sometimes, though, presenters are so passionate about their topic that they are blind to the kinds of objections that people may have. They think, 'How could people possibly disagree with my thinking on this?' If you fall into this category, you may need to consult people who are representative of your audience in order to gauge their mindset.

> **TIP**
>
> **Michelle says,**
>
> 'Whether your message is contentious or needs care in delivery or not, it's a good idea to work out what the objections might be when you are speaking, and plan how you will deal with or manage them — you will be amazed at what a difference it makes to your ability to persuade your audience. To be forewarned is to be forearmed!'

Once you have listed potential objections, you can decide which ones should receive airtime in the presentation and what you can say to address them.

As a presenter, once you know that some objections exist and, although unspoken, are very real for your audience, you have two main choices: you can ignore them and hope they go away, or you can address them and assist your audience to move forward with your message. If the objection is common to most of your audience, it is wise to manage it at Step 4 of your Persuasion Blueprint. Managing the objection will bring the problem or issue out in the open, help you solve the problem as best you can and allow you to continue to control the proceedings. In other words, it helps your audience move on from their objection and be more open to receiving your message than they might otherwise have been.

The objections you can expect

People can object to all sorts of things — from your content, to something personal about you, to the logistics of the event.

Let me give you some specific objections that your audience may have in presentations — whether they be face to face or virtual. And remember, they are mostly unstated objections that you have uncovered in your five-step analysis phase (chapter 2).

Audience objections may include:

- It's not broken, so why fix it?

- That's not how we do things around here.

- It's too early in the morning for this.

- It's too late in the day for this.

- I'm not going to get time to eat my lunch because of this.

- This time of day doesn't suit me.

- I'm too busy for this.

- This isn't a priority.

- We tried that 10 years ago and it didn't work then. Why would it work now?

- You wouldn't understand.

- You've never done my job.

- I already know this.

- I know more about this than you.

- I have no time to do this.

- There is no budget for this.

- There are no resources available.

- It's too expensive.

- This is not relevant to me.

- It's not a priority.

- It won't work.

- It's too hard.

- It's not in my job description.

- It's not my decision.

- It's not my problem.

- This is above my pay grade.

- It's not in the business plan.

Managing objections

I recommend that you use a specific technique to manage these unstated objections. It's called POO! It stands for pacing out objections.

Here is how you do it:

1. State the objection.

2. Say, 'and', 'so' or pause and say nothing.

3. Use the words 'actually' or 'in fact'.

4. Solve the objection.

5. Use the word 'because'.

See table 5.3 for the details on how you POO (a bit rude, I know!)

Table 5.3 Pacing out objections (POO)

Activity	Explanation
State the objection.	You might remember from the previous section that the way to build rapport with your audience is to be as similar to your audience as possible. So this is where you reflect that you know the audience is concerned about *XYZ*. It's important that you don't empathise with them if the objection they have is unfounded or unacceptable.
Say 'and', 'so', or simply pause and say nothing.	This is the tricky part of this technique because you may have noticed that many people say 'but' as their link from the problem to the solution. The thing about 'but' is that its meaning is 'except', 'other than' or 'on the contrary', so it's an emotive joining word that negates what you have just said. It is commonly considered a blocking word. Why would you say something and then negate it? That's ridiculous! And negating your audience's perspective is not great for ongoing rapport is it?
Say 'actually' or 'in fact'.	Copywriters have known for years that the use of these two words makes whatever follows more believable. It's worth a try, don't you think?

(continued)

Table 5.3 Pacing out objections (POO) (cont'd)

Activity	Explanation
Give your solution.	Your solution should be well thought through and acceptable to your audience. And often it's best if the solution is the opposite of the problem. For example, 'You may think that this is a waste of time, and in fact it will save you time because ...'
Use the word 'because'.	One of the easiest ways to compel your audience to action is to be specific. The more specific you are, the more credible your points, arguments or sales pitch will be. The simplest way to force yourself to be specific when using the POO technique is to say the word 'because'.

AVOIDING ALL SUBSTITUTES FOR 'BUT'

Maybe you agree 'but' is a blocking word, so you wonder about similar substitutes. 'However', 'although', and 'alternatively' are just as bad as 'but' because they also negate what you have just said. Using 'and', 'so' or a pause with your choice of 'actually' or 'in fact', are my best suggestions for joining words between steps 1 and 3 of the POO technique.

SOME EXAMPLES OF EFFECTIVE POO STATEMENTS

Here are a variety of examples that you can use to further understand how to use the POO technique yourself:

- 'Many people feel that a call centre is not necessary in our industry (pause). So today let's actually delve into the pros and cons of a call centre, and then together we can work out what we should do, because without considering both sides of the argument we can't be sure we will make the best decision.'

- 'You might be wondering what Company X can do that's better than all our competitors (pause). In fact, today's presentation will take you through the differences so you can make the best decision for your business, because understanding our competitors helps us pitch more confidently to our customers.'

- 'Some of what I am about to say will be difficult for you to hear because it relates to bonuses. And actually I'm going to explain the rationale behind our decision and share with you what we can all do to make this a better place to work, because lots of exciting opportunities are on our horizon.'

- 'You may already know some of what I am about to say; (pause) in fact, I thought I'd call on those of you with expertise to assist me in this presentation because your real-life examples will help everyone better understand this new process.'

- 'Some of you are very angry about the negative returns on your super this year. I know a number of you have turned up today to give us a piece of your mind, and others are simply confused and would like to understand what is going on in the investment market at present (pause). Actually, I'm a member of exactly the same funds as you, so I know how disappointing the results have been. Today's presentation has been designed to explain why our funds have performed as they have and to give you a chance to ask your questions of a panel of experts in the industry, because developing your knowledge is the best way for you to take charge of your financial future.'

ARE OBJECTIONS ALWAYS ANGRY?

Objections are not always angry or aggressive in their nature, although it depends on where you work and the nature of your presentation.

Objections can simply be a question or seeking clarification on a point. You could use this POO technique a lot in your everyday communication with others, couldn't you? I've heard of people who have used this technique to win arguments with their family members, to manage questions in an interview situation, and in negotiations.

TRY THIS

1. Go back to your Think/Feel/Do from your five-step analysis (chapter 2).

2. Use your analysis to direct your attention to the most concerning objections your audience will have about you, your message or your company, and the logistics of the meeting.

3. Write out the POO technique to manage the objections in your working example directly after the WIIFM statement at Step 4 of the Persuasion Blueprint.

4. Be careful not to write 'but' or 'however' into your script. These words creep in there even when you know not to say them!

Step 5: Control and relax your audience

Have you ever found yourself sitting in the audience at a meeting or conference presentation wondering, 'Do I have to have my camera on in this virtual meeting?', 'What credentials and experience does this speaker have?', 'What's the agenda and scope of this meeting?', 'How long is this going for and will there be catering?' or 'When can I ask questions or raise my concerns and opinions?'

As a presenter, have you ever had people interrupt you during your meetings with unrelated questions that take you off track? Or have you experienced people having side conversations that disrupt the rest of the group and draw everyone's attention away from you and your important message?

Some of the most common disruptions in business presentations are mobile phones ringing or people reading their text messages in what they think is a secretive way. (It makes me laugh that they believe you can't see them doing it!) Actions such as these indicate that the person is at least somewhat disengaged from your presentation. These interruptions can be very annoying and off-putting, for both the presenter and the rest of the audience. They can even make us feel nervous as presenters, especially when we don't know how to manage them or stop them happening in the first place.

Reducing disruptions and increasing people's attention

I believe that most inappropriate audience behaviour found in meetings, training courses and presentations (on- and offline) occurs because the presenter did not state their expectations of the audience, the time, the subject matter and the event in general. When you don't set the expectations or boundaries for your audience, they don't know the scope, time frame, logistics or anything about your experience or credentials. They are also not sure about what would be considered acceptable and unacceptable behaviour. As a result you can find yourself having to manage dysfunctional behaviour.

TIP

Michelle says,

'Most inappropriate audience behaviour occurs because of a lack of boundary-setting.'

With a move to virtual platforms, setting the ground rules has become even more important. If you need everyone's cameras on and their mute function on or off, for example, it's important you tell them so you can run your meeting properly.

So whether your audience is live or virtual, set the ground rules and boundaries early, along with all the details the audience needs to know, such as who you are, what your session is all about, what to expect and how to behave. Doing so will reduce disruptions, maintain order in your presentations and meetings and improve your audience's ability to listen and ultimately change their behaviour. Essentially, you will better control and relax your audience. Boundary-setting is otherwise known as framing.

SETTING BOUNDARIES

The following list outlines the most common boundaries, or frames, you should consider setting. Choose the ones that you feel are important in order to control and relax your audience.

Boundaries to consider include the following:

- your name, so people know how to address you

- your role, so people understand what you do

- your job title, so people know where you fit

- your department, so people understand which area you come from

- your company if you come from outside the company, so that the audience knows where you work

- if online, everyone has the camera on, so you can see their faces and connect

- if online, everyone turn the mute off, so that it is quick for people to respond to you (no-one likes it when you have to say, 'Jane, you're on mute. Jane! Jane, turn off your mute'; oh it's funny and annoying all in one!)

- if online, how to use the chat, reactions and polls

- if online, everyone turn the mute on, if you think people have distracting background noise

- your credentials, so people know why they should listen to you and believe you

- how long the presentation will run for, so people can manage their time

- whether there will be breaks and refreshments, so people can ensure their own comfort

- an indication of the content, so people know what you will be talking about

- the scope of the presentation, so people know what will not be discussed in this meeting or presentation

- the agenda, so people know what will be covered and the order in which you will deliver the message

- mobile phone etiquette, so disruptions are minimised

- when people can ask questions, so they can feel at ease about asking when they want to, or waiting until the end

- whether there will be a test, so people know how attentive they need to be!

- style, so people understand what is required of them — for example, will this be interactive today, or will you be delivering a slide presentation in the dark?

- whether people should take notes or whether there will be a handout, so they can manage their retention of knowledge.

Here is an example of some frames you might use in one of your presentations:

> My name is Michelle Bowden. I am the director of Michelle Bowden Enterprises. In the past two decades as a persuasive presentation skills expert, I have learned that anyone can be an exceptional presenter, no matter their personality or personal style. It's just a matter of knowing what you are supposed to do to be exceptional and then practising it! So today let's go through my top tips for exceptional presenting. This is going to be a highly interactive session, which means it would be excellent if you would please ask your questions throughout, and if you could switch your mobile to silent that would be wonderful for your colleagues.

KNOWING HOW MANY BOUNDARIES TO SET

The short answer to how many boundaries to set is as many as you need to — within reason, of course. The number of boundaries you set depends entirely on your audience. When you conduct your five-step analysis (chapter 2) you will be made aware (sometimes painfully aware!) of the potential areas of concern. These are the areas where people are potentially going to behave in a disruptive way and, therefore, need to be managed. So set as many boundaries as you need to for your audience to feel relaxed and so that you control the proceedings.

Luke's story

Luke works in a company where staff members are expected to go to many meetings that do not directly relate to their roles. As a result, they have started to bring their laptops along so they can do their 'real work' during the meetings!

Luke was so excited to learn about the importance of setting boundaries. He realised that if he doesn't ask his audience to put their laptops away, they will have them open throughout his session.

Now he knows to set the boundaries, people are wonderfully respectful and wouldn't dream of having their laptops open on the boardroom table in his presentations and meetings. A win for everyone concerned!

I suspect that if Luke were presenting online, he'd know now to frame expectations so people didn't do their other work while in his meetings!

WHAT IF YOU FORGET OR CHOOSE NOT TO SET BOUNDARIES?

If you don't remember or choose not to set the boundaries, people will be left wondering 'What's going on?' They will be distracted by their internal dialogue asking unanswered logistics questions such as 'When can I ask questions?' and 'How long will this go for?', and they may demonstrate undesirable behaviour, such as becoming distracted by their mobile phone, starting up side conversations or interrupting you unnecessarily.

When you do set boundaries, everyone in your audience knows you are credible. They know what to expect from the session and how they should behave for the meeting to be a success. This will lead to your audience feeling more relaxed and you will be better placed to maintain control — which, in turn, means you are more likely to maximise the likelihood of achieving your desired outcomes. Try this because it definitely works!

Outlining your credibility (without feeling like you're 'showing off')

Some people feel uncomfortable talking about their credentials — one of my clients said she felt like she was showing off, and hated sharing her skills and experience. She was looking for a clever way to establish her credibility in her presentation.

Yes, when someone stands out in front of a group of people or online and big notes themselves, it can make them look conceited. Have you ever been to a presentation where the person raved on and on about their credentials? 'I have this qualification and that qualification and I'm clever for the following reasons, blah, blah, blah.' (Yawn.)

Unfortunately, the result is that most of us don't want to discuss our credibility when we speak, because we don't want to give a negative impression. The problem is that if you don't give your credentials, your audience might be asking themselves, 'Who is this person and what do they know?' They may wonder about your credibility and question why you are presenting to them on your topic. This can have a negative impact on your ability to influence your audience. It is very important for you to give your credentials. You just need to give them in a way that's audience-focused, not self-indulgent or egotistical.

TIP

Michelle says,

'It's vital that you establish your credibility with your audience so they trust you and want to listen to your presentation.'

You can use a clever credibility formula to explain your credentials in a confident way that doesn't offend. Here it is:

In the x years I have worked as an x in the x, what I have learned is x [reflect audience pain)], and what this means for you is x.

You'll notice in the preceding formula that it says, 'reflect audience pain'. In other words, it's a good idea for you to mention the challenge, frustration, inconvenience that the audience is feeling. Show empathy by mentioning it and then solve it. This is clever because you are linking your credentials to the solving of your audience's pain. People will listen to you talking about yourself as long as you link your credentials to their pain and then solve it.

For example:

> In the 15 years I have worked in clinical research in the pharmaceutical industry, what I have learned is that it can be downright dangerous if we don't work with our medical investigators during clinical trials. So today I'll take you through a variety of ways to both communicate our requirements to our investigators, and to ensure that we remember to follow up with our clients to ensure ongoing patient safety.

> In the seven years I have worked in a variety of roles in human resources across industry, what I have learned is that people are often very sensitive about the title on their business card. What this means for you is we have engaged in some qualitative research to ascertain which titles we should adopt in our organisation, to give status and confidence to our people.

> In the three months I have solely focused on the [insert name] area in our business, I've come to realise that wastage and double handling are costing us time and money in a number of areas. The good news is that I've come up with three solutions to eradicate the double-ups and save ourselves both time and money.

Here's a different version of this credibility formula for you to try too:

> Recently I was speaking with x and they mentioned x, and it made me realise that x is a big problem for you at the moment. So I thought today we should go through how we can work on fixing this together.

Or you could try this way:

> I've had a passion for the area of [insert area] for some time now and I've spoken with senior people in our business, such as [name] and [name]. It's become obvious that there are a several areas of potential growth for us. In this meeting I'll share how we might make the most of these opportunities.

WHAT'S SO CLEVER ABOUT THE CREDIBILITY FORMULA?

The benefit of the credibility formula is that once you have explained something about yourself ('in the x years I have worked as an x, in the x, what I have learned is x [reflect audience pain]') you then move straight into telling the audience what they will derive from listening to you: 'and what this means for you is x'. In this frame, while the audience still hears you mention some of your experience, the conversation ceases to be about you and actually becomes more about the audience and what they will gain from your experience.

Remember: it's not about you — it's all about your audience.

Tamara's story

Tamara is a real success story in her organisation. At 31 years of age, she's already in the executive ranks of her company. She's very smart, talented and astute. However, because she's so young, people can tend to write her off and assume she's just 'a little girl' who isn't worth listening to.

Tamara explained to me that in the past she had been reluctant to talk about her experience and skills because she didn't want people to think she was vain. Her other concern was that people in her company should already know enough about her to realise she's not an executive for nothing! So why should she mention it again when they already know it?

After we chatted for a while, Tamara realised that it was entirely possible that people in her company didn't know her background.

(continued)

Because the credibility you mention about yourself should change and relate particularly to the issue being discussed, Tamara also realised that it was highly likely people had forgotten each of the relevant credentials she had, depending on the message she was delivering.

After learning how to use the credibility frame, Tamara now confidently adds in the relevant details (considering the issue being discussed) when she is communicating at work. She has found that people have started to sit up and listen and pay more attention to her when she says what she thinks in meetings. What a terrific shift!

TRY THIS

1. Go back to your Think/Feel/Do audience analysis in phase 1 (chapter 2).

2. Work out what frames you think you might need to use to control and relax your audience.

3. Write out the relevant frames for your working example. These go directly after your POO statement at Step 5 of the Persuasion Blueprint.

4. Be sure to include a credibility formula, using the guidance in this chapter, so that your audience knows why they should pay attention to you.

Step 6: Deliver the facts, figures and data

This step is where you cover the *What?* information of your presentation — that is, you define your topic, and deliver the facts, figures, research, information, statistics and insights. This is what many people would call the body of the presentation. This section can be quite short or very long, depending on your overall purpose and the needs of your audience. You would answer questions at this point for your audience such as, 'What is [the content being covered]?',

'What do I know about this?', 'What analysis or research has been conducted to come to this conclusion?', 'What are the facts of the matter?' and 'What statistics exist to back up my hypothesis?' Aim to cover the big picture first, and then narrow your focus to the overall principles and then the details. Make this section as interesting and creative as is appropriate in your workplace.

The best way to present statistics

Be sure to present the most important statistics first, followed by subsidiary points in decreasing order of importance. Use slides or a flip chart, a whiteboard (or even your iPad if presenting online) to show the statistics in nice big, clear writing.

Your audience will lose interest quickly, so show only the critical statistics that add value to your overall message. Remove all the non-critical data from your slides and make what's left as big as you can so the audience can see the point clearly from their seats (wherever they are in the room) or from their screens.

Handy tip: If you have lots of data and statistics and must present it all at once, don't be tempted to put all the data on a slide that's difficult to read. Instead, simply make a visually appealing handout and present your data on the handout.

Step 7: Explain the steps for implementing your ideas

This is where you explain the *How?* of your message. It's where you explain to your audience both the steps and the application of the content you have covered in the *What?* section of your presentation.

For example, if you are speaking about customer service, at this step you might explain to the audience:

- how to deliver great customer service
- the procedures you would like your audience to implement
- how to implement the new strategy you are trialling.

Research by educationalist Peter Sheal shows that your audience is 90 per cent more likely to remember your content if they say it and do it. So be sure to incorporate as many visual, auditory and kinesthetic techniques as possible into your presentation. (Kinesthetic refers to your sense of touch, your emotions and the movement of your muscles and joints. For more information on the different sensory channels, see chapter 14.)

If you're keen to engage your audience, the *How?* section is a good place for some interactive activities so that people can actually practise applying the content that has been discussed. For example, this is a good time to get your audience to

- turn to the person next to them and discuss what you have just said

- write something down that encourages them to think more deeply about the application of the content you have discussed

- move into a breakout room on your virtual platform to discuss

- perhaps even stand up and do something to practise using the skills you have just taught.

And always be sure that if you use an activity of any kind in your presentations (online or face to face), you debrief some of the findings by facilitating a question and answer session with your audience. That way the activity will always feel like it was a valuable part of your session and not simply an activity for the sake of an activity (which is very annoying to grown adults). For example, ask them 'What did you discuss?', 'What key points were you able to raise in your discussions?' or 'What did you learn from that experience?'

TIP

Michelle says,

'It's critical to debrief any interactivity or activities you set up with your audience so they feel meaningful.'

TRY THIS

1. Write down the logical steps your audience should take to implement your ideas.

2. Think of an interesting way to get your audience involved in your working example.

3. Plan out how you will instruct them to get involved.

Step 8: Provide any other information

In general, this step is where you address the needs of those people asking *What if?* and *What else?* It's the place in your presentation where you add in any extra information that you would like to cover that doesn't fit naturally into the other parts of the Persuasion Blueprint. It's also where you deliver the equivalent of a thank you to your audience and explain how they can stay in touch. To make this step a bit easier for you I suggest you divide it into three parts, as follows.

Step 8a: Other information

This is where you cover all those 'by the way…' points of interest. It's also where you can explore other applications and possibilities.

Step 8b: My pleasure

People often ask me when they should say, 'Thanks for coming' — and the answer is never! People often say 'thank you' at the start or the very finish of their presentations to be friendly and build rapport. The problem with this is that, by saying 'thank you', you're implying that your audience has just 'given' you something — and so you're thanking them for doing so. While this is a really nice thing to say and can help to build rapport, it implies that you now owe them. I recommend that you don't say 'thank you' at the end — your audience should be thanking you!

The alternative is to say something like:

- 'It's been my pleasure speaking with you today.'

- 'This has been fun!'

- 'I've enjoyed being with you today.'

- 'We've had a great session together.'

- 'This has been a terrific chance to discuss the important matter of xyz.'

Remember — you say this rapport-building statement to reflect your respect and thanks to your audience here, at Step 8 of the Persuasion Blueprint, not at the very end. The very end of your presentation is kept for your closing statement.

Step 8c: Contact details

This is where you put your contact details up on a slide, tell your audience your phone number, or explain how they can stay in touch and to contact you should they wish to discuss your presentation content further, once the presentation is over.

Giving your contact details at this time may seem odd. In fact, in my experience many presenters typically finish their presentation with a slide that tells the audience their contact details.

The reason it's good to place these contact details here (rather than at the very end, or in the framing at Step 5 of the Persuasion Blueprint), is that your contact details are important, but not as important as the next five steps leading to your close. I recommend you tuck them away at the beginning of the end to help you close in a memorable way with strength. (An example of how this works brilliantly in practice is provided in the next chapter.)

Step 9: Summarise your three key points

Now is the right time to remind the audience about your three key points. The reason I recommend three key points in a summary is because people remember things that come in threes. So your audience will remember your content more easily when you present your information to them in threes.

Adequately distilling your presentation to only the three main points can be harder than you might initially think. I suggest you make sure you go back to your Think/Feel/Do (chapter 2) and match your original intentions from your preparation with the content you plan to deliver.

Once you are sure that your intentions match your script, try to keep your summary to only three key messages to make it easy for your audience to remember your main points.

I also suggest that because you are in the *What if?* or *What else?* section of your presentation, you might choose to divide your three-part summary into one point from the *Why?*, one point from the *What?* and one point from the *How?* of the 4MAT System. This way you will re-engage all types of audience members.

Handy tip: I recommend you begin the summary section of your Persuasion Blueprint with the words, 'In summary'. When you say this at the start of the summary, people wake up! They often think something like, *Well, I haven't been listening that carefully, but this is the summary, so if I listen now it won't matter that I missed a bit.* Sad but true! If you are worried that when you say, 'In summary,' people might begin to pack up their things, or log off your virtual call, I recommend you say, 'In summary and before we close today'. That way people know that it's not the very end.

Step 10: Call your audience to action

Chapter 2 outlines the process of analysing your audience's current state and your desired state for them as a part of the Think/Feel/Do model. Now, at Step 10 of the Persuasion Blueprint, is where you tell your audience about the 'do' of your desired state that you planned in your analysis, way back at phase 1 of the presentation process.

After your audience has heard your summary, they are ready for you to call them to action. This step is where you explain what you need your audience to do now that they have listened to your message. The 'call to action' is often missing in the presentations I attend, so make sure you don't forget it. If you don't have a call to action, your audience won't know what you want them to do — so they won't do anything or they'll do their own thing. Don't be shy about asking for what you want. If you don't ask, you probably won't get it!

Here are some examples of the call to action:

- 'We are asking that you endorse our recommendations at the next board meeting in January.'

- 'We request that you embrace the new process changes, adhere to the new tasks and sequence, and execute these as per process timings.'

- 'Please go back to your desks and begin using the new process today.'

- 'I'd love to work with you; please choose me for this important development initiative.'

- 'Please report all faults to the hotline the minute your customers make you aware of them.'

- 'We look forward to hearing from you with your decision by next Wednesday.'

I enjoyed this call to action from Barack Obama on 24 July 2008:

> This is the moment when we must come together to save this planet. Let us resolve that we will not leave our children a world where the oceans rise and famine spreads and terrible storms devastate our lands.

Be sure you call your audience to action so they are crystal clear about what you expect of them now that they have listened to your message.

TRY THIS

1. Go back to your Think/Feel/Do analysis (chapter 2) where you initially planned your call to action in the 'do' section of the desired state.

2. Write your call to action for your working example after your summary so it's clear and unambiguous.

3. Remember the call to action goes at Step 10 of the Persuasion Blueprint.

Step 11: Manage questions and answers

The question and answer (Q&A) session of a presentation or online session is often the part that makes many presenters feel quite nervous. I think the nervousness comes from the uncertainty about what the audience might ask. I know that many people feel the Q&A is difficult to control, and no-one wants to look like a goose in front of their audience because they don't know how to answer a question.

Actually, my experience is that the Q&A is where you can really come out of yourself, convey your authentic self and showcase your intelligence and experience. Because you are often answering questions off the cuff and from your experience, you will find that you will probably speak more naturally and in a more relaxed manner, and come across as connected, sincere and authentic.

I believe it's a good idea for you to learn to facilitate the Q&A so you showcase your professional expertise. With a bit of planning and practice, you can make the Q&A section of your presentation an interesting and engaging part of your overall event. In my experience, it can actually be the best part of the presentation.

As the presenter, your role is generally to assist your audience to be relaxed, engaged and attentive throughout the Q&A — and there is a real art to it. So let's look at how you might ask for and then answer questions. Fun!

Encouraging your audience to ask some excellent questions

Have you ever asked your audience, 'Any questions?' and then had them stare blankly at you as though they were off with the fairies? The reason people don't respond well is because the question is too broad. So your audience's brains go into a massive spin-out trying to find something (in infinity) to ask, and it all becomes too massive and too hard — and no-one thinks of anything decent to ask you!

Let me explain further. If you're looking for some specific information on the internet, you need to type in the best key words for the search. If you type in key words that are too broad or not focused on the area you're interested in, you get a search result that doesn't provide the answers you need; whereas if you type the right key words, you get a much more useful search result. The same goes for eliciting questions from your audience.

As the presenter, you need to enter the best key words into your audience's brain so they can effortlessly search for a more specific response or question. This is called 'embedding search hooks', and it's where you tell the brain what to search for.

You can use something like the following script to help embed questions elegantly:

> Now it's time for some questions. For example, you may want to know more about x, or y, or maybe even z. Who would like to start? What questions do you have?

For example:

- 'You may have some questions. For example, you might like to ask me about the claims process, the specific clauses we are looking for, or maybe even the warning signs. Who would like to start? What questions do you have?'

- 'I'm looking forward to your questions. You might be wondering how we will deal with unexpected developments in our markets, or how we will track our performance, or even how we will prioritise between the different markets. Who would like to start? What questions do you have?'

Handy tip: You may remember from earlier in this chapter that some people have a preference to match and other prefer to mismatch. If you follow this sort of script, the mismatchers may ask you something entirely unrelated to the suggestions you've offered because they're clever and can tell that this is a bit of a set-up. To manage your mismatchers in the most effective way during the Q&A, you can put what I call an 'anything' question at 'y' of the template. For example:

You might have some questions at this time. Perhaps you'd like to know more about how we can access these tools, or about anything at all that we have discussed today. Maybe you'd even like to talk about the mechanisms we have in place for any bug resolutions. Who would like to begin the questions this afternoon?

You can see in this example that by saying 'anything', you're indicating that you're really happy to answer anything.

When you use this Q&A technique, you will reduce the weird silences, maintain the flow of your information and increase the chances of your audience asking you the exact question you'd like to answer!

Try this — it's great and it definitely works!

Answering questions like a professional

If you embed questions in your audience using the suggested script from the previous section, you will find you definitely get some questions rather than the usual silence. You need to know how to answer the questions so that you don't appear unprepared or less knowledgeable than you are. You don't want to seem foolish or incompetent. In fact, your ideal scenario during the Q&A is to showcase your professional expertise and respond to all the questions with confidence and ease — even if you don't always know the answer!

The Q&A really is the time to remain calm and inclusive of your entire audience. This way you'll be more likely to achieve what you want from the presentation.

You can use four steps to ensure you maintain rapport with everyone in the group throughout the Q&A section of your presentation. The steps are slightly different depending on whether you are presenting live or virtually.

ANSWERING A QUESTION IN A LIVE MEETING

Here are the four steps when answering a question in a face-to-face presentation:

1. *Acknowledge the question asker using their name:* Once you've waited for the questioner to finish asking their question, say something like, 'Thank you for your important question, Charlotte. And the reason it's important is because...' (Make your reason relate to the whole audience and their needs.) This is called 'giving status', and it's where you compliment the question asker and make them feel special. Giving status to an audience member causes a positive feeling in your audience, and encourages further questions because it demonstrates that you will reward questions. It also makes the question sound interesting to the whole audience and will draw them into wanting to know the answer.

2. *Paraphrase:* This is where you repeat the question in your own words. You do this in case the audience didn't hear the question and also to ensure that you heard the question and understood it correctly. Remember to also open your eye contact and body language out to the group as you repeat the question. You can use the 'Placater' posture (arms outstretched and palms up and open) and make sure your body demonstrates your intention to be inclusive. (I explain body postures in more detail in chapter 13.)

3. *Answer using the 4MAT structure:* Answer the question in an organised and structured way, so it's easy for everyone in your audience to understand your point. Stick to the relevant areas and remember to answer as succinctly as possible. If you can answer the question using a brief version of the 4MAT System (covering *Why?*, *What?*, *How?* and *What if?* or *What else?*) all the better!

4. *Check in:* Confirm that the questioner is happy with your answer. You might like to nod your head or give some direct eye contact. Or you could ask, 'How does that sound, Charlotte?' or 'Have I answered your question thoroughly enough, Charlotte?' This way if Charlotte is not happy with the answer she can help clarify with another question.

Handy tip: *Don't start your answer by asking, 'Did everyone hear Charlotte's question?' The reason is that most people probably didn't! Pointing this out makes either the audience members uncomfortable (because it's now obvious they were not listening) or Charlotte uncomfortable (because she didn't speak loudly or clearly enough). Simply repeat the question without checking whether people heard.*

ANSWERING A QUESTION IN A VIRTUAL MEETING

The four steps when answering a question in a virtual presentation are similar, but with just a few tweaks:

1. *Acknowledge the question asker using their name:* First wait for the questioner to finish their question (within reason, that is!), and then look right into your camera, imagining the face of the person to whom you are speaking, and say something like, 'Important question, Vijay, and the reason it's important is because...' Again, this is called giving status, and it makes people feel good. As in the previous example for live presenting, this approach also encourages further questions and, by making the question sound interesting to the whole audience, draws them into wanting to know the answer.

2. *Paraphrase:* This is where you repeat the question in your own words. You do this in case the online audience didn't hear the question and also to ensure that you heard the question and understood it correctly. Use the word, 'everyone' to wake everyone up and remind your virtual audience that you are talking to them all. For example, 'Everyone, what Vijay is asking is [repeat question]'.

3. *Answer using the 4MAT system:* Answer the question in an organised and structured way, so it's easy for everyone in

your audience to understand your point. Stick to the point and remember the famous comment from Thomas Jefferson, one of America's Founding Fathers: 'There's value in never using two words when only one will do'. Again, answer the question using a brief version of the 4MAT System if possible

4. *Check in:* Confirm that the questioner is happy with your answer. You could ask, 'How does that sound, Vijay?' or 'Have I answered your question thoroughly enough, Vijay?' This way, if Vijay is not happy with the answer, he can help clarify with another question.

I observed burns specialist Dr Fiona Wood AM presenting at the National Press Club in Canberra, Australia. Her presentation was excellent, engaging and absorbing — and her Q&A section was magnificent. I can't exactly quote what she said word for word, but she followed the four-step structure.

She said something to the effect of:

> Thank you for your question, Kerry. Kerry's question was *[here Dr Wood paraphrased the question and then paused]*. And the reason Kerry's question is relevant to all of you here is that I'm sure from time to time you have seen *[again Dr Wood paraphrased the issue, but in a completely new way]* happen. So you must also be wondering about the effect of...

Dr Wood repeated the issue Kerry raised again, and then answered the question. Finally, Dr Wood checked with Kerry that his question had been answered.

This was a great moment in the history of women presenting in business. Dr Wood's Q&A section had the entire audience sitting on the edge of their chairs, fascinated by everything she said! It was really splendid!

Answering something you've already covered

Ha! From time to time someone in your audience will ask you a question about something you've already covered. People simply don't listen to every single word we say all the time! Of course they will switch in and out of your message. My best tip for you is to be sure you don't say, 'As I said before, Margaret...' and make Margaret feel embarrassed — because now it's really obvious to Margaret (and everyone else in your audience) that Margaret wasn't listening! Be sure to respect your audience at all times. Just follow the four-step answer technique and answer briefly so you don't cause the rest of the audience (who were listening and know this is a repetition) to become bored.

Answering when you don't know the answer

If you don't know the answer to a question, keep the following in mind:

1. *Don't be defensive:* When you become stressed, you can't think straight. Remember it's all about the audience, so focus on them, smile authentically and be gracious. You can still go through the four-step answer technique, but in this case explain that you are going to have to look the answer up, research some more or discuss the issue with a colleague, and then you will come back to them with the answer.

2. *Don't fake it!* Your audience is smart and you will probably break rapport if they sense you are lying to them. Remember Friedrich Nietzsche's ominous words: 'I'm not upset that you lied to me, I'm upset that from now on I can't believe you'.

3. *Buy some time:* You can buy some time using psychotherapist Virginia Satir's Computer posture (also known by some as 'the thinker' — see chapter 13 for more). This is where you place one arm across your body with the other elbow resting on your hand and the other hand against your face. This slows down proceedings and gives you time to think about your answer. Then, either throw the question out to the group or postpone the answer. For example, simply explain you need time to look into the correct answer and will get back to them by a specific date.

Here are some examples of how to answer a question you don't have an immediate answer for:

*   'That's a good question, Georgia. *[pause]* I'm interested in what some of the rest of you here in the meeting today

think we could do to solve the dilemma Georgia raises about distribution of salary bonuses. *[pause]*

- 'That's an important question, Brady. *[pause]* I'd like to clarify the answer to your question with Chris from our technical department and I'll get back to you by Friday morning. Would that be okay with you, Brady? *[pause]*

Knowing who to look at when answering a question

When answering questions, either virtually or live, be careful of the 'moth-to-a-flame' syndrome. This is where you focus on the person who asked the question and exclude all others. Excluding the rest of your audience is almost certain to break rapport with the group at large and you will then have to try very hard to re-establish rapport. And all that singular attention and focus can also be potentially a bit too confronting for the question asker too. That's why the word 'everyone' is so important in virtual meetings. And in a live meeting, your eye contact with as many people as possible while you're answering questions says you're talking to everyone.

TIP

Michelle says,

'In a live meeting or presentation, try to look at as many of the people in the room as you can, so everyone feels included in your answer.'

Remembering the Q&A doesn't go at the end

The reason for placing your Q&A before the consequences and closing statement steps of your presentation — and not at the end of your presentation — is that sometimes, as you may know, audiences can take you off track with their questions. Whether you actually choose to answer these side-issue questions or not, your audience's attention will divert from your main message to the issues raised by the person asking the question.

When you are the presenter, you don't want your question askers to finish your presentation for you. What you want is for your audience to be really clear about what you want them to do, and about the positive and negative consequences of this action. You want to end with the final word. So that's why, after the Q&A section at Step 11 of the Persuasion Blueprint, you still have two more steps before you are finished.

TRY THIS

1. Think through the three things you'd like to embed as questions in your working example.

2. Write out your Q&A script.

3. Then write out some sample answers to the questions using the four-step answer technique.

4. Place this at Step 11 of the Persuasion Blueprint.

Step 12: Highlight negative and positive consequences

This is where you explain the negative and positive consequences of doing what you are asking. At this point in your presentation, you remind the audience about the things they will not achieve or the problems that could result from not proceeding, as well as the positive results or certain outcomes that can be achieved by moving towards your suggestion. Just like your WIIFM statement (Step 3 of the Persuasion Blueprint), this will stimulate both the people who move away from pain and the people who move towards reward.

For example:

- 'If we don't proceed with this project, the consequence will be x and y. When we do proceed, we will be able to achieve z within six months.'

- 'If we do nothing, inefficiencies will remain, frustrations will continue and customer disputes will increase. When we adopt the new process, we will certainly gain efficiency improvements, which means frustrations will be minimised and our customer disputes will reduce.'

TIP

Michelle says,

'Note that in this script you use the phrases, 'If we don't...' and 'When we do...'. In this way, you're highlighting the important implication that, of course, the audience will do as you have suggested.'

TRY THIS

1. Write out the negative and positive consequences for your working example.

2. Be sure to include 'if we don't and 'when we do' in your example script.

3. Place this at Step 12 of the Persuasion Blueprint.

Step 13: Close with a sizzle!

Have you ever been to a presentation where the presenter just finishes by saying 'Thanks' or 'That's it' or simply stares at you as you sit in their audience, hoping that you work out for yourself that they have come to the end of their presentation? Finishing your presentation like this will not allow you to maintain rapport with your audience — and it won't have you or your audience feeling very good about your presentation, either. It will leave everyone feeling flat.

You may agree that both the opening and the close of a presentation are critical to your overall presentation success. Your opening and close can also be the trickiest parts because knowing what to say can be difficult. I explain earlier in this chapter how to open your presentation. Let's now have a look at what needs to happen in your close, so that you finish with impact.

Perfecting your closing statement

The close is called the closing statement, and this is the final sentence of your presentation. It's the last thing you say so it's the last thing your audience hears — and can be the main thing they remember from your presentation.

Closing statements have a number of characteristics, including the following:

- *They're short and punchy:* They sell the sizzle of your message! They are exciting and motivational and are a bit like a slogan or a bumper sticker.

- *They're a signal:* They work as a sign to your audience that the presentation has come to an end. They link to your opening by reminding your audience of something you have said in your opening. In this way, they subtly help your audience realise that you are at the end of your message.

- *They're not a call to action:* You don't ask your audience for anything in your closing statement.

Here are some examples of strong closing statements.

- 'This is a game changer! And each of you is the Game Designer!'

- 'This is an exciting initiative for all of us. Our team ensures our customers receive the service they expect.'

- 'Customers are happier when they win prizes as part of their purchase, and we are here to make our customers happy.'

- 'ABC team takes care of your security. We have a real opportunity to make a significant improvement to the way we operate today.'

- 'ABC is a highly skilled technical group, working behind the scenes to guarantee Company X provides a great service for our customers.'

Avoiding another call to action

The reason you don't ask your audience to do something or give you something in the close is that in many cultures, and certainly in Australia (where I live), people don't like to be sold to. You may remember that you have already asked your audience for what you want at Step 10 of the Persuasion Blueprint — the step that is called the call to action. So you have already called your audience to action. They have heard you and they understand what you want from them, so you don't need to ask twice.

TRY THIS

1. Write a short, punchy closing statement for your working example.

2. Be sure that your closing statement links to your opening and ends your presentation with an obvious sizzle.

TOP TIPS
for scripting your presentation

- Consider all steps in the Persuasion Blueprint so you know what to say to your audience and maximise the likelihood of changing their behaviour — whether you're presenting online or live.

- Use the Persuasion Blueprint in the correct order unless you think that swapping the order will further increase your ability to influence your audience to do what you want.

- Ensure you open your presentation in a way that builds rapport. Inclusive statements reflect what your audience members already know to be true and, therefore, help you build strong rapport.

- Remember to motivate your audience using the WIIFM (What's in it for me?) language pattern: reduce, maintain and improve.

- Manage your audience's objections using the POO technique: state the objection, say 'and', 'so', or pause, try using the words 'actually' or 'in fact', lead to your solution, and finish with the word 'because' and a justification.

- Control and relax your audience using frames that set the boundaries, including explaining your credibility to give confidence to your audience.

- Cover the *What?* and *How?* sections of your presentation (Steps 6 and 7) as thoroughly as your audience needs.

- The audience may well have forgotten most of what you have said by the time you get to the end, so remember to articulate your three key messages in your summary.

- Remember to call your audience to action so they know what to do next.

- The Q&A is an opportunity for you to showcase your professional expertise, and can be just as controlled as the rest of your presentation.

- Make sure you include the negative and positive consequences.

- Don't say 'thank you' at the end of the presentation — instead, use a closing statement to conclude your presentation with a sizzle!

CHAPTER 6

Finalising your Persuasion Blueprint

In the previous chapter, I take you through all of the steps in my Persuasion Blueprint. In this chapter, I take you through an example script, to really see how all the steps play out and work together, and cover a few other aspects that may come up as you work through the steps.

Firstly, let's look at how my Persuasion Blueprint connects to the 4MAT System outlined in chapter 3.

Relating the Persuasion Blueprint to the 4MAT System

As covered in chapter 3, the 4MAT System is all about answering four main questions to increase the chances of all members of your audience having their needs meet. The four questions are *Why?*, *What?*, *How?* and *What if?* or *What else?* These four main questions are also answered through the steps of my Persuasion Blueprint.

Here's how the language patterns of the two systems relate:

- Steps 0 to 5 of the Persuasion Blueprint answer the *Why?* question.

- Step 6 answers the *What?* question.

- Step 7 answers the *How?* question.

- Steps 8 to 13 answer the *What if?* or *What else?* question.

Looking at an example script

Table 6.1 shows you a thorough five-step analysis process (refer to chapter 2) for a real presentation that was created by a client of mine. I have changed his real name to Steve at his request. The names of the organisation and departments have been also been changed.

Table 6.2 (overleaf) shows you the real-life presentation that was then created using the Persuasion Blueprint and in response to the practical application of the five-step analysis shown in table 6.1. You can use this example to get a sense of what a presentation looks like when it incorporates the five-step analysis, and when it flows from one step to the next.

Table 6.1 Five-step analysis

Step	Answer
Topic	Climate change
Goal	To convince the audience to care about the problem of climate change

Step	Answer
Purpose This is the interesting name of your presentation. Goes on the first slide and meeting invitation.	How we are going to solve climate change?
Leading statement • Key message • Often contentious • Must be reasonable	Climate change is real, urgent and can be solved.

Audience analysis

Current state:

- What do they *think* of me, my message, and my company/team?

- What do they *feel* about me, my message, and company/team?

- What is my audience *doing*?

Desired state:

- What do I want my audience to *think* about me (personal brand), my message and my company/team?

- What do I want my audience to *feel* about me, my message and my team/company?

- What do I want my audience to *do*? What is my call to action?

Current state:

- *Me:* Unknown, potentially not credible, biased (towards renewables).

- *Message:* Not sure what to believe or who to trust. Has a bias toward renewables rather than green energy.

- *Team/company:* Part of business that is slow moving and bureaucratic.

Desired state:

- *Me:* Interesting, smart, gets it.

- *Message:* This is important, truthful and within reach. Green energy is an excellent solution to the problem of climate change.

- *Team/company:* Doing incredible things for Australia.

Table 6.2 Fully worked example of the Persuasion Blueprint

Step	Statement	Category
0: Icebreaker	Our thin, fragile atmosphere sustains all known life in the universe. My name is Steve and I'm the CEO of Company X. Let's talk today about the existential threat that climate change poses, and how we are going to solve it.	
1: Build rapport	We know from scientists that humans are the cause of climate change. And the early indications of a changing climate are already evident. We also know that human ingenuity and inventions have solved many problems and created many opportunities throughout history.	
2: Assert perspective with leading statement	Climate change is real, urgent and entirely solvable.	
3: Motivate audience — WIIFM *reduce*	If we act decisively, we can *limit* the damage that we are doing.	
WIIFM *maintain*	We can *preserve* our way of life.	*Why?*
WIIFM *improve*	And we can *create* huge opportunities for ourselves and our children.	
4: Manage objections	I realise that you've heard this all before, and that we live in a 'post-truth' world.	
	I also understand that many of us feel disempowered or think Australia's role in this is insignificant compared to the likes of China and the United States.	
	And so … it's more important than ever that we pay attention to our scientists, realise we have some control and appreciate Australia's crucial role both morally and economically in solving this challenge.	
	Because nothing is more important.	
5: Control and relax audience with frames	I'd like to invite you to put away your phones for the next 10 minutes as we discuss the issue. Feel free to take some notes in the accompanying handout.	

Step	Statement	Category
6: Deliver facts, figures and data to answer the *What?* question	The increases in the Earth's temperature and the changes to our climate are caused by the build-up of CO_2 and other greenhouse gases in our atmosphere.	
	CO_2 concentrations are at their highest levels in at least 800 000 years — we are in uncharted territory.	
	Mean temperatures have already risen by 1.1 degrees since Industrialisation and, on current settings, we're on track for an overall warming of 2 to 2.5 degrees Celsius by the end of the century.	*What?*
	Adverse weather events are more frequent and more extreme. Sea levels are rising at an accelerating pace. And scientists tell us that these effects will continue for centuries if we don't reverse course soon.	
	I am the CEO of a company that has invested almost $2 billion in over 600 projects throughout Australia over the past decade, and we aim to repeat this success and more over the decade ahead.	
7: Explain the steps to answer the *How?* question	Renewable energy from solar and wind is now cheaper and more efficient than energy from fossil fuels such as coal, gas and oil. Last year the International Energy Agency stated that solar power is the cheapest form of energy generation in history. We must now deploy these technologies at scale throughout to transform our electricity system to one that is exclusively renewable.	*How?*
	The electrification of transport and heating will save us money as consumers, make our world safer and reduce emissions.	
	Battery storage and other energy storage technologies are needed to ensure we have energy when we need it. Costs do need to come down. And the good news is that the technology is advancing rapidly.	

(continued)

Table 6.2 Fully worked example of the Persuasion Blueprint (cont'd)

Step	Statement	Category
	We cannot get to net zero without carbon capture and storage. Methods are emerging to store carbon in our soils and permanently underground.	
	The manufacture of hydrogen by splitting water is technically possible and costs are projected to come down rapidly, helping to solve the remaining harder to abate sectors such as long-distance transport and heavy industry.	
8a: Provide other info	One more thing that may interest you is that carbon is not the only challenge. We need to reduce our methane emissions too. Methane is a powerful greenhouse gas that is responsible for around one-third of the warming we've experienced to date. We must stop fugitive emissions from fossil fuel supply chains, and we must deal with emissions from agriculture too.	*What if?* or *What else?*
8b: My pleasure	It has been my pleasure to talk to you today.	
8c: Contact details	I can be contacted via my LinkedIn profile or Twitter handle — both of which are on screen now.	
9: Summary	In summary	
Why	Climate change is a real and present danger, and we must act decisively now.	
What	It is happening because of our continued use of fossil fuels, from agriculture and from the choices we make as consumers.	
How	Climate change can be solved by deploying known technologies at scale, and by investing in R&D for the things that aren't yet solved.	
10: Call to action	You can help by learning about the solutions, making small changes to the way you live your lives, and by convincing your friends and family to do the same. Visit Company *X*'s website to learn more!	

Step	Statement	Category
11: Q&A (x, y, z)	We've got time for a few questions, so please raise your hand and a mic will be sent over to you. Perhaps you'd like to know what you personally can do or more about anything at all that's on your mind about climate change, or you may want to ask about a specific technology you've heard me talk about today.	
12: Highlight negative and positive consequences with 'if' and 'when'	If we don't act quickly to address this problem, we risk catastrophic climate impacts for decades and perhaps centuries ahead. When we take this seriously and act decisively, we can make the changes needed and protect our way of life and create enormous opportunities.	
13: Closing statement	Climate change is real, urgent and solvable.	

Isn't that just a terrific example?

Some final pointers

As you work on the final draft of your Persuasion Blueprint, a few remaining questions and aspects might pop up. The following sections aim to cover these areas.

Altering the steps

Have you ever seen those paint by numbers activities or colour by numbers apps? They're for people who want to learn how to create a beautiful artwork. The assumption with the paint by numbers activities is that the potential artist doesn't yet know how to paint an artwork by themselves, so they follow the number system and paint the sections as assigned. At the end of the process, the artist has created a painting! Yippee! Whether you are an artist or not, you can likely imagine that if you didn't know how to paint, the paint by numbers system would help you learn about how colours go together and what makes a beautiful painting.

My first degree out of school was a fine arts degree, so I don't need to 'paint by numbers' because I already know how to mix my paints and apply them to a canvas to create a work of art. (In fact, we have many of them hanging in our home.) I do have friends and family who have used paint by numbers activities, though, and to this day they have them hanging on the walls of their homes, all framed and fabulous and looking terrific. Guess what? You'd never know they had followed a simple, stepped approach in a logical manner to create that painting. And they aren't going to tell you they did it that way, either!

The process and the results are exactly the same with my Persuasion Blueprint. I have designed the Persuasion Blueprint to help you learn how to put certain language patterns and chunks of information together in a logical order so that you can be as engaging and influential as possible in all your presentations and meetings. The system is perfect for you if you feel you're not sure of how to do this for yourself with guaranteed results. You don't have to follow the Persuasion Blueprint perfectly. If you're not sure how to maximise the likelihood of changing your audience's behaviour, I recommend you follow the Persuasion Blueprint to the letter! This is the best way to make sure you achieve your desired outcome because the Persuasion Blueprint was created with an understanding of what the audience needs, not what is most comfortable for you.

> **TIP**
>
> **Michelle says,**
>
> 'The Persuasion Blueprint was created with an understanding of what your audience needs, not what is most comfortable for you.'

When you think that swapping the steps around will maximise the likelihood of achieving your outcomes, then go for it!

TRY THIS

1. Think of a presentation you have coming up, either online or in person.

2. Work through the five-step analysis model in chapter 2.

3. Then storyboard your presentation using the guidance in chapter 4.

4. Next, work through the steps from chapter 5 one at a time, and notice how influential your message is when it is crafted in this way.

You can also download a template for your presentation design from my website to help you — just go to www.michellebowden.com.au/howtopresent.

Using palm cards or notes

If you are really keen to engage your audience, then at least trying to deliver your presentation without using any notes or slides as a crutch is a good idea.

Just remember — your audience members are more likely to be convinced by what you say if they feel an affiliation with you and your message, and if you command credibility as the presenter. If you have to keep referring to your notes (or, worse, turning around to see what's on your slides or (if online) flicking your eyes around your screen), you suggest to your audience that you don't know your message well enough or that you do not respect your audience because you have not taken the required time to adequately prepare.

Regular reference to notes also causes you to break eye (or camera) contact and rapport with your audience, giving them opportunities to lose focus. This will have a direct impact on your credibility. So give some rehearsal a go (see chapter 9). Then try presenting with your notes to the side.

Using an electronic tablet for notes

Using a tablet such as an iPad to display your notes isn't a great idea, unless you can place everything on one screen. You will find that you become very distracted as you scroll on the tablet to find where you are up to (whether presenting online or face to face). You can easily lose your place and you will certainly break rapport with your audience when you're not looking at them enough. Another downside of using the tablet is that often the screen has a glare, which prevents you from seeing the text clearly.

What if you forget a point?

If you forget a point or go blank, it's important that you remember that it's not the end of the world. Great presenters lose their train of thought all the time and audience members typically don't notice little mistakes. Don't apologise or make a big deal about the fact you have forgotten something — audience members will then be distracted and track for further mistakes you might make! The audience wants you to be confident, so show them you are confident and move on to what is important.

If you have used the storyboard technique to design your presentation, you could look up and try to see an imaginary storyboard with your 4MAT System and sticky notes on the ceiling (above your eye line). This might stimulate your visual memory.

It's also important to remember to keep breathing right into your belly, so you keep your oxygen flowing. Remember, oxygen in your brain means increased clarity of thought.

Handy tip: If you still can't remember a point or where you're up to, then it's completely fine to take a drink of water and check your notes.

TOP TIPS

for finalising your Persuasion Blueprint

- The Persuasion Blueprint was created with an understanding of what the audience needs, not what is most comfortable for you.

- It's fine to change the steps around if you have completed a five-step analysis and know that the prescribed order is not the best one for your particular audience.

- If you're really keen to engage your audience, it's a good idea to at least try to deliver your presentation without using any notes or slides as a crutch.

- If you forget a point, don't apologise or make a big deal about the fact you have forgotten. Take a deep breath, drink some water, check your notes and just keep going!

CHAPTER 7

Watch your language!

Presenters regularly use a variety of statements or turns of phrase that are very clever and powerful, and engage their audience. Unfortunately, other statements can be quite a turn-off — and sometimes we're not even aware that we're using them. Let's first look at some of the common expressions that are off-putting to your audience — and good news, I will suggest an alternative for any of the common words or statements that I recommend you don't use. Later in this chapter, I then provide some tips and tricks for really firing up your language — and your audience — in all your virtual and face-to-face presentations.

Avoid turning your audience off

After all your planning, you don't want to turn your audience off by using words and phrases that reduce the rapport and confidence your audience feels towards you — or just plain annoy them. In the following sections, I run through some of these words and phrases, and what to use in their place.

'For those of you who don't know me ...'

This combination of words is not inclusive in nature. What about the people who do know you? I suggest you replace this option with something like, 'I have met some of you before and I look forward to getting to know everyone here today. My name is...' Or simply, 'My name is...' Or you could try, 'It's wonderful to see you here today. I'm [insert name].'

'Um', 'ah', 'like' and 'so' as filler words

Most presenters use a number of filler words when they don't know what to say, or to fill the quiet space that would be better served with a pause and a deep breath. Some of these words are 'um', 'ah', 'like' and 'so'. Using these filler words is not a great idea. As an alternative, remember to pause and breathe with confidence. Pause is powerful!

In one situation, 'so' is a good option — when you are managing objections (refer to chapter 5). In this context, 'so' is fine to use as an inoffensive, unemotive joining word instead of 'but' or 'however', which negate what you have just said.

TIP

Michelle says,

'It is close to impossible to remove filler words when you present unless you remove them from your everyday conversation.'

TRY THIS

1. Consider whether you regularly use filler words such as 'um', 'ah', 'like' and 'so' when you communicate.

2. Make a plan to pause and breathe instead of saying words that don't work for you or your audience.

3. If you're not sure what you say when you present, ask a trusted colleague or friend to listen out for some of these habits.

4. Make a plan to remove filler words from your everyday conversations today!

'Okay', 'basically', 'obviously', 'you know?' and 'alright?'

Certain words can make your audience disagree with you. Avoiding these words is a good idea, because you want your audience to be in rapport with you for as much of your presentation as possible.

What are these words, you ask? They are 'okay', 'basically', 'obviously', 'you know?', and 'alright?'

When you say these words, the people in your audience who are predisposed to mismatch your ideas (refer to chapter 5) may say to themselves, 'No, it isn't!' or 'No, I don't!' These words encourage them to start looking for other parts of your message that might be inconsistent or inaccurate in some way.

Consider replacing these words with a pause and a diaphragmatic breath. You will find you can eventually eliminate this habit when you speak.

'You' versus 'I'

Presenters commonly say phrases such as, 'I think...', 'I want you to...' or 'I need you to...' when they present. Before using such phrases yourself, stop and think about your audience. How do you think your audience feels when you say 'I' this or 'I' that? Please remember, if you take one main point away from this book make sure it is this: It's not about you. It's all about the audience!

When you think about it, it makes sense, doesn't it? Your audience isn't generally that interested in what you think, what you want or what you need. Your audience is more caught up with what they think, what they want and what they need!

When you communicate in presentations (online or live) and even more generally at work, make sure you use words that include, incorporate or bring in your audience. Help them feel that you are there for them, not separate from them, and not demanding of them.

When people feel included, and equal or similar, they will generally feel a stronger rapport or connection with you. This means they will be more likely to do what you want and change their behaviour if you ask them to.

Instead of saying, 'I think', 'I want' or 'I need' — which may appear self-centred, self-indulgent and demanding, and not audience-focused — try saying 'you', 'your', 'our', 'together', 'we' and (my favourite choice) 'let's'.

TIP

Michelle says,

'Don't forget: It's not about you. It's all about the audience.'

TRY THIS

1. Ask a trusted adviser if you say, 'okay', 'basically', 'obviously', 'you know?', or 'alright?' when you present.

2. Consider whether you should incorporate words such as 'you', 'your', 'we' and 'our' in your working example.

3. Make a plan to pause and breathe instead of saying words that don't work for you or your audience.

Using electrifying, polished language in your presentation

Why is it that some people are more charismatic as leaders than others? In fact, why are you influenced by some people, and not by others? Why is it that you believe the speeches of certain leaders and not others? And what is it that makes politicians such as John F Kennedy, Martin Luther King Jr or Barack Obama so memorable?

Of course, communication isn't the only important characteristic of an effective leader, but it's certainly one of the top characteristics, wouldn't you say? Intelligence and empathy, and the ability to develop an effective strategy and see a plan to fruition, are fundamental for a great leader. And great leaders also inspire, excite and motivate — and nothing inspires, excites and motivates people like a great presentation.

> **TIP**
>
> **Michelle says,**
>
> 'Great leaders inspire, excite and motivate.'

As well as avoiding words and phrases that make your audience tune out (or, worse, turn them off), you can also add in some words and language tricks that make your message more powerful — and improve how much of that message your audience takes away with them. The following sections outline some of these.

Using definite language

'Confident' is a word that many of us would like our audiences to say or think about us as presenters. As the author Samuel Johnson wisely said, 'Self-confidence is the first requisite to great undertakings.' One way to engender that confidence is through the words we choose to use.

Unfortunately, presenters often use a number of less confident words to soften their message (sometimes without even realising it). These unconfident words — such as 'hope', 'guess', 'trying' and 'might' — send the message that you aren't quite sure about what you are saying. Coming across as confident and convincing to your audience is going to be difficult if your language is not strong and definite. Some alternative expressions are 'it will', 'it is', 'I'm sure' and 'I know'.

So when you are communicating at work, try to use definite language as often as possible.

Adding power words

Power words are action verbs. They are words that you can use to help make your statements stronger. By using strong action verbs, your words become clearer and more concise, because you're not having to add adjectives or adverbs to clarify. I suggest you consider using some relevant power words in your presentation so you increase the strength of your message.

Here are some examples of power words. For a full list, visit my website at www.michellebowden.com.au/howtopresent.

Abbreviated	Activated	Advertised
Abolished	Adapted	Advocated
Absorbed	Addressed	Affected
Accelerated	Adjusted	Aided
Accompanied	Administered	Allocated
Accomplished	Admitted	Amended
Achieved	Adopted	Amplified
Acquired	Advanced	Analysed

Anticipated	Benchmarked	Collected
Applied	Benefited	Combined
Appointed	Billed	Committed
Assessed	Blocked	Communicated
Assigned	Bolstered	Completed
Assisted	Boosted	Composed
Assumed	Captured	Conceived
Attained	Cast	Conceptualised
Attracted	Challenged	Condensed
Audited	Changed	Conducted
Augmented	Channelled	Conserved
Authorised	Circulated	Consolidated
Automated	Clarified	Critiqued
Awarded	Classified	Cultivated
Balanced	Coached	Customised
Bargained	Collaborated	Dealt

TRY THIS

1. Go back to your working example and be sure you have used inclusive and definite language throughout your script.

2. Include some power words in your working example too.

Working in linguistic techniques

A number of linguistic devices or techniques are used by great orators to motivate and inspire. These techniques are alliteration, conduplicatio, epistrophe, anaphora and tricolon. They help embed your key messages and inspire your audience. And the good news is that you can use them too!

In the following sections, I show you how you can develop a love of the English language to help paint evocative images with your words. More importantly, you can captivate your audiences by using these wonderful linguistic devices in your presentations. Although some people consider these techniques 'advanced', they are actually fast, easy and powerful things to try. Okay — let's get started.

TIP

Michelle says,

'Language is a magical tool that has the power to captivate, mesmerise and inspire your audience.'

USING ALLITERATION

You may remember learning about alliteration at school. Alliteration is where you repeat the same consonant sound at the beginning of two or more words in close succession. The purpose of alliteration is to create a consistent pattern that catches the mind's eye and focuses the audience's attention. It's used frequently in news headlines, corporate names, literary titles, advertising and nursery rhymes. If you, like me, can still remember your nursery rhymes (even though you may not have been a child for a while), you no doubt already realise that alliteration helps your audience remember your key points — because it's catchy. Repeating the same or a similar letter is not sufficient; you must use a repetition of sound.

You can use alliteration to emphasise a key message or phrase, and fix it in your audience's mind. Alliteration is commonly used in poetry and tongue twisters. It is also sometimes used in advertising taglines and business names to make them more memorable, such as Krispy Kreme and Coca-Cola.

Well-known examples of alliteration include some famous tongue-twisters:

- Peter Piper picked a peck of pickled peppers.

- She sells seashells by the seashore.

- Round the rugged rock the ragged rascal ran.

And numerous examples of alliteration have been a part of corporate speak for years. Some simple examples are 'boom or bust', 'sink or swim', 'back to basics', 'balance the books' and, of course, 'perfect preparation prevents poor performance'.

Both US president John F Kennedy and civil rights leader Martin Luther King Jr were known to use alliteration well. And in the 2004 Democratic National Convention keynote speech that brought Barack Obama to prominence, Obama said, 'Do we participate in a politics of cynicism or do we participate in a politics of hope?' In 1985 the *Wall Street Journal* adopted the slogan 'The daily diary of the American dream', while the *Washington Post* adopted 'Democracy dies in darkness' in 2017.

If you're keen to try to use some alliteration, I suggest you plan out the purpose of your presentation using the five-step analysis process (refer to chapter 2), then design your message using the 4MAT System (chapter 3) and storyboarding (chapter 4), and finally add the Persuasion Blueprint (chapter 5). Be as clear as possible on your key messages. Once you have narrowed down your key messages and written out what you want to say, go over your notes with a fine-toothed comb, looking for places where you could use alliteration to embed your key messages and make them more memorable.

Handy tip: Work within your own personal style and pattern of speech when adding any linguistic tricks into your presentation to ensure they sound natural and unforced. Then try it out!

USING CONDUPLICATIO

Conduplicatio sounds like a made-up word. Actually it is the repetition of a key word or words in successive sentences or phrases.

Here is an example of conduplicatio:

> *Success* is what we are aiming for in this business. When we achieve *success*, we will all feel immense, overwhelming gratification. Because it is in the achievement of *success* that our long hours, persistence and sacrifices are justified.

US senator and presidential candidate Robert F Kennedy also used conduplicatio when he said the following after the assassination of Martin Luther King Jr in 1968:

> So I ask you tonight to return home, to say *a prayer* for the family of Martin Luther King... but more importantly to say *a prayer* for our own country, which all of us love — *a prayer* for understanding and that compassion of which I spoke.

USING EPISTROPHE

Epistrophe is the repetition of a word or phrase at the end of every clause.

Barack Obama's famous 2008 New Hampshire speech provides an example of epistrophe, in his repetition of the sentence 'Yes, we can'. You may remember that these words echoed around the globe, rallying supporters far and wide:

> It was a creed written into the founding documents that declared the destiny of a nation.
>
> *Yes, we can.*
>
> It was whispered by slaves and abolitionists as they blazed a trail towards freedom through the darkest of nights.
>
> *Yes, we can.*

It was sung by immigrants as they struck out for distant shores and pioneers who pushed westward against an unforgiving wilderness.

Yes, we can.

USING ANAPHORA

Anaphora is one of my favourite techniques and I use it all the time as a speaker and in my business pitches. This is when you deliberately repeat the same word (or words) at the beginning of successive phrases or sentences. It's one of the most commonly used rhetorical techniques and you will hear it used regularly by politicians. The untrained speaker might think it repetitive. And, yes, it is meant to be repetitive — its repetitiveness is what makes it effective. You may know of the famous speech from 1940 by British prime minister Winston Churchill in which he repeated the words 'we shall':

> *We shall fight* on the beaches, *we shall fight* on the landing grounds, *we shall fight* in the fields and in the streets, *we shall fight* in the hills; *we shall* never surrender.

And here's another example from Steve Jobs, the famous Apple CEO. In his Stamford Commencement speech in 2005, Jobs said:

> *You have to trust* that the dots will somehow connect in your future. *You have to trust* in something — your gut, destiny, life.

And, of course, Martin Luther King Jr's 'I have a dream' speech of 1963 used this powerful linguistic device too. Here is an extract:

> ...*I have a dream* that one day this nation will rise up and live out the true meaning of its creed: We hold these truths to be self-evident, that all men are created equal. *I have a dream* that one day on the red hills of Georgia, the sons of former slaves and the sons of former slave owners will be able to sit down together at a table of brotherhood. *I have a dream* that one day even the

state of Mississippi, a state sweltering with the heat of injustice, sweltering with the heat of oppression, will be transformed...

Julia Gillard even used the technique twice at the start of her (unscripted and now famous) 'misogyny' speech in parliament in 2012:

> *I will not* be lectured about sexism and misogyny by this man. *I will not*. And the Government *will not* be lectured about sexism and misogyny by this man. *Not* now, *not* ever.

And here's an example from one of my clients:

> *The more* we target the right customers, *the more* we will sell and *the more* profit we will make.

USING TRICOLON

Tricolon is also known as the rule of three. No-one seems to know why the human brain is able to absorb and remember information more effectively when it is presented in threes. Again, this technique is something that inspiring leaders use in their speeches, and in your presentations it will help you to stand out as a charismatic, inspirational, powerful presenter (see what I did there?).

According to some commentators, 22 tricolons were used in Barack Obama's inauguration speech alone, and 14 in his 2009 speech in Prague (to take two speeches at random).

Here's an example for you:

> I stand here today humbled by the task before us, grateful for the trust you have bestowed, mindful of the sacrifices borne by our ancestors.

You can no doubt spot plenty of opportunities to use any or all of these linguistic devices in your business presentation. Let's say you have originally written, 'These KPIs are going to be a stretch for many of us'. You can see that this is a bit of a 'nothing' way to express the point. To make this point more inspiring, all you need to do is add a tricolon. That is, add two more aspects to the word 'stretch'. For example:

These KPIs are going to be a **challenge**. These KPIs are going to be a real **stretch** for many of us. And, yes, these KPIs are going to be a **wonderful** way for us to really achieve something exciting, real and meaningful this quarter!

See how it works? In addition, I added anaphora at the start and added an extra tricolon at the conclusion of the point with 'exciting, real and meaningful'. You can have a lot of fun with this once you get going!

Here's another example. You might be planning to say to your manager that you'd really like to work on a specific project. But if you're sick of asking for more responsibility and being ignored, overlooked or passed over — in fact, if you're sick of feeling like you have way more knowledge, skills and abilities than people give you credit for — why not use an anaphora and two tricolons like this:

This project is something I'd like to work on very much. This project would utilise the skills I've developed in my role so far, and this project would give me a chance to show you how committed, excited and capable I am of achieving results for our team.

I mean, really, how could they say no?

Let's say you were going to say in your presentation, 'This year was a tough year and even so we all pulled together to achieve a pleasing result'. Now this is okay as a statement, but it's not very memorable.

Break the single sentence into three sentences, and begin with something more memorable. In this example, I've used tricolon and anaphora together:

We pulled together even though it was a tough year. We pulled together and formed a cohesive team. We pulled together and produced a very pleasing result of 5 per cent earnings, and now we're set for an exciting, stimulating and results-focused fourth quarter.

Actually, if you look again, you will see that I've used these linguistic devices in a variety of places throughout this book — can you spot them?

Michelle says,

'Language has the power to make you worthy of remark – language has the power to make you remarkable.'

Using these devices in your workplace presentations

Despite the fact that many people use these clever linguistic devices with such elegance, mastery and artfulness, it's pretty common for people to feel scared of using them because they are worried about sounding artificial, false or dramatic. Here are some tips for using any or all of these powerful linguistic devices:

- Write out your presentation script (as you would usually do).

- Then go over your script and see where you can introduce the various linguistic devices.

- For alliteration, work out if you can change some words so that three or more words have the same first letter.

- For epistrophe, try repetition of the final words.

- For tricolon, all you need to do is look through your script for places you have used a noun, a verb or an adjective, and simply add two more!

- For anaphora, decide where you might repeat the first few words of a sentence.

It's truly not as difficult as it might seem at first. Have some fun with this!

Michelle says,

'Combine these clever language patterns with dynamic vocal delivery and a strong, anchored posture and you're on the way to having the engagement, charisma and influence you desire!'

TRY THIS

Take some time now to work these linguistic devices into the script for your next presentation, and notice what an improvement this makes to your overall effectiveness.

Using rhetorical questions

Another exciting way to make your presentation — and your message — stand out and be memorable is through the use of rhetorical questions.

What is a rhetorical question? A rhetorical question is a question that you ask and then answer yourself. Ha ha! See what I did there? You don't expect your audience to answer it out loud. You do pause and give the audience a moment to think about what the answer might be before answering.

Rhetorical questions are a clever engagement technique because as long as the audience is listening to you when you ask the question, no other thought can co-exist in their mind, except the answer to your question. Let me show you. You might ask, 'Why is this important?' As long as your audience is listening, the only thing your audience can think about right now is, *Yes, why is this important?* As a result, the audience is more likely to concentrate and listen to what you have to say.

Why not use the questions from the 4MAT System to guide your use of rhetorical questions? For example:

- Why is this important?

- Why should we do this?

- What's in it for you to approve this idea?

- What is the challenge?

- What is our recommended solution?

- What is the issue on the table?

- Who is involved?

- When should we take action?

- How might we solve this?

- How will we fix this?

- What are the next steps?

- What do we need to do now?

- What if we don't act now?

- What happens once you agree with the proposal to proceed?

- How are we going to achieve this?

- What if we don't do this as requested?

My recommendation is that you use as many rhetorical questions as seems natural in your presentation.

TIP

Michelle says,

'Remember to place a slight pause after your rhetorical question to make your audience more likely to try to answer it in their mind.'

TRY THIS

- Plan out where you might be able to ask some rhetorical questions in your presentation.

- Practise delivering your rhetorical question so that you use the correct mini-pause before you answer, and the correct vocal intonation so you really engage your audience.

TOP TIPS
for watching your language

- Pause and breathe diaphragmatically instead of using filler words that break rapport with your audience.

- Ensure the words you say help your audience to agree rather than disagree with you. Try to avoid saying 'okay', 'basically', 'obviously', 'you know?' and 'alright?'

- Use audience-focused, inclusive language throughout your presentations, such as 'you', 'your', 'our', 'together', 'we'.

- Try some definite language, such as 'it is', 'I know', 'it will', so you appear confident and sure of yourself.

- Add power words to help you increase the strength of your message.

- Consider using linguistic devices such as alliteration, conduplicatio, epistrophe, anaphora, tricolon and rhetorical questions to ensure your messages are even more memorable for your audience.

CHAPTER 8

The art of storytelling

Stories have been with us since time began. They are a wonderful way for you to convey your message so your audience finds you interesting, engaging and memorable. As my good friend — and personal branding expert — Monica Rosenfeld says, 'Stories give us the opportunity to break down barriers, stir conversation and inspire positive change.'

A technique for telling memorable stories

The three main storytelling techniques are the 'hero's journey', the 'magic formula' story and the Persuasion Blueprint.

I covered the Persuasion Blueprint in great detail in chapter 5 and you may like to go back and read that chapter with a 'storytelling' filter in your mind.

The hero's journey is the model that movie makers follow in movies from *Pretty Woman* to *Harry Potter*. It is a wonderful structure if you've got the time and patience to follow all of the steps.

When it comes to telling captivating and memorable stories in business presentations — live or online — you can't go past the magic formula storytelling technique. This technique was developed by writer Dale Carnegie, who authored the famous book *How to Win Friends and Influence People*.

The magic formula for storytelling is a really simple technique to use. You simply cover three main aspects:

1. *Incident:* Tell the story — this is where you deliver a short, interesting account (the incident) to your audience.

2. *Point:* Some storytellers tell the story, tell the story and tell the story — and you sit there thinking, *Get to the point!* It's really important that you deliver the point of your story. Don't assume it's obvious to your audience.

3. *Benefit:* This is where you link your story and the point of your story with the people in your audience.

TIP

Michelle says,

'A story told well is compelling for your audience and can help you convey your key messages more effectively.'

Magic formula storytelling example

In my presentations, I sometimes tell a story about a fund manager delivering a boring, self-focused, 'blah, blah, blah' presentation. In the following sections, I include my script for this story, broken into the three sections of the magic formula for storytelling, to show how I tell the story, make my point and make the link between the story and my audience.

INCIDENT: TELL THE STORY

I once observed a fund manager present to a group of financial planners at a conference. His role was to influence the planners in the room to invest their clients' money in his fund. He made the classic mistake of putting up the first slide, with a small group of numbers printed neatly in the bottom right hand corner. It said 1/46! So what? Well, the presentation was only going to last 45 minutes! The speaker was going to show more than one technical slide per minute.

What followed is what is commonly known as subjecting the audience to 'death by PowerPoint' — too many slides, with too much information that people couldn't read even if they tried.

It's common for people to use their slides as a way of moving the focus from themselves. The problem with this approach is that the audience often doesn't respond well. As I watched the audience to see how they would respond, I saw people writing notes to each other and even folding paper aeroplanes. Eleven people got up to go to the bathroom during his presentation, even though the lunch break immediately followed. I would bet my house on the fact that no-one heard what he said, no-one cared what he said and no-one would have decided to invest in his fund on the basis of his presentation.

POINT: DELIVER THE POINT OF YOUR STORY FOR ALL AUDIENCE MEMBERS

It doesn't matter how good your message is if no-one's listening. The fund manager could have convinced so many of the audience to choose his fund. Unfortunately, because he was so self-focused, and unable to adapt when he must surely have seen that people weren't listening to him, the opportunity was lost!

BENEFIT: LINK THE INCIDENT AND POINT TO YOUR AUDIENCE

Make sure you don't do the same thing to your audiences when you present. Know your audience. Consider what they want and give it to them. Keep your slides simple, connect with the real-life humans in the room and change your strategy if people start walking out!

Other important considerations when telling stories

Here are some key points to ensure you make good use of stories in your presentation:

- Love your story and tell it like you own it!

- Talk with your audience not at them.

- Keep the story short.

- Make sure the story is relevant.

- When you tell your stories, use gestures that reinforce your story and add life to the characters or incidents you are describing (see chapter 13), as well as emotive language and vocal emphasis (see chapter 12), so the story is exciting for your audience. This will ensure you pull your audience into the story with you.

- Aim to create a referential index shift. This is a fancy term for the storyteller's reference becoming the reference of the audience member. In other words — your story becomes their story!

- Practise with your friends before delivering your anecdote to a business audience. Your friends love you and will be more forgiving!

- Listen to other storytellers as much as possible. You will learn heaps about what to do and what not to do. A wonderful source for well-told stories and exceptional presenters is at www.TED.com.

Handy tip: One way to shake up your storytelling from time to time is to start in the middle of the story where the action is. This technique is clever because you're telling your story from the most exciting part and your audience is drawn into the plot immediately. You just hint at something unexpected or captivating and then go back to the start, so they understand how you got there. It's a nice way to create suspense and memorability. For example, 'The audience erupted with a standing ovation. They stood, they applauded, and they nearly lifted the conference centre roof with the noise of their ear-splitting enthusiasm and praise for the speaker. What had she done to achieve such a reaction? Let's go back to the beginning...'

Understanding what works as a story

By story, I mean any of the following:

- anecdote
- metaphor (discussed later in the chapter)
- analogy (discussed later in the chapter)
- example
- case study
- legend
- fairytale
- myth
- fable.

Just stick to the magic formula, and each of these will be especially meaningful and engaging for your audience.

You can find stories in:

- your personal and professional life
- magazines
- newspapers

- journals

- movies

- fables

- your family and friends, and other people's lives (with their permission, of course)

- your clients' experiences (again with their permission)

- children's stories.

In particular you are looking for:

- challenges you or your clients or colleagues overcame

- successes you or your clients or colleagues achieved.

When looking for stories to add value to your presentation, think about the moments that stand out in your life. If the incident is something you thought to mention to another person, it's probably a story, even if you didn't at first realise it.

TIP

Michelle says,

'Make sure your stories are always true and always yours—not someone else's story that you pretend is yours! Remember, your audience is smart and when your story is not true you will almost certainly give it away with your body language, and so lose credibility and break rapport with your audience.'

Remember—stories help your audience connect with the key messages in your presentation and they help to bring out your personality. When you tell a story, you are giving people a glimpse of who you are. The audience will enjoy seeing a part of you when you tell stories.

Ruchika's story

Ruchika is a senior manager in a pharmaceutical company. Her role involves updating internal stakeholders about upcoming conferences that she organises for them.

Ruchika is an outgoing, likeable character with a very strong personality — a real character! She's a natural storyteller, but for most of her career Ruchika kept her business presentations strictly professional — no stories, no humour, no fun! She thought stories were for her personal life rather than her professional life.

Ruchika presented at a meeting some years ago where she was given feedback from her immediate manager that she was 'aloof' when she presented to her colleagues. Her manager said she should find a way to better 'connect' with her audience if she wanted to rise up the ladder in the organisation. This feedback was hard for Ruchika to take because she was a naturally engaging sort of person — she was to all intents and purposes the opposite of aloof.

Ruchika realised that, in an attempt to be seen as credible, professional and experienced, she had removed her personality from her presentations. She came to me to learn how to get more 'Ruchika' into her presentations. After structuring her message using the Persuasion Blueprint, Ruchika was ready to insert some stories. She used the magic formula story method to tell three quick, relevant stories in her next internal presentation and was delighted to receive feedback from her manager that she was no longer 'aloof' — instead she was 'Ruchika' when she presented. A magical result!

TRY THIS

- Spend some time thinking about all the stories you could tell. Turn them into 'magic formula' stories, making sure you include an incident, point and benefit.

- Practise telling your magic formula stories to people who will support your storytelling journey!

Exploring storytelling techniques

Once you have the basic three-part structure for your story, you can enrich it with techniques such as metaphor and analogy — and through adding some humour. The following sections show you how.

Using metaphor

A metaphor is a figure of speech that asserts that a subject is similar in some way to an otherwise unrelated object or subject, without using the word 'like' to join the two things.

In reality, the two seemingly unrelated objects or subjects actually have something in common. A famous example of a metaphor is the saying (from Shakespeare's *As You Like It*), 'All the world's a stage'. Why is this a metaphor? Because the world is not a stage, and a stage is not the world. The world and the stage are unrelated at first thought. However, when you put them together they do share something in common and they help you to understand something extra about the qualities of both objects.

You can see from this example that metaphors most often link things we can sense with intangible thoughts or concepts. The world is an intangible concept but the stage has very tangible characteristics — we can see it and feel it.

Metaphors work for a number of reasons:

- They convey a picture, object or meaning quickly — with only a few words.

- They help explain something that would otherwise take way too many words to explain clearly and simply (or is too intangible to describe).

- We react more readily to the emotional and visual than to the rational, and metaphors often have an emotive or visual component.

- Metaphors create an association between two tangible things to better convey how something looks, sounds, smells, works or moves.

Here are some tips for making metaphors work in your presentations:

- Be patient — crafting powerful metaphors takes time, patience and deep consideration, even for really experienced presenters.

- Work out your main message or theme.

- Develop some metaphors that will convey your meaning.

- Make them short and sweet.

- Don't use too many, and steer clear of annoying metaphors that you hear people overusing, such as 'at the risk of the pot calling the kettle black'.

- Stick to one theme — metaphors should make your key message more vivid.

- Steer away from clichés that make your audience cringe.

- Consider placing the metaphor in your icebreaker or opening, again in the body of your message (the *What?* or *How?* sections at Steps 6 and 7), and again at or near your close.

The founder of Revlon, Charles Revson, is reported to have used the following metaphor to help people understand the cosmetic company's approach: 'In the factory we make cosmetics. In the store we sell hope'.

My brilliant client Alexandre Rappoport from Salesforce used the metaphor of space in a client demo presentation. He talked about reaching the chosen planet one destination at a time 'aiming for Mars first — not Neptune'. He included related elements, such as the spaceship that would get you there, the challenges the pilots face and the trajectory of the journey. He had a prop of a spaceship, his slides had space images and the whole experience was an immersive space metaphor. Incredibly memorable. Definitely repeatable. His client will buy his concept — no doubt in my mind.

Using analogy

An analogy is a comparison of certain similarities between things that are otherwise different, with the word 'like' joining them. An analogy is typically used to explain complex or abstract concepts rather than simple ideas.

Analogies are more memorable than simple facts or statistics, and your job as the presenter is to make your message memorable for the audience.

Here are some tips for making analogies work in your presentations:

- Remember that crafting powerful analogies takes time, patience and deep consideration, even for really experienced presenters.
- Work out which subjects in your presentation need to be reinforced with an analogy.
- Consider the key qualities of the subject that needs reinforcing.
- Think of an object, animal, place, person or artefact that has the same qualities as the qualities of your subject.
- Use the word 'like' to link the two subjects.
- Don't use too many analogies in the one presentation.
- Place the analogy in the correct spot in your presentation.

In 2012, Barack Obama used the following analogy to describe the debt crisis in the United States:

It's like somebody goes to a restaurant, orders a big steak dinner, a martini and all that stuff, then just as you're sitting down they leave and accuse you of running up the tab.

Zoe's story

Zoe works in the learning and development section of a financial institution. Her role is to explain concepts such as direct debit, income protection insurance and debt protection to her colleagues, who then sell those products to their customer base around the world.

Zoe was struggling to make these subjects interesting to the participants who sat in her debt protection training courses. She came to me for some advice. Essentially she wanted to add some sparkle to her presentations and use some techniques to make this fairly boring finance content sound interesting and engaging. She also needed them to remember the key points of her message so they would sell more!

We came up with a metaphor combined with analogy that's been used many times in workplace presentations — the tree. Zoe explained to her audience that the roots of the tree were like the hard work you do to earn your income, and the trunk is the income everyone earns, which is strong, robust and finite in nature. She further explained that the branches of the tree were like the essential items everyone has to buy with their income (such as food, housing, transport), and the leaves were the material possessions, the treats, rewards and uplifts (such as holidays, clothes, new cars and jewellery) that their clients want to buy with their money.

Zoe used a slide in the opening of her presentation with a picture of a beautiful, healthy, abundant apple tree. At this time, she used the metaphor 'protect your orchard' (with the word 'orchard' replacing the word 'income' in this sense). Then when she reached the *What?* (or Step 6) section of her presentation, she described the tree analogy clearly and in detail. Her call to action was then 'I encourage you to help our clients protect their orchards', with another beautiful slide of an apple orchard with rows and rows of abundant apple trees.

Zoe found that through the use of this clever tree metaphor, coupled with the analogy (all the parts of the tree are 'like' something), she was better able to explain her complex content and hold the attention of her audience. Thanks to this combination of metaphor and analogy

(continued)

Zoe was worthy of remark — many of her training participants now mention to her that they remember her teaching clearly and that they also use that combination of analogy and metaphor when explaining the concept of debt protection to their clients.

What a terrific result! You can achieve similar results if you take the time to weave metaphor and analogy into your presentations.

Using humour

Humour can be anything from a cheeky smile to a one-liner or a hilarious joke. Well-used humour is engaging, interactive and a delight for your audience. Humour can make your message really engaging, entertaining and memorable for your audience. Just be careful to use it wisely.

Here are my top 10 tips to using humour in a workplace presentation:

1. Write your presentation with the serious content first, and then add humour at the beginning, the end and adjacent to your serious points.

2. Be natural — don't force the humour.

3. Know who you are and use the humour that best suits your style.

4. Remember that the use of humour should be for the audience, not so you can show off.

5. Some forms of humour aren't appropriate in a business context. Think about it from your audience's perspective and make the best choice for them. Using humour that might upset or offend anyone in your audience is not a good idea, because it will cause a negative ripple. (For more information on the ripple effect, see chapter 15.)

6. Let your face do the talking — smile, let your eyes sparkle and laugh at yourself if it's authentic.

7. Use idioms (words, phrases or expressions that cannot be taken literally — for example, 'break a leg') to inject little doses of humour. You can use these especially in your stories when you are recounting what one person said to another — for example, 'And my mum said to me, you're driving me up the wall'.

8. Remember that a joke has a set-up and a punchline. Jokes can sound like a riddle. You can search online for jokes by topic if you're looking for a specific joke about a specific subject. Be sure you practise jokes with your friends. They love you and will laugh regardless of how funny you are, and you will only improve at joke telling from there!

9. Irony is a value-neutral use of words to convey a meaning that is the opposite of its literal meaning. A common example of the use of verbal irony is the scenario of a man staring out a window looking at a miserably muddy rainy day and remarking, 'Lovely day for a stroll'. This remark is ironic because it expresses the opposite of the circumstances. Irony can be very funny when used appropriately, whereas sarcasm is an attempt at belittling the person — such as, 'Oh no, you're not fat!' Sarcasm, it is said, is the lowest form of wit, so it's best to stay away from sarcasm, preserve your rapport and avoid negative ripples in your audience.

10. It doesn't matter if the audience doesn't laugh — sometimes it's a sign they are listening intently to what you're saying, which can ultimately be a compliment.

Using exaggeration

Exaggeration is a type of humour. Exaggeration is the expansion or reduction of the details of a situation. You've likely seen how cartoonists do this, especially when drawing politicians. For example, cartoonists often give former Australian prime minister Julia Gillard a huge pointy nose like a crazy bird. And they often made former Australian prime minister John Howard's eyebrows look like a ferret was lying across his forehead! Former US President Donald Trump is given a bright orange face and very big hair. It's funny because, despite the exaggeration — and sometimes because of it — the character is still recognisable.

The key to using exaggeration is to inflate or deflate whatever you are talking about so much that it is obviously an exaggeration — otherwise, you run the risk of it being not always obvious and that's not very funny.

Annabelle's story

Annabelle is a keynote speaker who specialises in negotiation. She exaggerates in the following way: 'Who would like to open future negotiations so that your stakeholders are sitting on the edge of their chairs, completely engaged, and they can't wait to hear your offer?' Then she asks, 'And who would like to be able to speak up and influence people at work, at home — in fact, all the time, every day of the year?' And then she says, 'And who would like to win all the deals they enter into for the rest of their life — in infinity!'

Get it? 'In infinity!' Exaggerating like this is funny to most people, as long as you've built rapport first. Because Annabelle exaggerates a little bit for the first two questions, it just gets funnier when she says 'in infinity'.

Handy tip: Don't use exaggeration as the immediate opening or close to your presentations. You can use it once you have credibility and rapport, and you know the group are with you, so to speak.

TRY THIS

- Consider where you might use some humour and exaggeration in your presentation to liven it up and make it more entertaining.
- Be sure your humour and exaggeration are appropriate for your topic and your audience.
- Smile and enjoy it! Remember, smile and the world smiles with you!

TOP TIPS
for the art of storytelling

- Stories have been with us since time began. They are a wonderful way for you to convey your message so your audience finds you interesting and engaging.

- A story told well is compelling for your audience, meaning storytelling can also help you convey your key messages.

- To captivate your audience, stories are best told using the 'magic formula' for storytelling, with an incident, point and benefit.

- Any of the following can employ the same magic formula story technique: anecdotes, metaphors, analogies, examples, case studies, legends, fairytales, myths and fables.

- You can effectively tell stories in a variety of places in your presentation.

- Metaphors and analogies are more memorable than simple facts or statistics, and our job as the presenter is to make our message memorable for the audience.

- Humour can be anything from a cheeky smile through to a one-liner or a joke with a set-up and a punchline. Well-used humour is engaging, interactive and a delight for your audience. Just be careful you use it wisely.

- Exaggeration is the expansion or reduction of the details of a situation and belongs in the middle rather than the opening or close of your presentation.

Phase 3: Delivery

Captivate your audience

CHAPTER 9

Warm up your mind

Do you typically find yourself running from one meeting at work to another (whether these meetings are online or in person), with very little time to think about what you need to say in the meeting, much less what you want to achieve?

When it comes to presenting with confidence, you can do a number of clever things to prepare yourself. This chapter explains how to get ready for an exceptional virtual or face-to-face presentation.

Yes, unfortunately, you do need to rehearse

If you are nervous about going blank, or waffling on, or getting pulled off track by strong audience members, or if you're keen to come across as a confident, engaging and compelling presenter, it's a good idea to warm up your mind and rehearse before presenting. In my experience, exceptional presenters rehearse! And then they rehearse and then they rehearse. They take a leaf out of civil rights leader Martin Luther King Jr's book: 'Whatever your life's work is, do it well. A man should do his job so well that the living, the dead and the unborn could do it no better.' Gender bias aside, you get the point — exceptional presenters rehearse until they can't get it wrong. A typical executive who engages me to coach them would rehearse (especially their opening and close) between 50 and 100 times for important events.

TIP

Michelle says,

'Exceptional presenters rehearse until they can't get it wrong.'

Now I can hear you saying, 'Really? 100 times?' As William Shakespeare said, 'All things are ready, if our minds be so.' Don't be intimidated by this rehearsal number, just know this is what exceptional presenters do. If you want to be exceptional, you need to do it too. And don't worry about it needing to be 100 formal rehearsals: all those little practices you do in the car, the shower and walking around the supermarket count towards knowing what you want to say. Just remember — the more you run through your presentation, the clearer and more seamless your delivery will be, and the more you will embed your message with your audience. Interestingly, the more you rehearse, the more unscripted, natural and authentic you will sound.

Rehearsing versus rote learning

Rehearsing is not the same as rote learning your presentation. Rote learning is where you learn your script word for word. It's the way many of us learned our multiplication tables, for instance. This method is not recommended for presenters because of the way our brains work. Research by cognitive psychologist George A Miller asserts that our brain can only remember between five and nine things at once, so rote learning only works when you have loads of time to practice. (Or, like the Australian households of the 1970s and the old times-tables charts many of us grew up with, you have a copy of your script on the back of your toilet door!)

Rehearsing is where you run through your key messages over and over again, so you embed the general gist of your message. (Sometimes the result is that you will end up, almost accidentally, committing some of the parts of your message to memory.)

While you may inadvertently memorise some of your content, you will find that, with rehearsal, you deliver most of your message in a different way each time and the result is that you sound more natural. I am guessing that you are too busy in your life to try to completely rote learn your presentations before delivery.

TIP

Michelle says,

'When you use the storyboarding process (refer to chapter 4) to elicit and order your key messages, you have already begun the process of remembering what you want to say in your presentation.'

How to rehearse

I suggest you find a variety of places to practise your presentations. The greater the number of locations you rehearse in, the more comfortable you will feel presenting in the actual location of your presentation — no matter where it is. Book a variety of meeting rooms over the course of a week at work if you're in the office; have a few turns in front of your bathroom mirror at home; go out into the garden for a practice if you can; and then try delivering your message in a variety of other rooms in your home. I know — it sounds a bit crazy, doesn't it? Well, it works!

Exceptional presenters rehearse and rehearse and rehearse. They rehearse until they can't get it wrong. And that's why they get such awesome results!

Maree's story

Maree is a senior executive who has worked with me for retrenchment, restructure and results announcements. We've worked on change-management messages and takeover or merger presentations for many years.

Maree had an important presentation to make to about 800 people who worked for a company (Company X) that her organisation had just acquired. These people were unhappy about being taken over. The acquiring organisation put on a conference to welcome and induct the new staff. Both the conference and the acquisition were seen as unwelcome disruptions by everyone at Company X, from the managing director through to the junior staff.

Maree's role was to explain the new and exciting marketing campaign that would launch the new brand for Company X to the Australian public and put Company X on the map. She knew, despite the fact that this was an exciting venture, her audience would be reluctant listeners and she would have to do some fast-talking to influence them.

Maree rehearsed the beginning and end of her presentation over 100 times. Yes, you read that correctly — over 100 times! She rehearsed in the office, at home, and she even did some rehearsing with my children and me in my home before flying to the conference! She also rehearsed over and over again in the aircraft on the way to the conference.

As a result of all that rehearsal, Maree was extremely confident as she presented her message. When she was finished she sat down next to the managing director of the company that had just been acquired, feeling joyous and relieved. And to her satisfaction, the managing director turned to her and whispered, 'I had heard you were an amazing business person; I had no idea you were such an amazing presenter as well!'

Needless to say, Maree called me immediately to relay the story. She was thrilled and delighted that all her efforts had paid off.

> **TIP**
>
> **Michelle says,**
>
> 'Successful presenters rehearse, then they rehearse, then they rehearse some more - until they simply can't get it wrong! And that's why they achieve such awesome results!'

TRY THIS

- Once your presentation is completely designed, make some time to rehearse.

- Ensure you choose a variety of locations for your rehearsal.

Using the power of your mind to manage your nerves

Many of the best presenters use the power of positive thinking before they present. They imagine themselves as successful, confident, engaging presenters, and are often delighted with the results. Others imagine themselves as something or someone else. (Remember — this technique is about finding the parts of you that you want to emphasise. You should never try to deceive your audience and pretend to be something or someone you are not.)

Let's look at some examples:

- A tall guy with a massive ego projected an image of a gentle giant onto his stage before presenting.

- A fellow with an irritating accent projected the image of a gorgeous, handsome, charismatic presenter.

- A woman I know thinks of the warm rays of the sun and instantly feels the warmth in her personality coming through.

- A friend of mine who is a fellow presenter watches Jim Carrey movies before an event, and he says this makes him more entertaining.

Another aspect of positive thinking in your presentation is the way you choose to describe the nervousness. Have you ever stopped to think that, whether you are nervous or excited, you have exactly the same physiological experience? In fact, the only thing that determines whether it's a negative or positive experience is the word you choose to use to describe it. As William Shakespeare said, 'There is nothing either good or bad, but thinking makes it so'.

If you have ever been bungy jumping, abseiling, parachuting, white-water rafting, climbing, caving, scuba diving or parasailing, you know full well that people pay money to experience the feeling we get when we present!

And when they are doing those adventure-type sports, they don't call the feeling nervousness. They call it excitement, energy, exhilaration, thrill, joy, arousal, pleasure, stimulation or enthusiasm.

TIP

Michelle says,

'Don't keep telling yourself you're "nervous". Reframe the word nervous and instead say, "I am ready, I'm excited, I'm alive!"'

Handy tip: In our family we call this feeling 'funny tummy', and we even draw a smiley face on our stomachs with washable bath crayons (yes, I know—too much fun!) to reframe how we feel in the moment! It's so clever because it reframes in our minds that the experience most people call nervousness is, in fact, a positive thing. I've been known to ask executives I work with to draw smiley faces on their stomachs too! It is bizarre. It works—it makes them relax and smile. And, by the way—there's something quite funny about knowing you have a smiley face drawn under your business shirt that no-one knows is there!

Which word will you choose?

The question to ask yourself is this: which word do you want to use? If you continue to call the feeling before you present nervousness,

I'm not sure you're really that serious about making presenting an enjoyable experience for yourself.

Remember, one definition of insanity is doing the same thing over and over again and expecting a different result! So it's quite simple really: change the word and change the experience. Go on — do it right now!

Changing the word and calling it 'funny tummy' (or whatever word you prefer) doesn't mean you won't feel the adrenaline. You know, we have the genes of cave dwellers and you'll still get the fight or flight response. The good news is that giving it a different name, like 'funny tummy', really works! It makes you relax and smile.

TRY THIS

1. Come up with a new word to describe the feeling of adrenaline that you get before presenting, and change the experience to a positive one for yourself.

2. Which word are you going to choose? Write it down right now and put it somewhere you will see it before you present!

Understanding the impact of personality on nervousness

Another advanced technique is available for reducing your nerves, maintaining your ability to convey your message and improving your ability to present and achieve results.

You may know that we each have a different combination of personality filters that make up who we are. These filters can put labels on our differences and help us to understand why people act the way they do.

Working out our own filters enables us to have self-respect and self-confidence. This enhanced self-acceptance empowers us to make necessary changes to the way we approach people and tasks. It gives us a greater ability to devise strategies for dealing with difficult or frustrating people and situations, and allows us to communicate with others more effectively.

The filter I am going to explain to you is called the 'standards sort' — it determines the way you approach tasks. I bet you'll have a bit of a laugh at yourself (or your boss, colleagues or partner) as you keep reading.

Which one are you: perfect or excellent?

If you have what is known as a 'perfection sort', you look for perfection — an absence of flaws or mistakes. You drive for high standards and remarkable performances. And you find it easy to see a flaw in your own performance and in the performance of others.

You can tend to set unrealistically high goals and short time frames, and prefer to view the end product as the criteria for assessment. You need to complete tasks in a way that satisfies your criteria perfectly.

You tend to treat yourself and others with harsh judgement for any shortcomings. You typically have a future orientation, which can be obsessive. You can feel continually frustrated and dissatisfied. And, sadly, if you have a perfectionist sort, anything less than perfect equals failure. This puts you under a considerable amount of pressure.

If you have what is known as an 'excellence sort', you will be looking for the best you can do with the circumstances and situations that present. You look for what can work. You do the best with what you have and are happy with that. You tend to set goals in small steps, so you can appreciate the progress and successes along the way, and operate practically and pragmatically with goals. You will view the process and journey as being as important as the end product — life is a journey, not a destination! You are not too tough on yourself and appreciate the diverse variables in the process. The downside of an excellence sort is that you can deny what is really happening, ignore the real problems and constraints, and lose sight of the big picture. You sometimes have a lack of drive and motivation and, as a result, can suffer from low standards and a 'near enough is good enough' attitude.

Most people are stuck with the personality filters they have! Experts suggest that a significant life event or lots of personal effort is required to shift your filters or preferences. So that means, regardless of whether your preference is a perfection or excellence sort — good for you, enjoy it. Make the most of it, because they both have strengths and weaknesses. Be sure to manage yourself so you and the people around you get you at your best.

You can change something related to your standards sort, and this is the magic key to nerve-free presenting!

Is your apple rotten?

We all have a core question. Your core question is the question that drives you and determines your attitude to the task at hand. Combine your understanding of perfection or excellence with your core question and you have the answer to reducing your nerves and enjoying presenting in business!

Here's how it works. If you have a perfection filter, your core question is more likely to be driving for a perfect result. For example, 'How can I be perfect?' 'Will I be the best in the room?' How can I make sure I don't stuff anything up?' These are retracted, self-focused core questions that will put the focus back on you and will make you nervous.

If you have an excellence filter, your core question is more likely to be driving you to do the best you can with what you have. For example, 'How can I do the best I can today for this group, knowing what I know?' or 'How can I help these people better understand?' You can hear the acceptance that you should try your best and you can only do what you can do. These are extended, others-focused core questions that will maintain your focus on the audience and reduce your nerves.

Changing your core question

You can, most definitely, change your core question and devise one that works for you. Regardless of whether your preference is perfection or excellence, you can choose to have an audience-focused, excellence core question. Why not plan one right now for your future presentations?

TRY THIS

Questions to ask yourself and reflect upon:

1. Do you have a perfection or excellence sort?

2. Think about your perfection or excellence filter and your core question for a few days.

3. Is your core question sabotaging you and preventing you from being the best presenter you can be?

4. Or is your core question setting you up to be an interesting, engaging presenter who enjoys speaking to groups?

TOP TIPS
for warming up your mind

- It's important to warm up your mind, your body and your voice before presenting.

- Rehearsal is a good way to warm up your mind, and the more you rehearse the more unscripted and natural you will sound.

- Rehearsing is not the same as rote learning. Rote learning is where you learn your script word for word, and rehearsing is where you run through your key messages using different words each time.

- Find a variety of places to rehearse so the room you actually present in is just one more location.

- Harness the power of positive thinking to keep control of your nerves.

- Find a word other than 'nervous' so you reframe the experience and make presenting a positive experience – change the word and change the experience.

- Your core question is the deep, inner question that is driving your presentation.

- Regardless of your preference for perfection or excellence, be sure that you have a core question that enables you to be your best.

CHAPTER 10

Warm up your body and voice

If an athlete competed at a sporting event without warming up, you'd likely expect two things to happen:

- They injure themselves.

- They perform at less than their potential.

It's the same when you are presenting. Whether your presentation is online or in person, it's very important to warm up your mind through rehearsal (refer to chapter 9), and to warm up your body and voice with physical exercises and vocal warm-ups. Warm-ups do a number of things for you: they prepare your mouth and brain, they help you use your adrenaline wisely, and they help you feel ready and pumped before an event.

So let's get to work on warming up.

TIP

Michelle says,

'Vocal warm-ups prepare your mouth and brain, help use up your adrenaline wisely, and help you feel ready and pumped before an event.'

Warm up your body

Your voice and your ability to convey confidence is a reflection of your entire physical and mental being. Did you realise that tension in your body restricts your ability to use your voice effectively and can make you look and feel very nervous? Conversely, feeling nervous is very difficult when your body is relaxed. The way you relax your body is to warm it up!

You can do some wonderful exercises to warm up your body, including the ones I've included in the following sections.

Stretch

If you stretch out your limbs, you will find you feel loose and ready for anything. I'm a Soprano 2 in a women's choir and we do this every time before we sing. You can do it before you present too.

Let's stretch your body:

1. Place your left arm above your head.

2. Stretch your left arm over your head and bend slightly over to the right side of your body to expand the left side of your ribcage.

3. Place your right hand on your left side.

4. Now breathe — right down to your bottom. Do you know what I mean? Breathe so deeply into your body it feels like the breath is going into your bottom! Feel the ribs open on the stretched left side.

5. Drop your left arm and swap to the other side.

6. Take your right arm and place it over your head.

7. Stretch it over to the left side and bend slightly to the left, so you expand the right side of your ribcage.

8. Place your left hand on your right side.

9. Now breathe into your bottom again. Well done!

Tense and relax

Tensing and relaxing various body areas twice in quick succession releases the tension from that body area. To do this, stand up and tense and relax one body area at a time, twice in quick succession. Start with your eyes and face, and then feet, calves, thighs, bottom, stomach, pectorals, shoulders and hands. The more nervous you feel, the more you should do this before you present.

The following provides some special pointers for the eyes, feet and hands.

THE EYES

We don't usually notice when our eye muscles become tense. The following exercise is great for people who work at a computer for much of the day.

Find a way to look outside and imagine a firefighter is climbing a ladder to rescue a little animal stranded at the top of a house. Focus on the firefighter as they climb all the way up the ladder. Observe the feeling in the muscles behind and around your eyes. Follow this person with your eyes — up and up — until they get to the top. They have saved the little animal and are now bringing it back to the ground. Keep following them with your eyes. Now they are at the bottom. Relax your eyes and if you want to, let them close. Notice how different they feel.

THE FEET

Imagine you are at the beach, with no shoes on, standing on a pebbly spot of the ground. Making very slight movements as you stand and focus on your feet, imagine that you are walking on the beach with the sharp pebbles underfoot, and imagine you can feel them under your bare feet. Pick your way carefully over them. Ouch! That one was sharp! Observe the tension in your feet. Now walk on to the soft sand. Really feel the difference. Then lie down and let your feet relax completely.

THE HANDS

Have you ever made a snowball? Imagine you are picking up snow and patting the hard, cold snow into a firm snowball. You want to throw it at someone, so you are in a hurry. (If you've never made a snowball, imagining you're patting wet sand into a ball also works!)

As you quickly make your snowball, notice the tension in your hands. Then drop them and let them relax beside your body or (if you're lying down) on the bed or floor beside you, and notice how warm, soft and loose they feel. It is the simple things that can make all the difference in ensuring your mind and body are working in harmony.

These warm-ups will help prepare your body by loosening up your limbs and using up some of your adrenaline. Try these simple techniques the next time you feel you need to relax before a presentation!

Warm up your voice

You know how some people stand out when they present because their voice is like liquid chocolate? I frequently observe that these people with fantastic voices are more likely to get what they want.

In our society, we tend to associate credibility and authority with people who have a rich, resonant vocal quality. In fact, many of us know someone who has a strong, rich, resonant voice. Maybe it's an actor, such as Chris Hemsworth or Cate Blanchett, or a radio personality. At some point, you may have found yourself wishing that you could enhance your vocal quality and projection so you were more confident, compelling and persuasive in your life.

Well, it is possible — in fact, it's easy to have the voice of your dreams! It's my experience with the many executives I have coached that creating a rich, resonant, influential voice is completely possible and is a very rewarding journey

Having the voice of your dreams is a journey. Remember — your voice is a powerful tool that must be warmed up to ensure you perform at your best and so you don't injure yourself. Just as you need to relax your body to feel physically confident, you also need to relax your throat, jaw, tongue and the other areas of your face to help you speak with a confident, powerful and resonant voice. The way you do this is to warm up.

TIP

Michelle says,

'Having the voice of your dreams—one that's rich, resonant and influential—is possible.'

Sarah's story

Sarah is a very intelligent woman in business who contacted me after missing out on a number of workplace promotions. She is intelligent, beautifully dressed and has an open, warm demeanour. Sarah's problem was that when she spoke, her voice could be shrill and aggravating. Oh my goodness—her voice could sound like a cat on heat! Aargh! You know the sound: a high-pitched screeching sound that stays with you for quite some hours after you meet the person responsible!

Sarah realised that if she could change her voice, she would be more likely to influence people. She learned how to warm up the power and resonance of her voice. In effect, we recreated her vocal identity. Now her voice is professional and attractive and matches her professional, attractive personal presentation. What a great result!

So let's get to work on the main vocal areas you can warm up. They are:

- breath
- vocal quality
- articulation.

The breath

Did you realise that, as an adult, you have probably forgotten how to breathe correctly? Children know how to breathe well instinctively — and they can use that breath to really scream when they want to, especially newborn babies! Yet most of us have unlearned our perfect breathing. As a result, when we find ourselves in a situation of conflict or discomfort, many of us revert to chest breathing that is shallow and unfulfilling.

When you breathe from your chest during a presentation, your voice becomes high-pitched and tinny in quality. This is not a great voice for others to listen to, and it's not very credible or believable. This means it's not great for influencing others, either! The other negative side effect of chest breathing is that you will find it difficult to retain your clarity of thought, because your oxygen won't circulate as effectively to your brain unless you breathe nice and deeply.

Correct breathing is fundamental to a strong, powerful voice. A strong voice requires lots of constant air from the lungs to maintain sufficient pressure on the vocal cords. When you're presenting, it has the other awesome result of helping you feel energised, focused and relaxed. Terrific!

The thing to remember when you breathe is this: when you breathe in, your diaphragm should contract and move downwards, allowing more air to flow into your lungs. When you breathe out, your diaphragm should relax and move upwards. Try this lying down to ensure you are practising correctly. Allow your belly to rise as you breathe in and your diaphragm contracts, and to fall as your breathe out. Try to do this consciously at least 10 times a day. It will eventually become second nature.

Naomi's story

Naomi came to me because she had begun fainting in her presentations at work. Yes, you read it correctly! She used to faint every time she spoke to a large group of employees.

She would just collapse on the floor in front of everyone. Imagine how embarrassing that would be. In the corporate world, they call this a CLM (career-limiting move)! During her presentations, her breathing was shallow rather than diaphragmatic, and she had no confidence in the structure of her message or her delivery skills.

We worked together to help Naomi learn how to structure her presentation so she felt confident delivering her message. We also spent some time on Naomi's breathing. She needed to re-learn how to breathe deeply so she was centred and calm. And she rehearsed her delivery many times too.

You will be pleased to know that after this simple coaching, she performed brilliantly at her next big event. And she has received standing ovations, and has been head-hunted at least twice since we worked together. She continues to contact me with stories of her ongoing presentation and career success.

WARMING UP YOUR BREATHING

You can do many exercises to warm up your breathing. I think the easiest one is called the coffee plunger.

Here's how it works:

1. Place one hand on your belly, with your thumb on your belly button and the rest of your hand over your tummy.

2. Place the other hand on your upper chest (the bony part of your chest just under your neck).

3. Visualise pulling the coffee plunger up from the lower abdomen as you breathe in and then pushing the plunger down on the out breath.

That's the coffee plunger. Great work!

Vocal quality

Vocal quality is what you may know as your tone, or the resonance of your voice. And, as already mentioned, we associate people who have a rich, resonant vocal quality with also having authority. A great way to achieve this richness is to warm up your voice and tone with the yawn and hum.

YAWN

To warm up your vocal quality, you must yawn. Forget the manners you were taught by your parents. When I say 'yawn', I don't mean a polite little yawn with your lips together and hand across your mouth — I mean YAWN! Have a big, open mouth. You want the air to come out unobstructed. The noise is not contrived or forced; it's just the natural, loud sound you'd make if you were doing an unobstructed huge yawn. Allow your tongue to touch the back of your bottom front teeth, and then move into a sigh. Great work!

HUM

The second thing you can do is hummmmmm! The thing to focus on when you hum is the vibrations you cause. Take a good deep breath and then direct the hum to the front of your mouth; if your lips and nose start to tickle, you know you're on the right track. The key to this is to create lots of space inside your mouth. The roof of your mouth should be raised and not touching your tongue. In turn, try sending the vibrations to the top of your head, the back of your neck and to your upper chest, and put your hands on these spots to see if they are actually vibrating.

Articulation

Articulation is the crispness and clarity of your words. Clear, crisp articulation is possible when you warm up your jaw, tongue, lips and face. You can do this with jaw relaxation, kiss/grin, orange/pea, horse neigh and tongue in cheek! Here's how.

JAW RELAXATION

Imagine you have some very sticky caramels in your mouth and you're chewing them well. They are sticking to your teeth. Work this great chunk of caramel out of your teeth. Notice what is happening.

Then rest and drop your jaw. Let it relax, and become quite soft and loose. Notice the different feeling of complete release of the jaw muscles. Wonderful!

KISS/GRIN

Kiss your lips in a pout. Stick the lips right out in front of you. Go on! Pucker up! Now grin. Stretch your lips into a cheesy grin, showing all your teeth, and feel your cheeks almost touch your eyes. Repeat this over and over again! Well done!

ORANGE/PEA

Make your lips into a green pea. You know the little green vegetable? Purse your lips together and make the opening at the tips of your lips into the shape of a pea. Then, with a surprised face, make the shape of an orange with your mouth. With this exercise, your lips are going from tensed together in a pout to a big, open, round shape. Do this five times and make sure you really exaggerate!

HORSE NEIGH

Neigh like a horse! What more can I say?

TONGUE IN CHEEK

Place your tongue against the inside of your left cheek and say, 'I am an amazing presenter with beautiful vocal quality and commanding stage presence'. Say this three times. Then, swap and do it three times with your tongue in the other cheek. Too funny! You'd better try this one in a secluded location, don't you think?

Using tongue twisters to warm up

If you'd like to check how well you are warmed up, consider trying a variety of tongue twisters. Tongue twisters are another effective way to warm up your articulation and to test your degree of vocal warmth, especially if you do the tongue twisters that have a mix of different consonants and vowel combinations.

Here is a sample of some of my favourite tongue twisters:

- Six sick hicks nick six slick bricks with picks and sticks.

- How can a clam cram in a clean cream can?

- Rush the washing Russell, rush the washing Russell.

- Thirty-three thirsty, thundering thoroughbreds thumped Mr Thurber on Thursday.

- Lift the ladder later, lisped Lester; Lester lisped, lift the ladder later.

- The big black bug bled black blood!

Warm-ups create a rich, resonant voice. If you do these warm-ups before a sales meeting, internal presentation (online or face to face) or any other important event, you will sound more credible and authoritative, and be more likely to get what you want. The effects of the warm-up can last for anything between an hour and a whole day, depending on how much talking you are doing. So get cracking and do the exercises in the bathroom and the car.

Handy tip: I often find a private room, somewhere far from the conference room at the hotel where I'm presenting a keynote speech. And I do all these exercises. I urge you to do the same. I wish you every success as you find the vocal influence within you!

TIP

Michelle says,

'With vocal warm-ups, you will sound more credible and authoritative — and that means you are more likely to get what you want!'

TRY THIS

Try some of the warm-ups presented in this chapter and notice the difference in your vocal quality before and after you warm up.

TOP TIPS
for warming up your body and voice

- Tension in your body restricts your ability to use your voice effectively and can make you look and feel very nervous.

- Warm-up exercises help prepare your body for presenting by loosening up your limbs and using up some of your adrenaline.

- In our society, we tend to associate credibility and authority with people who have a rich, resonant vocal quality. You can use warm-up exercises to develop this vocal quality.

- Your voice is a powerful tool that must be warmed up to ensure you perform at your best and that you don't injure yourself.

- You can warm up your breathing, your vocal quality and your articulation with a variety of exercises, such as the tense and relax, kiss/grin, and tongue twisters.

- You can warm up anywhere you won't feel embarrassed yawning with your mouth wide open!

- If you warm up, you will come across as credible and persuasive, and be more likely to get what you want.

CHAPTER 11

Managing your nerves

Have you ever sat in a presentation as an audience member and thought to yourself that it wouldn't matter if you just got up and left, or turned your camera off, because the presenter didn't look at you once? It's as if they didn't realise you were even there! In these situations, the presenter often spends more time looking at their slides and talking at you than meeting your needs and connecting with you. It's really just another 'blah, blah, blah' scenario, isn't it?

To make sure you create a wonderful connection with your audience and don't fall into the same trap, when it's time to deliver your presentation it's essential to remember: *It's not about me. It's all about the audience!*

TIP

Michelle says,

'Remember: It's not about you. It's all about the audience!'

April's story

I went to a presentation run by a presenter called April. I was one of around 200 people in the room. I didn't know the presenter personally, yet by the end of the presentation I felt as though I was one of her friends.

As she spoke to all of us, I had a powerful sense that I was the only person in the room. I felt completely and utterly mesmerised by her message and compelled to take action because it was like being in a personal mentoring session, rather than in a room full of hundreds of people. Have you ever had an experience like that yourself?

April focused on giving me direct, sincere, connected eye contact. She looked at me as though I was important and special, the way my friends look at me when I am talking with them in a coffee shop. It was an excellent experience because I found I achieved much better value in her session than in similar sessions run by other presenters. I listened attentively and was captivated and engaged. I knew on reflection that April's deep connection to me through her eye contact was responsible for encouraging me to listen carefully, process the key messages and get the best value from her presentation.

Great presenters connect with their audience members like this all the time. I believe it is this skill of connecting that sets the exceptional presenters apart from the good ones. And the good news is that anyone can master this skill when they present. Yes, especially you!

'Extending the self' to reduce nerves and connect with your audience

To develop a real connection with your audience, I suggest you try a technique called 'extending the self'. This is a powerful technique for reducing nervousness because it takes your focus off your nerves and puts your attention on your audience, which in turn enhances your connection or rapport with them.

The idea behind this technique is that most people have some sort of symptom that indicates nervousness — perhaps a sick feeling, or a flushed face, shaky legs or a dry mouth. Others become hot and perspire profusely when they are nervous.

If you focus on yourself, you will become very aware of your nervous symptoms, and will probably get even more nervous. If, on the other hand, you are fully focused on your audience and, therefore, less aware of yourself, your body may still be nervous but you won't be as aware of it.

The technique of placing your focus fully on your audience increases the connection they feel with you, and dramatically reduces your own sense of nervousness. Remember: it's not about you. It's all about the audience!

What extending the self does for you and your audience

Extending the self and connecting with your audience is important for several reasons. You will be:

- more engaging
- more convincing
- more likely to emphasise key words and points
- louder
- in a position to enjoy your presentation
- less nervous because your audience-focus prevents you from wallowing in self-awareness
- more likely to achieve a more natural vocal range (where your voice goes up and down in natural and interesting way).

This last point is important. You can't get a conversational vocal range unless you make eye contact — when you are not looking at your audience, your voice flattens out.

If you extend the self, your audience will:

- feel more involved and engaged

- understand your message better

- be less likely to switch off and more likely to concentrate on your message

- be more confident in you as a credible source of information.

Working on extending the self

Extending the self is somewhat tricky and even some of the greatest public speakers don't do it very well. Once you do work out how to do it, you will be an engaging, confident, charismatic presenter every time.

When it's time to deliver your presentation, as always, focus first on the audience. Then you can focus on extending the self:

1. Claim your space confidently and charismatically at the head of the meeting table or in the centre of the room or stage where you are presenting.

2. Imagine a bubble is around you and your audience.

3. Throw your attention out into the bubble.

4. Look into the whites of your audience's eyes, rather than skimming their heads or pretending to look at them. Know that they are real, live humans, and you have the wonderful opportunity to engage and help them. You will notice that you also see their bodies, their clothes and their expressions.

Handy tip: When presenting online you must look into the camera at all times—otherwise, you'll either be seen as having shifty eyes, or people will only see the top of your head! (See chapter 20 for more on this.) You can still imagine the bubble around you and your audience. Unfortunately, you can't see their eyes. So what do you do? I recommend that you imagine the whites of their eyes. Picture the faces of the actual people attending your virtual meeting inside your camera lens (no matter how small it is). And look into your camera as though you are looking at the real people.

Extending the self helps you really connect with your audience. Remember that your audience is made up of real live humans, and you have the wonderful opportunity to influence and help them. This takes your focus off yourself and your nerves, and places your attention on the audience — which, in turn, enhances your connection or rapport with them.

TIP

Michelle says,

'Some people call that moment where you sense the connection between you and one other person in the audience the "click". It's what you should be aiming for with every live presentation.'

Look at everyone in your audience

In a live meeting everyone needs to feel connected to you as a person, even the people who don't look up from their notes! Just keep trying to connect with everyone. Eventually they will look up and remain engaged.

Don't look from one person to the next in a linear order. If you do so, you will look like you have been on a really bad presentation skills training course! Ha! The tip for eye contact is to look from one person to another as though you were looking from one point of a star to the opposite point of the star, as shown in figure 11.1 (overleaf).

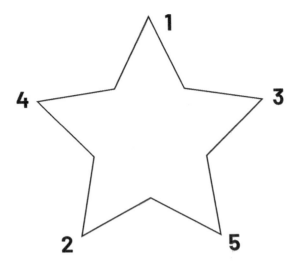

Figure 11.1 Pattern for making eye contact across your audience

TRY THIS

Spend a few moments trying different types of focus.

1. Try to retract the self. This is the opposite of the technique I am suggesting you use. It is where you feel as though you are inside a skinny bubble all by yourself. No-one is in the bubble with you. Stand up and walk around the room in a completely self-focused manner. Become aware of your breathing, the feel of your clothes against your skin, your hair against your face – you're totally self-centred, self-conscious and self-aware.

2. Now change your focus to an extended state. Become aware of everything going on around you. Notice the intricacy of the flooring, the quality of the air and your surroundings.

3. Consider how each of these different states feels and what that might mean for your presentations.

In presentations, all sorts of things can happen to make you retract. For example, the projector bulb might blow, or someone will ask you a disconcerting question or walk in late or let their phone ring.

When these things happen, we often retract the self, and it can be difficult to extend your attention back to the people in your audience. For this reason, practising moving from a retracted state to an extended state at random times in your life is worthwhile. Then you'll be thoroughly trained in how to re-extend the self should you retract the self in a presentation.

TRY THIS

Practise changing from a retracted to an extended state at the click of a finger. Being able to switch your focus from a retracted state to an extended state in a second will help you reduce your nerves when all the distracting things happen in your presentation and you accidentally become retracted.

Do you currently extend the self when you present?

1. If you answered yes, what will you continue doing?

2. If you answered no, what will you start doing right now to make presenting more fun and to connect more fully with your audience?

3. Spend some time writing down your goals and place them where you will see them before an important presentation or communication.

Don't imagine your audience naked!

Imagining your audience naked is a very common recommendation for dealing with nerves. Please don't do it! Yuck! Extending the self is quite different from picturing your audience naked. No offence: I think at best you will laugh and at worst you'll be sick! There are certainly people we present to, especially at work, who we really don't want to think of naked! The consequence of imagining your audience naked might be that you feel powerful. That is, 'I am clothed and you are naked, so I feel I have power over you'. But even if you do happen to feel this way, it's not actually a good thing, because it will also mean you could come across as arrogant, condescending or egotistical. You will break rapport and be less likely to influence your audience.

Extending the self is about an equal, two-way communication between you and your audience. It's not about a power exchange. I recommend extending the self as an effective way to manage your nerves and connect beautifully with your audience.

Handy tip: If you are nervous about presenting to a 'group' my advice is to remember that it's physiologically impossible to present to a group. You only have one set of eyes and, generally speaking, they look in the same direction! Remember this: In any given moment, it's just me and one other. *Focus on just one person at a time—this may be less daunting than thinking you're speaking to a group.*

TOP TIPS
for managing your nerves

- Remember: it's not about you. It's all about the audience!

- Extending the self is an effective way to manage your nerves and connect beautifully with your audience.

- Extending takes your focus off yourself and your nerves and puts your attention on the audience, which in turn enhances your connection or rapport with them.

- To extend the self, imagine a bubble is around you and your audience. You are also in the bubble. Connect with every individual in the audience, one at a time.

- Use the star method of making eye contact, and be sure to look at everyone in the audience — even the people not looking at you.

- In a virtual presentation you can still extend the self, just imagine you can see the real people in your audience.

CHAPTER 12

Speak with confidence

I explain in chapter 9 that the quality of your voice reflects your emotional state, your belief in yourself and your overall health and ability to manage stress. We often think of people who have a rich, resonant tonality as powerful, authoritative and credible.

Think about how much more credible you find the presenter with a strong radio voice, compared to the one with the Elmer Fudd–style high-pitched, unconfident voice. ('Watch the woad, wabbit!') You also no doubt know how difficult it is to listen to a presenter with a flat, boring monotonous voice. And it's just as difficult to listen to someone who is trying too hard to sound interesting. Someone who is trying too hard will sound inauthentic (like they are trying to trick their audience), resulting in the audience looking for the next trick.

In this chapter, I take you through ways to ensure you speak with confidence and use your voice effectively — whether presenting online or in person — to embed your credibility and message with your audience.

Using your voice effectively when you present

If you want to be engaging and convincing when you speak, it's important that you strive for a natural variety of pitch, speed and volume. Pitch is the highs and lows in your voice. Speed is all the different tempos between fast and slow. And volume is the variety between loud and soft.

TIP

Michelle says,

'To ensure you are not boring, you should use a variety of pitch, speed and volume in one presentation.'

The key is to use the most appropriate vocal variety for the message. For example, at times speaking in a slow, soft voice is powerful; at other times, speeding up and using a higher pitch is a good idea. Work out what you think is the best thing to do to get your message across and, whatever it is, do that.

Using pauses

Pausing is critical for exceptional presenting. As writer Mark Twain rightly said, 'The right word may be effective, but no word was ever as effective as a rightly timed pause'. People in your audience need time to hear what you have said, make sense of it and come to their own conclusions before you move on to the next point. They do this when you pause and say nothing.

TIP

Michelle says,

'Pause is powerful! Be sure to pause often so your audience has time to make sense of your point.'

Pausing will help you breathe deeply and diaphragmatically, which in turn will help you relax and maintain control of yourself as you present. Pausing will also help reduce your need to 'click' your saliva or make a 'tut' sound, because you will be better able to swallow your saliva if you pause.

It's a good idea to plan your pauses in advance. Locate some of the more important places in your presentation where pauses should occur and make a plan to ensure you do take a pause and a diaphragmatic breath. Make sure you practise with the pauses in the right place when you are rehearsing.

Emphasising key words

Emphasising key words when you present is also a good idea. This helps your audience know what's important and get a strong sense of your emotional objective, or the vibe you're aiming to create.

TIP

Michelle says,

'When you emphasise key words, you create interest in particular parts of your message.'

John's story

John is the managing director of a global corporation. He has bought and sold numerous businesses in his time and is a self-made man. John is considered an expert in his field. He is a low-key, relaxed and likeable guy.

John needed to present to some internal stakeholders and some clients at a conference run by his company. When we did his Think/Feel/Do analysis (chapter 2), John realised he wanted to shift his audience from thinking he was low-key to describing him as passionate, compelling and exciting.

(continued)

He designed some beautiful, evocative slides, rehearsed the delivery of his message many times (including in front of some of his direct reports, who gave him feedback on how to improve his delivery), and he warmed up his voice using the exercises in this book (refer to chapter 10). He did his vocal warm-ups three times. Yes, you read it correctly — three times from start to finish! He then delivered his message with some vocal emphasis on all the words that helped him convey his emotional objective (passionate, compelling and exciting).

At the end of his presentation, he was given feedback that he was the best presenter at the conference. He was described as exciting, compelling and interesting. And the audience was excited about his message. This was a great result for John.

He put his success down to three things:

1. Rehearsing his content left him feeling confident and ready for anything.

2. Vocal warm-ups greatly improved the sound of his voice, and this resulted in a further increase in his self-confidence.

3. Emphasising key words helped him convey his emotional objective as he spoke.

I recommend you do the same. Remember to rehearse, warm up your voice and be sure to emphasise the key emotional words in your presentation.

Making use of technology for in-person presentations

Using a microphone when speaking either online or face-to-face is a great idea. You can let the mic do its job and make your performance easier for you and your audience. The mic projects your voice so you don't need to strain, and it creates a pleasant, even, smooth sound so it's easier for your audience to listen to you. Remember — the best sound system is one the audience doesn't notice.

In a live presentation you don't want to be stuck behind a podium with a microphone, though. For this reason, I recommend using either a lapel or headset microphone.

Using a lapel microphone

Have you ever seen a presenter trip over the cord of their microphone like a circus performer? Or heard that high-pitched interference squeal or the spitting sounds that are the result of poor microphone skills? Don't let this be you! Instead, take advantage of a lapel mic — and know how to use it.

Ensure that all technical aspects of your presentation are thought through and that you have assistance standing by. For those unaccustomed, it is simple to behave naturally with a lapel microphone as long as you follow these steps:

1. *Check the equipment first:* Be sure to arrive in plenty of time so you can test your equipment and talk to the sound technicians well before the presentation begins. I always bring chocolate for the sound technicians when I speak at a conference. Whether you sound good or not is in their control!

2. *Wear a belt:* The transmitters for lapel mics are best clipped onto your belt, so remember to wear one. Remember to thread the cord through your shirt and tuck the surplus cords down into your trousers or skirt.

3. *Wear appropriate jewellery:* Ensure any earrings or other jewellery don't jingle around and make an annoying tapping sound into the microphone. Choose earrings and jewellery that will remain still on your ears.

4. *Position the microphone carefully:* Keep the head of the microphone low enough to avoid the spitting sounds, but high enough so it projects your voice. (Roughly 5 to 10 centimetres from the tip of your chin is best.)

5. *Check your frequencies:* Ensure that the audio speakers are set to different frequencies so they don't clash when you walk and speak.

6. *Use mute as required:* I recommend you check where the on/off and mute buttons are. Remember to mute the sound if you go to the toilet! I've experienced many times the embarrassment of a fellow speaker who forgets to switch their microphone to mute before going to the toilet, only to entertain their audience with their trickling sounds! As a professional speaker, I always ask the sound technicians if I can control my own mute buttons. If you are unaccustomed to speaking with a microphone, you may prefer to let the sound people manage this for you. They will turn you on and off, so you can focus on the more important job of saying what you mean to say in a confident, clear, charismatic way!

7. *Be natural:* Speak in your natural voice; don't strain or push the sound towards the audience.

8. *Have a back-up plan:* Remember, you are the presenter, so you control your space. If something goes wrong with your microphone, don't ignore it and hope it will go away. Have a back-up on hand (either another lapel mic or a hand-held microphone) that you can use immediately. And make sure you have either brought your own replacement batteries or asked the sound technicians to have them ready just in case. Maintain your composure no matter what happens with your equipment. Continue your eye contact with your audience so you keep up your connection with them, and just keep going as soon as the mic problem has been resolved.

9. *Take care if you walk around with a microphone:* You can't always walk anywhere you want if you are wearing a mic. Rehearse with the microphone if you can. On some stages and with certain sound systems, if you walk too close to the speakers they will let off a piercing interference squeal that is very uncomfortable for your audience. That means you must rehearse with the microphone and test to see if there is anywhere you can't stand — so as to avoid that dreadful squealing sound.

Handy tip: If you have more than one presenter, ensure you have two microphones and have the second person wired up well before you finish your presentation. A seamless transition from one speaker to another often goes unnoticed. A messy transition will have you looking unprofessional and disrespectful.

Using a headset microphone

A headset microphone is, as the name implies, a microphone that you wear on your head. It is an excellent alternative to a lapel mic.

Headsets have been around for years in musical theatre and have become more and more popular with conference speakers. A headset mic typically has a strap or piece of soft wire that hooks over one or both of your ears, with the microphone stretching down across your left or right cheek. Most headset microphones come with a comprehensive fitting guide to allow you to achieve the most comfortable and effective placement for your microphone.

Simply place the headset wireframe around your head so that it sits horizontally across the back of your head and the ends of the wireframe fit over and in front of your ears. Make sure it feels comfortable and stable. Move your head around to be sure it won't fall off your ear! If the headset feels loose or uncomfortable, carefully bend the sides of the wireframe to make it tighter or looser. You may choose to use elastic tape to secure it once and for all. The angle of the wireframe earpieces may also need adjustment. Make sure you place the headset mic a short distance above, below or to the side of your mouth so it projects your voice and not your breath.

TRY THIS

1. If you can, borrow a lapel microphone from your human resources or marketing department and practise setting it up and speaking with it.

2. Ensure you wear it well: position the mic appropriately (see the tips in this chapter).

3. Experiment with it so you become like old friends with the lapel microphone.

TOP TIPS
for speaking with confidence

- A smooth, confident voice is within us all.

- When your voice sounds confident, your audience is more likely to relax and listen.

- Use the most appropriate vocal variety for the message. If you want to be engaging and convincing when you speak, strive for a variety of natural pitch, speed and volume.

- A pause is powerful and necessary for your audience. Pausing is where your audience catches up with you!

- Pausing will help you breathe deeply and diaphragmatically, which helps you relax and maintain control of yourself as you present.

- The best sound system is the one the audience doesn't even notice.

- If you use a lapel or headset microphone, ensure you tuck all surplus cords inside your clothing.

- The transmitters for lapel mics are best clipped onto your belt, so remember to wear one.

- Rehearse with the microphone if you can.

- If you have more than one presenter, ensure you have two microphones and have the second person wired up well before you finish your presentation.

CHAPTER 13

Congruent body language

Your body plays a fundamental role in the believability of your message — as dancer and choreographer Martha Graham said, 'The body never lies'. I remember going to a presentation where the CEO said, 'We have an open-door policy', while making a gesture with his hands where they moved from the centre of his body with his palms down to the outside of his hips. We call this body posture 'the Leveller' (I discuss this in more detail later in this chapter). The Leveller is not an ideal posture to do when trying to invite your audience to connect with you, because it is a no-nonsense, 'don't argue with me' type of posture! By using this gesture, the CEO effectively cancelled out his words. I thought to myself at the time that his true thoughts about the open-door policy were revealed in the gesture he did! Have you ever seen something like that?

Psychologist Albert Mehrabian's research into verbal and non-verbal messages suggests that in face-to-face communication we apportion only 7 per cent of the meaning of the message to the actual words that are said. Another 38 per cent of the meaning derives from the tonality (the way you say the words), and 55 per cent of the meaning comes from body language (how you move your body).

And you may know, we use body language as the final test for deciding on the congruence and authenticity of a presenter. In this chapter, I give you everything you need to pass this final test. (Note that the information in the following sections relates more to face-to-face presentations. For tips when presenting virtually, including help with eye contact and engaging your audience, see chapter 20.)

> **TIP**
>
> **Michelle says,**
>
> 'Congruent body language — body language that matches the words being spoken — is critical if you want to build and maintain strong rapport and influence your audience.'

Understanding body language

I have divided body language into three main areas:

- eye contact
- stance
- gestures.

The following sections look at each of these three areas of body language during face-to-face presentations in more detail.

Eye contact

In live presentations, it's essential that you focus on the different members of your audience as much as possible and, importantly, as much as they need you to. Some people don't like you to give them too much eye contact, so take their lead and don't look at them as much as some of the other people. Others in your audience require a lot of eye contact, so it's a great idea to look at them more! As a general rule, it's a good idea to give individually appropriate eye contact to all of the different people in your audience.

In addition, looking into the eyes of the people in your audience is important because it:

- helps you connect with your audience

- stops the audience switching off and doing something else

- reduces your nerves.

In the following sections, I run through a couple of common difficulties with maintaining eye contact.

'WHAT IF MY AUDIENCE IS VERY BIG, OR IF IT'S DARK AND I CAN'T SEE THEM?'

If you have a large audience, or it's dark and you have spotlights in your eyes, the key is to really look at as many people as possible. Mix this up with looking into the other sections of your audience where people's faces aren't clear. Imagine the faces of the audience so it looks and feels like you really can see their eyes. Make sure this is as genuine as possible.

TIP

Michelle says,

'When presenting with spotlights, make sure you don't squint into the light. Open your eyes and focus through the light so you connect with your audience.'

Better still, ask the organiser to always have 'full house lights on' when you are presenting. That's the jargon for all the lights on. If you have the lights on, you'll better see your audience members' eyes, you'll better connect — and you'll avoid the migraine headache that can be the result of staring into stage lights.

'I HATE PEOPLE LOOKING AT ME WHEN I PRESENT — WHAT CAN I DO?'

If you feel this way you are most definitely not alone! This is one of the most common obstacles for presenters. Here are some tips that may help:

- The audience takes about nine seconds to make an initial assessment of you. They look at superficial things such as your hair, make-up, spectacles, accessories, clothes and shoes, and judge you in that moment.

- Once they have made their initial assessment, they take about another 25 seconds to validate their original thoughts and feelings about you. This involves listening to your voice, and watching your body movements, facial expressions and energy.

- Then they go back to thinking about themselves!

In other words, the audience is there for themselves, not for you. They are going to assess you in those first few seconds and then, provided everything is okay — which, of course, it will be — they go back to working out how your message can help them in their life. They are not really looking at you at all!

Don't think of your presentation as a presentation to a group — which is a scary thought for many. Looking at a whole group is not possible in the one moment. You can only look properly at one person at a time. You can't properly look at someone in the whites of their eyes and look at everyone else at the same time. Just focus on the whites of the eyes of one person at a time (refer to chapter 11 for more).

TIP

Michelle says,

'Remind yourself: "In any given moment in my presentation, it's just me and one other person".'

TRY THIS

1. Next time you present, be really aware that you are sharing your eye contact around with everyone in your audience.

2. Start to become aware of which people in your audience like you to look at them a lot, and which people would prefer you gave them less of your eye contact. Follow their lead and do what's best for your audience.

Stance

Most presenters are at their most nervous at the start and finish of their presentation. Can you relate to that? The middle of the presentation can also cause some concern for you if conflict or discomfort arises. During these times you should consider standing in what is called the 'natural' stance.

This is where you stand symmetrically, with your weight equally on both feet. It's called the natural stance because it's how we learned to stand when we were little. It was the way we automatically stood when we were all first learning to hold up our own body and before learning to walk.

TIP

Michelle says,

'The natural stance will help put you and your audience at ease.'

Interestingly, though, research by psychologist Robert Cialdini suggests that in Western society we are attracted to patterns of asymmetry. Although most of us stood in the natural stance when we were little children, when we hit adolescence we mostly unlearned the natural stance in favour of more asymmetrical casual postures such as the lean (where you put your weight into one hip and one foot at a time).

TIP

Michelle says,

'If you want your audience to think of you as confident and professional, the natural stance is the best choice for you.'

WHY THE NATURAL STANCE IS EFFECTIVE

Standing symmetrically in the natural stance helps you breathe diaphragmatically instead of using chest breathing. (For more about the importance of deep breathing and the links to a strong voice, see chapter 10.) The natural stance also helps you look and feel solid and more confident as you stand and address your audience. If you're standing when presenting online, you can use this stance for virtual presenting in the same way you would in a live presentation. It's a really simple stance to master.

Here's what to do:

1. Place your feet under the bones of your hips.

2. Ensure your weight is fully over both of your feet equally.

3. Slightly relax your knees.

4. Imagine a bowl of your favourite drink all around your pelvis that is full to the brim. (I don't know about you, I wouldn't want to spill a single drop over the sides!)

5. Brace your core — your deep-down tummy muscles.

6. Relax your shoulders (this is very important so you don't look or feel stiff).

7. Ensure your head is to the front.

OTHER CHOICES WHEN STANDING

The natural stance is for the times when you need to look and feel credible, strong and unflustered — such as at the start of your presentation when your audience is deciding whether to trust you or not. At other times in your presentation you will choose to stand in a lean with your weight into one hip, because you want to come across as more casual and approachable.

Michelle says,

'Be sure to stand in a way that sends the right message to your audience.'

USING THE TYPICAL STANCES

You've likely also used some other common stances — or seen them in other presenters. Some are helpful, and others detract from your message.

Table 13.1 shows some typical stances.

Table 13.1 Some typical stances

	Stance	Meaning
	The Prince Philip	As the name implies, this stance has been taught and used by presenters far and wide since Prince Philip, Duke of Edinburgh and the husband of Queen Elizabeth II, was a young man. It is where you stand tall with your hands held together behind your back. The benefit of this stance is that you seem confident. The downside is that you can appear arrogant or as though you might be hiding something behind your back.
	Crossed arms	This is where you cross your arms in front of your body. If your message lends itself to this stance at times, then by all means do so with your body. This stance can indicate that you are closed-minded or inflexible. If this is incongruent with your message, this stance is not a good choice.
	The 'fig leaf', 'crotch clutch' or 'reluctant nudist'	This position, where you stand with your hands covering your crotch, is a stance you should definitely avoid. I notice that board members are commonly photographed in this stance! This stance makes everyone look at the one part of your body you would probably rather they didn't. I'll say no more!

TRY THIS

1. Try the natural stance. Follow the steps listed in this chapter and notice whether the natural stance still feels natural or not.

2. Make a plan to practise standing in the natural stance whenever appropriate, even when you're not presenting. This will help you feel more natural when you use it in a presentation.

3. Ask a friend who attends one of your business presentations to give you some feedback about your stance. Make a plan to correct any habits that don't maximise the chance of influencing your audience.

MOVING AROUND WHEN PRESENTING

Yes, it's a great idea to move around the stage when presenting. Just be sure that you always stand in the correct place on your stage and remember to either stand still or move with a purpose to your next position.

TIP

Michelle says,

'Either stand still or move with a purpose.'

When deciding where to stand in the room during face-to-face or virtual presenting, keep in mind that certain areas on the floor represent the past, present and future.

In Western society, we read left to right. This means that as we sit in an audience we see what's on our left as our past and what's on our right as our future. When presenting, you need to remember that you are facing in the opposite direction to your audience. This means you need to move in a counterintuitive way — in the way that is congruent for your audience but incongruent for you. The way you work this out is to ask yourself: What is correct for my audience?' Do what makes sense for them, not you.

Here's how to use the 'past', 'present' and 'future' positions when presenting live or online:

- *Past:* Because we recognise that the audience's left is their past, when you talk about competitors, past events or bad results, you should stand to the audience's left, in their past. I suggest you aim to stand to the audience's past for the 'reduce' section in your WIIFM statement, when you raise the POO (not the solution), and for the negative consequences at Step 12 of your Persuasion Blueprint. (Refer to chapter 5 for more on all of these sections and steps.)

- *Present:* Because the audience's present is the centre of the room, when you are delivering important information you should stand in the middle of the stage or presentation area. The middle is also known as the 'hot spot'. Your hot spot (or centre of intelligence) is where you deliver facts, data and information that are not to be questioned, such as your leading statement (Step 2) and your call to action (Step 10) from the Persuasion Blueprint.

- *Future:* We recognise the audience's right as their future. So when you talk about future-focused things and positive results, you should stand to the audience's right, in their future. I suggest you aim to stand in the audience's future for the 'improve' section in your WIIFM statement, your solution to the POO, and for your positive consequences (Step 12) of the Persuasion Blueprint.

Handy tip: The same guidelines apply for gestures and eye contact. When you gesture to your audience's left, you signal that your message is past-focused, bad news or competitor related. When you gesture to your audience's right, you signal that the words you are saying are future-focused, great news or something to look forward to. You can do the same with your eye contact, moving from the audience's left to their right.

Considering how and where you move in this way is not actually as complicated as it sounds. Try it a few times and I guarantee you will find it adds that extra dimension of authenticity to your message for your audience.

TIP

Michelle says,

'When presenting on a stage, be sure to enter from the audience's left (or past) and exit to the audience's right (or future).'

TRY THIS

1. Think a bit about your audience's past, present and future.

2. Make a plan to ensure that you stand in the correct place and time when you next present, based on the kind of content you're presenting at different points.

Gestures: what to do with your hands

People will be stimulated by you as a presenter and will understand your message more fully if you use your hands cleverly. In live and online presentations, I believe it's important that you use your hands to reinforce your message and maximise the likelihood of changing your audience's behaviour.

Can you gesture too much? Absolutely! It's very possible to move your hands so much that your audience becomes distracted by your movement or entranced by your activity to the detriment of their ability to listen. So remember to put your hands down by your sides (called 'cleaning the slate') between gestures to give your audience a break every now and then!

USING INFORMAL AND FORMAL GESTURES

The two main types of gestures are informal and formal ones.

Informal gesturing is often referred to as talking with your hands. These gestures are unrehearsed.

TIP

Michelle says,

'It's completely okay to gesture informally, as long as you put your arms back down by your sides for a rest every now and then.'

Formal gestures are rehearsed, often in front of a mirror. The purpose of a formal gesture is to emphasise a point that is important. Well-delivered gestures can replace the need for some of your PowerPoint slides. An example of a formal gesture is when you count something with your fingers at the same time as you say the words 'one', 'two' and 'three', or when you stretch your arms out, with your palms up, to your audience while saying, 'It's up to you'.

Two things are important to remember when you gesture formally in a live meeting:

1. Practise in front of the mirror to refine the gesture and ensure that it is strong and congruent with the message you want to send. I call this having energy through to the ends of your fingertips. Make sure you don't use any 'limp fish' gestures.

2. Ensure lots of air is under your armpits to increase visibility when you gesture! In other words, make your gestures big enough for people to get your point.

I cover what to do when you gesture in a virtual meeting in chapter 20.

GESTURES AND MEANING

Author and family therapist Virginia Satir noted that a number of gestures have particular meaning. These gestures or postures can create certain reactions or responses in your audience. Table 13.2 (overleaf) outlines these gestures and their meanings.

Table 13.2 Some common body postures and their meanings

	Body posture	Meaning
	Blamer	Characterised by a pointed, often stabbing finger, and sometimes with a forward body posture. This gesture can be seen as aggressive, so it's wise to use it sparingly. As a general rule, I recommend you open your palm to soften the impact if you choose to use this gesture.
	Placater	This is a symmetrical, open posture with arms outstretched and palms upturned. I recommend you use this gesture when you want the audience to feel you are open to their point of view. For example, 'What questions do you have?'
	Computer	Characterised by one hand on the chin with the other arm folded across the chest holding the elbow. This is recommended when you want to either send a message that you are thinking, or when you want your audience to think about something. For example, 'Let me think about that'.
	Distracter	This is an asymmetrical posture, often off balance, and characterised by frenetic energy or lots of moving around. Overused, this posture is, as the name suggests, distracting. Used well, this posture can be entertaining and energising for the audience.

	Body posture	Meaning
	Leveller	Another symmetrical posture. The leveller is characterised by arms outstretched and palms open and facing downward. It often goes with an outward movement of both hands from the front of the body to the sides of the body. It's a gesture you should use when you are either making an important point or when you are saying something that is not for negotiation. For example, you would say, 'That's how it must be' with this sort of gesture.

USING PAST, PRESENT AND FUTURE POSITIONS WHEN YOU GESTURE

It is important to gesture in a way that supports your message. So, depending on what you are saying, your gesture should move from the audience's left to right or from their right to left, based on the areas that represent the past, present and future in space, on the floor and on the stage. As mentioned earlier in this chapter, the audience's left is their past, so for past events or bad news, gesture to their left. The audience's right is their future, so for future-focused things and positive results, gesture to the audience's right.

IF YOU DON'T GESTURE

If you don't gesture, your audience may not receive as much visual stimulation as they need and this could result in them losing concentration. Well-delivered gestures will definitely reduce the likelihood of you being perceived as a presenter who is just saying 'blah, blah, blah'. For more information on the need to gesture, see the next chapter, which explains in more detail why certain types of learners need more or less gesturing from the presenter. Also see chapter 20 for more on effective gesturing in online presentations.

Using a lectern

I'll be honest with you: I'm not a big fan of the lectern. Presenting is such an excellent way to showcase your professional expertise and connect with your audience. Standing behind a lectern when presenting in person takes away some of your expertise and ability to connect. A lectern says, 'I'm up here with this barrier between you and me, and anyway I need to keep reading my notes'. Please aim to be the person who wears a microphone and stands in the middle of the presentation space to confidently engage the audience — not behind the lectern.

TIP

Michelle says,

'Where possible, come out from behind the lectern, with no barriers between you and your audience.'

If after reading this you still want to use the lectern, be sure to at least start (that is, when delivering Steps 0 to 5 of the Persuasion Blueprint) in the middle of the stage, in the 'hot spot', and away from the lectern. The hot spot is the best place for you to stand when your aim is to build rapport and engage with your audience. You can then stand behind the lectern for Steps 6 and 7 of the Persuasion Blueprint, and then move back to the hot spot, or middle of the room or stage, for your close (Steps 8 to 13 of your Persuasion Blueprint).

TRY THIS

1. Rehearse your gestures until they look really natural.

2. Run through your presentation and notice the occasions where you could move across the floor from past to future. Make a note of those places, so you move effectively every time you deliver this presentation.

The role of smiling

Smiling plays a very important role in presenting, and this is true for both in-person and virtual presentations. It has many benefits — not least of which is that it makes you feel good! Smiling makes you more attractive, improves the immune system, reduces stress and makes you seem more confident.

TIP

Michelle says,

'Guess what? You just might find that if you smile more, you will make yourself feel happier and more confident!'

Remember that your role as the presenter is to ensure your face, words and body movements are congruent with your overall emotional objective, or emotional intention, from one moment to the next in your presentation. So if your intention is to have the audience feeling happy and uplifted, a smile is a great choice. If, on the other hand, your objective is to have your audience feeling concerned or fearful of certain consequences, then be sure that you are authentically connected to your message and lose the smile.

TIP

Michelle says,

'Make sure you smile when necessary to convey the appropriate emotional objective.'

TOP TIPS
for congruent body language

- It's important to give appropriate eye contact to individual members of your audience. Focus on the different members of your audience as much as possible and, importantly, as much as they need you to.

- Your body also plays a fundamental role in the believability of your message.

- At the start and finish of your presentation, and when you are under pressure in your presentation or just want to be seen as credible, try the natural stance — feet under your hips, brace muscles engaged.

- The two main types of gestures are informal and formal. Informal gesturing is where you talk with your hands, while formal gesturing is rehearsed and involves lots of air under the armpits.

- Formal gestures can replace slides.

- Put your hands down by your side and 'clean the slate' between all your gestures to give the audience a visual break every now and then.

- Your audience's left is their past, their right is their future, and the centre of the room or presentation space is the centre of intelligence, where you deliver your important facts and data.

- Do what's necessary with your body to maximise the chances of influencing your audience.

- Make sure you smile when necessary to convey the appropriate emotional objective.

CHAPTER 14

Engage and entertain

When it comes to presenting we know that audiences are made up of people who have a variety of personality filters. One of the more relevant filters to understand when you are presenting, running meetings, influencing people or facilitating groups — online or live — relates to the way people process and sort information.

Have you ever sat in a presentation or meeting feeling so bored you were nearly asleep? Or have you ever been to a presentation where the presenter was just not on your wavelength, where it sounded to you as though they were just saying 'blah, blah, blah'? Maybe you have had an experience where you were speaking with someone and their eyes glazed over and you felt as though you might as well have been saying 'blah, blah, blah' to them? Surely not!

There is a significant reason for feeling this way during an unstimulating or boring presentation. The reason is probably that the presenter was not attending enough to your visual, auditory or kinesthetic preferences. So let's make sure you don't make the same mistake in your presentations!

Engaging with your audience is all about flexibility. We know that the ability to build rapport and get along with people is very important in both business and personal relationships. We also know that it is easier to build rapport with people who demonstrate the same or similar characteristics to us — people who are like ourselves. Building rapport with people who are not like us becomes more difficult. When we don't understand others, we often find it difficult to relate effectively to them — and find it even harder to influence these people in a workplace meeting or presentation setting.

If you have ever wished you could be more engaging and stimulate the whole of your audience more effectively throughout your online or face-to-face presentations, keep on reading.

Engaging and stimulating your audience

Let's quickly run through the differences between the visual, auditory and kinesthetic audience members. Once you know what these preferences are, you can consider how to keep each of the different styles completely engaged in your presentation.

Visual preference

Most audiences include people who favour their sight and visuals for processing and storing information or memories. In other words, they favour their visual channel. These are the people who:

- seem to take a lot of pride in their appearance

- often have an organised, neat, orderly desk

- like to see what you mean

- make decisions based on how things look

- have trouble remembering verbal conversations or presentations

- are less distracted by noisy interferences because they focus less on their auditory channel.

TIPS FOR STIMULATING THE AUDIENCE'S VISUAL PREFERENCE

People with a visual preference need visual displays to be engaged by your message, to stay alert and to understand your point easily. You can use the following to ensure you stimulate these people:

- *Visual aids:* Use visual aids such as slides and make sure your slides have clear, simple graphs and beautiful, modern images or pictures — and not too many words! Also try wall charts, video, posters, flipcharts, a whiteboard, banners, handouts and props. Each of these options creates visual stimulation.

- *Movement:* Use gestures, stance and movement with a purpose across the floor, especially when you are telling a story. Bring your story to life!

- *Icons:* Use the hand up, smiley face and other icons on your virtual platform, where appropriate, to keep people listening.

- *Precision:* Pay attention to the detail in your personal appearance. Shine your shoes, brush your hair, iron your clothes well, tuck your shirt in properly and, for the lipstick wearers, make sure you reapply it throughout the day!

- *Speed:* People with a visual preference tend to process information quickly and will be frustrated by time-wasting, so make sure you speak quickly at times and keep your message moving.

- *Reinforcement:* Give people with a visual preference some form of written reinforcement of your content, such as handouts, web addresses and back-up information.

- *Eye contact:* Ensure you give people with a visual preference lots of your eye contact.

- *Background:* In a virtual presentation, pay attention to your background. Is it the right colour, design and vibe for your event?

- *Language:* Use visually based language. The following lists some visual words for you to consider.

Aim	Foresight	Paint a picture
Appear	Frame	Pattern
Bird's-eye view	Glaze	Perspective
Blank	Glance	Picture
Blind	Glare	Portray
Blur	Glow	Reveal
Bright	Hazy	Round
Brilliant	Hindsight	Reflect
Clear	Horizon	See
Cloudy	Illuminate	Sketch
Colour	Imagine	Short-sighted
Dark	Insight	Sight for sore eyes
Dim	Light	Show
Diagram	Look	Shine
Disillusion	Luminous	Take a peek
Draw	Mirror	Tunnel vision
Dull	Obscure	Watch
Eclipse	Observe	View
Envision	Outlook	Vivid
Enlighten	Overshadow	Visualise
Flash	Oversight	Vision
Focus	Overview	

TRY THIS

Go back to the presentation you have been working on while reading this book and ensure you have some visual words and some visual strategies planned throughout.

TIP

Michelle says,

'Always keep those people with a visual preference engaged and entertained in your presentation.'

Auditory preference

Most audiences also include people who favour their sense of hearing and vocals for processing and storing information or memories. They favour their auditory channel.

These are the people who:

- don't always look at you when listening — they will turn their head and use their ears as their primary information-gathering channel

- are easily distracted by noise

- breathe from the middle of the chest

- have the gift of the gab

- articulate their words beautifully and they use different pitch, volume and speed.

TIPS FOR STIMULATING THE AUDITORY PREFERENCE IN YOUR AUDIENCE

Use the following to ensure you stimulate people with an auditory preference:

- *Appropriate eye contact:* These people need to focus on their ears and listening when you communicate with them. Don't be put off if they turn their eyes away from you and their ear towards you. You can build rapport with them by matching their body language and giving the visual people in the room more of your eye contact.

- *Warmed up voice:* Pay attention to the way you say your words. Warm up your articulation with techniques such as the kiss/grin, orange/pea and the horse neigh. Warm up your tone by yawning with a big, open mouth. (Refer to chapter 10 for more on these techniques.)

- *Variety:* Use vocal variety (speed, pitch and volume) and emphasise key words (refer to chapter 12).

- *Linguistic tricks:* Try some alliteration, anaphora, tricolon, conduplicatio, epistrophe and rhetorical questions to spark their interest. (See chapter 6 for more information on using these exciting inclusions in an exceptional presentation.)

- *Onomatopoeia:* Some onomatopoeia can be exciting for them, too. Do you remember this from school? 'Kapow!' and 'Boom!'

- *Patience:* Don't expect immediate responses. People with an auditory preference typically need time to reflect and discuss your content before making decisions.

- *Spoken feedback:* Give those members of your audience with auditory preference spoken feedback to reinforce behaviour. And let them talk. They will understand your message better if they are given the chance to discuss their perspective.

- *Music:* Try to use appropriate music to either open or close your presentation.

- *Audio tracks:* The audio in a video or just pure audio is wonderful for these people.

- *Questions:* Ask your audience members some questions and get them to answer either one at a time or in groups so that everyone has a turn.

- *Microphone:* Whether live or online, ensure that your voice is being enhanced with the right microphone for the event.

- *Language:* Use auditory-type language. The following outlines some auditory words for you to consider.

Acclaim	Discuss	Quiet as a mouse
Aloud	Echo	Resounding
Amplify	Exclaim	Retort
Announce	Harmony	Rhythm
Argue	Hear	Rings a bell
Articulate	Hiss	Say
Audible	Hush	Scream
Beat	Listen	Shout
Boom	Loud	Silent
Buzz	Melody	Snap
Cacophony	Mention	Sound
Call	Music	Squeal
Chant	Mute	State
Chime	Noise	Swear
Clang	On another note	Talk
Clear as a bell	Pronounce	Verbalise
Click	Propose	Voice an opinion
Deaf	Purrs like a kitten	Volume
Describe	Question	Whisper

Michelle says,

'It's a great idea to work in some music throughout your meeting and especially during any breakout sessions.'

USING MUSIC IN PRESENTATIONS

If you have ever wished your conferences, training programs or meetings could be more engaging so that attendees felt stimulated and entertained (and, before they know it, it's time for dinner), then try using music in all the breaks and for appropriate activities. If possible, hire a professional sound system from a reputable provider for face-to-face presentations. In bigger meetings, and if you have some extra budget, it's much easier if you can get the audiovisual experts to manage the music for you from the back of the room.

To choose some music for activities (whether your presentation is online or in-person), pick songs with particular messages or beats that set the mood of the activity. Start with popular music with one beat per second (roughly in time with the human heartbeat). Keep in mind that, the more out-there you go with your choice, the more likely you are going to offend someone. In breaks, play upbeat songs that match the theme of the event for you. As a very simple example, at a team-building event you might play 'We are family' by Sister Sledge.

Michelle says,

'Music can make a big difference to the ambience and energy levels of your audience. Plan the music to suit the mood you wish to create.'

Handy tip: When you are using music, remember to fade the track out at the end of activities (that is, turn the music down slowly) rather than simply pressing the stop button and surprising people with a jolt! If you are playing a particular theme song to call your audience back from the breaks, let the song come to its natural end and then stop it. The purpose of using the same song to denote the end of a break is to signify the start of something new and interesting and to give people time to resettle in their seats.

TRY THIS

Go back to your presentation and ensure you have included some auditory words and planned some auditory strategies throughout to keep the people with an auditory preference engaged and entertained.

Kinesthetic preference

Most audiences will also include people who favour their touch, movement and emotions for processing and storing information or memories. These people favour their kinesthetic channel.

These are the people who:

- breathe from the bottom of their lungs
- move and talk slowly
- dress for comfort
- are often referred to as 'touchy-feely' and respond well to touching and physical sensations
- can tend to stand very close and often touch you when they talk
- often seem fidgety in the meeting — they click pens, tap their legs and take lot of notes.

TIPS FOR STIMULATING THE KINESTHETIC PREFERENCE IN YOUR AUDIENCE

You can use the following to stimulate your audience members who have a kinesthetic preference:

- *Patience:* When you question people, don't expect an immediate response. Kinesthetics need time to sort through your message in their own way. They need time to focus, think about and process your information. Coming to a decision on the spot is difficult, because they often need to mull it over.

- *Comfortable environment:* Build strong rapport with your language, dress and room set-up. Consider the chairs, the aspect and the temperature of the room. Make sure the environment is as comfortable as possible.

- *Physicality:* Audience members with a kinesthetic preference respond well to handshakes, smiling and other appropriate physical approaches.

- *Touch:* Give out things to touch and explore physically, such as samples, examples and handouts. Stress balls and fuzzy-wuzzies are also perfect.

- *Reduced distractions:* Don't give out pens that click! The people with a kinesthetic preference will find a way to tap, knock, bang or click whatever writing implement you give them (much to the annoyance of people with a visual or auditory preference).

- *Emotion:* Tell stories that evoke emotions, and use anecdotes, case studies, examples, metaphors and analogies. And be sure to remember to actually tell your audience why you love this subject — it's contagious!

- *Movement:* Ensure you build in activities, moving around, talking and interacting, or these people will become very restless and will distract others. This is one reason many of the top corporate trainers ask participants to regularly change positions and sit in a different chair.

- *Participation:* Give people with a kinesthetic preference a chance to jump into activities and talk through how they feel about your content. This will help connect them with your content and move them to a decision.

- *Online breakouts, polls and chat:* These online functions help kinesthetic learners stay engaged. Use them as often as you can and just be sure to be firm with instructions so they don't distract.

- *Imagery:* Search online photo libraries for some emotive, evocative images you can use in your slides, rather than just using words.

- *Warmth:* Compliment your audience and cause as many positive ripples, or good feelings, across your audience as possible throughout your presentation. (See chapter 15 for a more thorough explanation of ripples in your presentation.)

- *Smile:* Your authentic smile causes a kinesthetic reaction in your audience and is an indication you are warm and making a big effort to connect. It also shows you enjoy your subject.

- *Names:* The greatest sound is that of your own name! Make sure you use people's names as often as appropriate.

- *Language:* Use kinesthetic language, such as the following.

Activate	Block	Delightful
Affection	Catch	Drive
Agitate	Cemented	Emotional
Annoy	Compress	Excited
Anxious	Concrete	Extend
Attach	Connect	Exuberant
Backing	Complacent	Fall
Balance	Cool	Fed up
Blend	Cut	Feel

Firm foundation	Jarring	Point
Flat	Joyful	Pull some strings
Get hold of	Lift	Push
Get in touch with	Lonely	Reach
Hang in there	Loose	Resist
Hand in hand	Love	Rigid
Happy	Kick	Rough
Hard	Massage	Sharp as a tack
Heated argument	Merge	Shocking
Hit	Mix	Smooth operator
Hold	Move	Solid
Horrified	Passive	Support
Hurt	Pressured	Tap into

TRY THIS

Go back to your presentation and ensure you have some kinesthetic words and some kinesthetic strategies planned throughout so you keep the people with a kinesthetic preference engaged and entertained.

By using the strategies outlined through this chapter, you will be more likely to build rapport with everyone in your audience. You will be more entertaining and engaging, and the audience will listen more actively to you.

This means you will be increasing the likelihood of achieving your presentation outcomes. (For much more information on persuading different types of people throughout all aspects of your life, see my book *How to Persuade: The skills you need to get what you want*, also published by Wiley.)

TOP TIPS
for engaging and entertaining

Audiences are made up of people with a variety of personality filters, which explain the different ways we process and sort information.

- Some important filters that you should understand and pay attention to when you are delivering a presentation are the visual, auditory and kinesthetic filters.

- You can use a variety of methods to stimulate the visual, auditory and kinesthetic preferences of your audience members.

CHAPTER 15

Dealing with difficult people

The ability to deal with difficult people in a way that is respectful for all concerned is the sign of a truly exceptional presenter. Maybe in the past your presentation has been hijacked by people in your audience who were behaving in a dysfunctional way. If that has happened to you, I wonder how you managed the problem at the time. Was it easy for you to regain control, or did you find yourself freaking out and feeling very uncomfortable or even angry?

I recommend you pay attention to disruptive behaviour and nip it in the bud as soon as you can to ensure the smooth running of your meeting or presentation — whether it be online or offline.

Keeping your audience on side

Have you ever been in a presentation where the presenter either accidentally or willingly insulted an audience member and, before you knew it, the whole group had turned against the presenter?

If you answered yes to this question, what you experienced is called the 'ripple effect'. When you throw a stone into a pond, the concentric circles ripple out — and it's the same when you present. You can create your own metaphorical concentric circles by either insulting or complimenting your audience members. By either insulting or complimenting your audience members, the ripples you create will be either positive or negative, depending on what you have said or done as the presenter.

Excellent presenters send out hundreds of positive ripples in a single event. Unskilled presenters can cause many negative ripples without even realising it — and then they ask themselves, 'What was wrong with that audience?' In this instance, the presenter often doesn't realise that they caused one or more negative ripples.

TIP

Michelle says,

'Unskilled presenters can cause many negative ripples in their presentation and then wonder, "What was wrong with that audience?"'

Creating positive and negative ripples

Positive ripples are caused by:

- complimenting, rewarding or acknowledging the audience or a member of your audience by smiling and shaking hands in a respectful way
- making people in your audience feel important and special — known as 'giving status'.

Negative ripples are caused by:

- rudeness or insensitivity to an audience or audience member
- ignoring someone too many times, or withholding eye contact
- humiliating, offending or embarrassing an audience member.

TIP

Michelle says,

'Excellent presenters send out hundreds of positive ripples in a single presentation.'

Natasha's story

Natasha is a fellow speaker who was recounting an experience she had as an audience member in a conference.

The presenter was a world-class speaker, and it seemed the power had gone to their head. Any time anyone in the audience asked a question that indicated they were unclear about the point or unsure of the theory, the speaker would ridicule them with a joke or a put-down comment and a big laugh. When the speaker laughed, they looked to the rest of the audience to get their buy-in to the put-down.

Natasha became increasingly uncomfortable and eventually chose not to question or comment. Essentially, she shut down and switched off. She reflected that, as she did so, some other members of the audience noticed her discomfort and started giving her smiles and words of kindness to try to help ease the discomfort. The number of people distracted by this activity grew to about a third of the audience in no time. If a third of the audience were focused on Natasha, what were they not focused on? Exactly — they were not paying attention to the speaker.

Finally, the speaker realised the ramifications of their insensitivity and began to try to draw both the group members and Natasha back into the presentation. Unfortunately, the audience remained offended at the presenter's treatment of their colleagues: they refused to budge and chose not to listen properly for the rest of the presentation.

Handy tip: Remember that presenting is not about your ego. It's about getting into the audience's shoes and helping them relax and listen, so they can understand your message and change their behaviour. Respect your audience. Give 'love' at all times and manage both the positive and negative ripples in your audience.

Fixing a negative ripple

As long as you are not a really rude presenter who doesn't care at all about your audience, it's very easy to fix a negative ripple if you cause one accidentally. All you need to do is refocus on connecting with the individuals in the group and then purposefully cause a whole lot of positive ripples — using compliments, smiles and inclusive statements — to counteract the negativity. You will find that the audience will be on your side again quick smart.

TIP

Michelle says,

'Remember: presenting is not about you, it's all about the audience. Make sure at all times that you are conscious of the ripples you create. Respect your audience and master your craft.'

Managing difficult behaviour without causing negative ripples

Perhaps you have had difficult audience behaviour in your meetings, conferences or presentations (either online or face to face). Examples can include side conversations, or a person who really loves the sound of their own voice and keeps calling out ideas or asking inappropriate questions that don't add to the learning for the whole group. What did you do at the time? Did it work? Do you know what to do to make sure you minimise the amount of your energy you have to spend on managing the group, so you can spend more of your effort in connecting with the audience and influencing their behaviour?

The following sections outline some tips for managing difficult behaviour.

Build rapport

Ensure at all times that you maintain your 100 per cent rapport. Don't sound annoyed because, if you do, you've lost your control. Remember, people are not their behaviour. So while the person's behaviour might seem to be dysfunctional, that doesn't mean they are a dysfunctional person.

Turn to a friend

In this technique, you suggest to the audience that they each turn to the person next to them and discuss three key things that are related to your subject. When you do this, it's important that you give at least one example. You could ask your audience to discuss the three things they most want from the project under discussion, the three concerns they have about the project, or the three blockages they believe exist in relation to the project. And make sure you explain what you are asking the group to do in three different ways. This way they will be more likely to do what you are asking.

While the audience is doing what you asked them to do, you can spend time attending to the people causing the disruption. Once you have addressed the disruption, you can re-claim your space and debrief the activity you sent the rest of the group to do. By this time, they will generally have forgotten there was a disruption in the first place!

TIP

Michelle says,

'When it comes to facilitating group activity, remember that the first time you ask your audience to do something they generally don't listen, the second time they hear you but don't understand, and the third time they hear and understand.'

Use physical proximity

Walk close to the person causing the disruption without turning your head or looking at them. Remember never to face front-on to them. Your physical proximity is often enough to help people realise their interruptions are unwanted at this time.

Hand it over to the audience

This is a version of the 'turn to a friend' idea. Use the energy of your audience and give permission to everyone to talk about something with the person next to them. For example, 'Okay everyone, please talk to the person next to you and find out their concerns about the project plan to date — you have 2 minutes.' This way you have controlled the way the audience members go to the activity, and now you can control them turning their attention back to you when you say the time for the activity is up.

Call the behaviour

This is where you smile authentically, relax your body and then articulate what the person is doing that is unacceptable. For example, if Shirley was interrupting Heath's question you might say, 'Your point is relevant Shirley, and I'm conscious of not interrupting Heath'. Or if Brian was asking too many questions and taking the group off-track, you might say, 'Ah, yes, another question from you Brian'.

While many of us would regularly employ this technique with our close family and friends, it is the most risky of the techniques because you need strong rapport with the whole audience to carry it out. If you can't use this technique well, you might cause a negative ripple that could significantly break rapport. Be careful and choose wisely.

Ignore the problem

Sometimes ignoring the problem is the best strategy. Occasionally, if you ignore the problem it simply goes away. I will cross my fingers for you!

Use pre-framing

This is where you approach the person (who you know is going to be disruptive based on past performance) before the presentation and ask for their assistance during your meeting or presentation. This interaction might be a presentation that uses the four questions from the 4MAT System (*Why?*, *What?*, *How?* and *What if?* or *What else?* — refer to chapter 3) in its own right, or you might use the POO technique or pacing and leading to achieve this outcome (chapter 5).

TRY THIS

1. Think back to your most recent presentations. Was there any difficult behaviour that you wish you could have managed better? What do you think you might do differently next time?

2. Think about a presentation you have coming up. Who is going to be there? Do you expect any particular behaviour from the people who will be there? Can you plan for anything in advance?

TOP TIPS
for dealing with difficult people

- Pay attention to disruptive behaviour and nip it in the bud as soon as you can to ensure the smooth running of your meetings or presentation.

- Presenters can cause both positive and negative ripples in their audience.

- Excellent presenters send out hundreds of positive ripples in a single event: they compliment, smile, acknowledge and give status to the audience.

- Unskilled presenters can cause many negative ripples in their presentation: they demonstrate rudeness and insensitivity and ignore or offend the audience.

- Skilled presenters can counteract a negative ripple with some positive ripples.

- You can use specific strategies to help manage disruptive behaviour in your presentations.

CHAPTER 16

Using visual aids

Slides are an invaluable, powerful and exciting tool for creating visual aids that transform average speakers into masterful presenters. Or are they? Slides have become so dreadful and torturous that the phrase 'death by PowerPoint' was coined. In fact, statistician and professor emeritus Edward Tufte is quoted as saying, 'We've drifted into this presentation mode without realising the cost to the content and the audience in the process'. Let's make sure you don't cause death by PowerPoint when you present. Use your slides to set yourself up as the best (online or live) presenter you can be!

Take the test: will your slides be lethal?

Are you guilty of the 'kid in a toy shop' syndrome, where your enthusiasm for your newfound slide mastery is clouding your judgement as a presenter? Have you thought enough about the need to concentrate more on your verbal and non-verbal communication than your visual aids?

Try the following test to assess your use of slides:

- Do you lack confidence as a presenter? Would you be horrified at the thought of presenting to an audience without slides?

- Are you guilty of using slides to take the focus off yourself?

- Do you use slides as convenient palm cards?

- Do you find yourself looking back at your slides to remember what to say?

- Do you use PowerPoint to write your presentation?

- Do you try to use the entire functionality of PowerPoint as a way of improving your presentation?

- Do you always use the standard deck that your head office provided without any changes?

If you find yourself answering 'yes' to these questions, you've likely been relying on slides to carry you as a presenter, rather than using them simply as a visual aid to highlight the key messages for your audience. You may have great technical skill in designing slides, but it may well be at the expense of developing your ability to communicate with your audience and properly connect with them.

TIP

Michelle says,

'Please don't cause "death by PowerPoint": don't set yourself up to use slides as a lethal weapon!'

The purpose of slides

I believe the main reason many people don't use slides to their advantage is that they don't know how to. Delivering your message with confidence and charisma is simple, as long as you don't use slides that disengage your audience.

The purpose of slides for all presentations — online or face to face — is to reinforce your key messages, not to remind you, the presenter, what to say next. Slides have the potential to create a visual, kinesthetic and maybe even an auditory connection between your audience and your message. In other words, they help stimulate your audience in a variety of ways that will help them to remember your content.

Here are my top tips for designing slides to help you set yourself up as a powerful presenter who uses slides as an aid to influence your audience to your way of thinking, not as a script:

- Ask yourself the critical question, 'Is this the best way to visually reinforce this point?' If the answer is yes, then keep it in your presentation. If the answer is no, then fix it, delete it or start again.

- Replace words with pictures whenever possible. And make sure you only use one image per slide. Have your chosen image 'bleed to the edges', unless you're contrasting something — in which case, it's okay to use two images side by side.

- Use clever, beautiful images, not overused, tired ones.

- Use dark text on a light background, a minimum font size of 30 point and choose an easy-to-read font such as Times New Roman or Verdana.

- Don't use underlining, italics, bold or shadows on your fonts — change the colour if you must highlight a word.

- Use only the key words on your slides.

- Remove bullet point slides where possible. A great tip is to take each bullet point and make it into its own slide with the bullet point as the heading and a gorgeous image that delivers your point. As an example, let's say you have a bullet point slide that has three bullets. Turn this into three slides.

- Only reproduce the important parts of graphs and supplement with a handout if more details are needed.

- Colour-code graphs so people see the point of the graph easily from a distance.

- Ensure your transitions from one slide to the next don't distract the audience.

- If you use sound clips, ensure they add value, rather than distract from the message.

Michelle says,

'You don't need agenda, questions, "thank you" or "the end" slides. You should replace these unnecessary slides with your direct, connected eye contact and a rehearsed gesture.'

'But everyone in my company uses lots of busy slides...'

Yes, I know exactly what you mean. I've certainly seen the best and worst of slide presentations. If you are trying to use simple slides and supplement your slides with gestures, flipcharts, handouts and whiteboard work, when no-one else in your company does it that way, it's very possible you could feel isolated — and this can be a scary thing!

If you feel you are all alone trying to improve your use of slides, you may like to speak with the marketing department in your company and suggest some alternatives for slide use in your company. This is important, because if your company has very strict rules and guidelines for the use of certain fonts, colours and templates, you will need to get permission to change anything.

Or perhaps you could chat to your own manager and make some changes in your immediate team — if the rules aren't too strict where you work.

Or what about trying just a few of the techniques and slowly implementing changes into the way you design your slides?

Michelle says,

'It's critical that you use slides as a visual aid, not as your script. Be bold and stand out for the right reasons!'

Susan's story

Susan is a doctor. She was offered the opportunity to speak on melanoma to a group of claims consultants and underwriters. She created a limited number of beautiful slides, including one slide describing how hard it is to find the one case of pre-existing terminal melanoma that shouldn't be underwritten.

She could have used all sorts of dreadful graphs, charts, forms and templates to illustrate the point. Instead of bombarding the audience with too much information that they couldn't read on the slides from their seats in an audience of more than 500 people, she used a picture of lots of beautifully coloured Smarties, with one dark brown Smartie in the middle.

The point was made so clearly: 'It's like trying to find the one brown Smartie in the pack.' There was no need for all the boring forms and templates.

The audience got the point in 10 seconds. That is what slides are for. Susan was given feedback that her presentation was exceptional.

Presenting technical information

An engineer in one of my training programs said to the group (and to me), 'But I'm an engineer. I don't have to be interesting!' Aargh! Are you serious? This is a classic misconception! This engineer is not the first person in a program of mine who thinks that his superior intelligence, his technically robust subject matter and his overloaded slides are enough to wow an audience.

Surely the people who present the most technical and driest content need to try the hardest to be interesting. People often think that their expertise and information will sell itself. This is actually not true.

If you think about it, we do know deep down that 100 slides with tiny print and diagrams that we couldn't read in an hour (if we had a spare hour!) isn't going to make any message worth listening to, much less one that is engaging or persuasive for an audience.

Sadly, most business presentations are still mind-numbingly dull and boring. As a presentation skills trainer for many decades, I have seen thousands of technical presentations. Most people would be lucky to stay awake in them, even with an energy drink or a strong coffee at the ready. And I think it's such a shame because, in most cases, the presenter was a true subject matter expert — they just didn't know how to showcase their professional expertise in a way that was exciting for their audience.

TIP

Michelle says,

'It doesn't matter how smart you are, how robust your research is, or how conclusive your opinion is if no-one is listening!'

Make sure your delivery is engaging, with lots of direct, connected eye contact, clear audience-focused messages and excellent slides that help your audience to focus on your key messages. This way, people will want to listen to your message, no matter how technical or dry it is.

Top tips for technical presentations

The tips and guidelines you have already read throughout this book for creating fabulous presentations (particularly the Persuasion Blueprint outlined in chapter 5) also apply if you have technical information to impart. Anyone can be an exceptional presenter. It's just a matter of knowing what to do, and doing it.

Here are my top tips for presenting technical information:

- *Know your audience:* Your technical area probably affects every aspect of the business you're in. Remember that just because you know the minute details related to your role doesn't mean that the people you're speaking to know about your topic. You must understand the level of knowledge and the roles of the people you're presenting to so you can tweak your message and put things in a way that your audience understands.

- *Build rapport:* People like people who are like themselves. So find a way of using your dress, body language, voice and language patterns so you are as similar to as many people in the audience as possible. That way, you will be in rapport from the start.

- *Motivate your audience:* Most people go to way too many meetings that are a complete waste of time. Remember that your role is to motivate your audience to listen from the very start — otherwise, they may not!

- *Manage any objections:* Spend some time thinking about all the objections your audience may have to your content. What questions will they ask and what are the different answers you could give? To be forewarned is to be forearmed.

- *Set the guidelines:* Make sure your audience knows the boundaries of your presentation. What will be covered and what won't? Should they complete pre-reading so they don't get left behind when you get into the details? Should they turn their phone to silent? How long will it last and when should they ask questions? Setting the boundaries will help you avoid chaos.

- *Rehearse:* Exceptional presenters rehearse the opening and close of their presentations many, many times.

- *Use a whiteboard or flipchart as well as slides:* Draw pictures. Your audience will love to see your images created organically in front of them on a whiteboard or flipchart. And you'll look so clever if you can draw your graphs and pictures free-hand and on the spot.

- *Love your content:* People often say to me that they don't know how to make their topic interesting because it's so boring or dry. Well, if you think it's boring and dry, what is your audience going to think? Find the parts of your message that you are passionate about and make sure you highlight those parts with vocal emphasis (be louder or more energetic at certain times).

- *Be yourself:* Don't talk with the audience as if they are some scary, judgemental bunch wanting to find your information boring, or are too stupid to understand your point if you speak at a reasonable pace. Instead chat with them as though they are your old friends.

- *Make your presentation a discussion with your audience:* In most situations, people would rather be part of a discussion than be talked at. Don't rely entirely on your slides and don't just read what's on the screen. Remember — you are a real live human being and your role is to connect with the real live human beings in your audience.

- *Evoke emotions and motivate:* People are more likely to change their thinking or behaviour if you tell stories or use analogies that are related to your subject and that evoke emotion.

- *Don't assume you need slides:* A common assumption when you're giving a presentation is that you must use slides. That's not true. My client Salesforce teaches all their salespeople the skill of whiteboarding. It makes them more real and connected, and showcases their expertise better than a pre-designed slide deck. Yes, it sets them apart. A short talk with the use of a whiteboard, flipchart or detailed handout may be the best way to get your points across. My advice is to use slides as an aid for your audience to remind them of your three key points. Use other visual aids, such as gestures, facial expressions and body movement, too.

- *Use illustrations, not bullets:* It's easier to tell a story when you use pictures and graphics instead of bullet points. Pictures and graphics, pie charts and tables can be a better way to convey your message, and they help your audience too. When using images, make sure the image takes up the whole screen — right to the edges.

- *Prepare, prepare, prepare!* Remember — exceptional presenters rehearse until they can't get it wrong. Effective presentations have to be planned out, thought through, and refined for days, if not weeks, in the lead-up to your presentation. Preparing your material well in advance gives you time to fine-tune certain aspects and to program your subconscious regarding the flow and general message of your presentation. This way your delivery will sound more natural.

- *You don't need to be over the top:* Don't worry about being a charismatic comedian! Be yourself and talk about what you know. Your authenticity, trustworthiness and integrity will be evident to your audience, making them better placed to connect with you and buy your concept or idea. You will also be more comfortable with yourself, able to relax and deliver a stronger presentation.

Use these tips when presenting technical information and notice your audience sitting up and listening with interest!

Handy tip: Some of these rules change when you are presenting virtually rather than face to face. For specific tips on engaging a virtual audience, see chapter 20.

Brad's story

Brad is a passionate young medical specialist and consultant. He has presented around the world at medical conferences for the past few years.

When he first began speaking, he was told that he should stay under the radar and present the way everyone else did. He was told to follow protocol and read out his long, wordy and complicated essay to the audience word for word and rely heavily on slides with no or little eye contact — because 'that's how we do things around here'. Brad is very motivated to become a world leader in his chosen field. He did as he was told for a few years and then increasingly noticed that hardly anyone was listening to his presentations. What a surprise!

(continued)

Brad decided presenting at these conferences was pointless if no-one was going to listen to him speak! He realised that life is too short to keep acting as though his ideas were not important or worth listening to. He decided he didn't want to hide his exciting medical findings and opinions on slides that were covered in hundreds of words in tiny 8-point fonts. He realised that if he wanted funding for his research projects, he would need to have his audience on the edge of their seats bursting to hear what he had to say next!

Brad came to me looking for some tips for spicing up his presentations. His brief to me was that he wanted to go against the grain and stand out! Awesome — I love a brief like that!

I showed Brad how to think about the presentation from his audience's perspective — to think about what they needed to hear from him. We spent some time applying my Persuasion Blueprint to his content. And I provided Brad with the slide design tips listed on the previous pages.

He was quite worried that the audience would reject his new approach. After all, it was a big change from the boring 'blah, blah, blah' papers that the audience was used to. In fact, Brad need not have worried. He received a standing ovation on his very first attempt at the new style and has gone on to be a world leader in his field. He is commonly asked to speak at medical conferences. People in his industry know what he thinks; they listen when he speaks; and they can feel his passion for his subject. They generally applaud him loudly. A tremendous result!

TIP

Michelle says,

'There are no excuses for being a boring presenter — none at all!'

Using handouts

I mentioned earlier in this chapter that handouts can be a wonderful alternative to slides. Handouts are great if your audience is a size you can manage. In meetings and small presentations, handouts are a good idea, especially for complex patterns and information, such as an organisational chart or a series of comparative graphs that no-one will be able to see on a slide.

The question is when should you give out the handout? Typically, it's a good idea to have all handouts on people's chairs or in front of them on their table before your presentation starts. This way you won't have to waste people's time handing them out, and you won't annoy all the people sitting in the back if they have to wait for the handouts to get to them (especially annoying if the audience is very big). If your presentation is online, make sure you email any handouts and attachments beforehand.

Handy tip: If you're worried about people reading ahead with the handout (and not listening to you), consider having a number of people to assist you to hand it out at the correct time in your agenda if you're presenting in person. Alternatively, remember the skill of framing (refer to chapter 5) and use your words to guide people's attention between the handout and yourself. (This works for both online and offline presentations.)

For example:

- *'Please look at page 7 of the handout, where you will see a schematic of the current network configuration compared with the proposed configuration.'*

- *'You will find the schematic in your handouts, and may I ask that you don't turn to it just yet? That way you will understand the rationale before going to the comparison. Thank you.'*

TIP

Michelle says,

'A handout is a terrific idea for content-heavy diagrams that your audience wouldn't be able to read as a slide.'

Setting up before your presentation

Now that you have beautifully designed slides, if you're presenting in person the next thing to consider is your room set-up. When you are using slides in your presentation, be sure to arrive early and set up the room properly.

Set up the room to increase the chances of your audience members being excited to be there with you! Three things you should remember to do when presenting face to face are:

1. Set up your screen to the side.

2. Keep the lights on.

3. Manage your own distractions.

Set the screen up to the side

Incorrect positioning of the screen, projector and lectern for a presentation is the first big mistake that many presenters make when they decide to use slides. If, like most corporate presenters, you want to use slides, it is critical that you don't let the slide equipment (furniture, cords and so on) trap you, creating a self-induced invisible wall that acts as a barrier between you and the audience.

You may remember from chapter 13 that the middle of the stage is known as the 'hot spot'. It is your centre of influence, the point from which you are best able to project your image as a confident, credible presenter. So set up your room with the screens and projector to the side, so you can stand in the middle of the stage with confidence and charisma. This is referred to as claiming your space.

In a large room, you would ideally have two screens, one on each side of the stage, so audience members can relax and see you and the slides from all directions!

Handy tip: If your corporate office has the flat-screen TVs fixed to the centre of the wall, or the projector positioned in the centre, you'll need to blank your slides a lot more often and make sure nothing is distracting people behind you when you need them to focus on what you are saying. Keep reading for tips on blanking your screen.

Michelle says,

'If you must use a lectern, position it slightly off centre on the opposite side of the stage to the projector screen. This set-up allows you to travel from the centre of the stage (or hot spot) to the lectern periodically, if and when you need to refer to your notes.'

Keep the lights on

Have you ever been to a presentation where the presenter turned off the lights? What did you do? Did you sleep? Or did you vague out? Maybe you think you were listening intently, but can you recall the content?

Actually two responses are common during a presentation with slides when the lights go out:

1. The audience sleeps — either metaphorically or actually! This is clearly not okay.

2. The audience is captivated by the slides and blocks out the presenter. You're probably aware of doing this at a movie? Once the lights go down, you bond with the screen or film. This is only a good choice if you are selling an idea via the slides and you want your audience to bond with the screen. If you do this, ensure that, once the slides are finished and the lights are back on, you re-engage your audience (whites-of-the-eyes eye contact and human to human) and close the sale.

It's certainly true that when the lights are on people feel more inclined to pay attention.

If the audience can't see your slides with the lights on, redesign them or replace them with a flipchart, whiteboard or some handouts.

Manage your own distractions

Setting the room up correctly will maximise the benefits of using slides, and also help you manage your own distractions. I discuss room set-up in detail in the next chapter.

How well do audiences look and listen concurrently?

Many business presenters create an interesting phenomenon when they simultaneously use slides and talk to their audience — and the audience members become unsure of where to look. So they end up flicking their gaze from the presenter to the slides and back again as if they were at a tennis game!

Working with other researchers at the University of New South Wales, educational psychologist Professor John Sweller developed a concept known as 'cognitive load theory'. This theory suggests that the human brain processes and retains more information if the information is digested in *either* verbal or written formats, not both simultaneously.

The research found that diagrams, charts and graphs can be useful, but should be used carefully. It also found too much load on the mind occurs when a presenter reads out the words that are written on their slides. This decreases the audience's ability to fully comprehend what is being presented.

If you have graphs, diagrams, bullet points or words on your slides, it is important to understand Professor Sweller's theory of cognitive load. To avoid cognitive load, or what I call 'split attention', ensure your audience is clear that they should either be looking at you (as you claim your space and engage them from your hot spot with either a simple image behind you or the screen or screen image blanked out), or looking at the screen (as you stand out of the way and allow them time to read the slide).

Handy tip: If presenting in person, use the 'B' key on the keypad of your computer, or the <blank> button on your remote control to blank out the *screen. Pressing it a second time reveals the image again on screen. This is ideal for blanking out the slides when you are engaging the group with your eye contact.*

Operating the slides for face-to-face presentations

Few of us have someone we can bring to our presentation event to help us with our slides. And a lot of presenters don't like the idea of handing over the control of their visual aids to someone else anyway. In these cases, you can either use the remote control to operate the slides or manually change the slides on the computer.

Conference keynote speakers generally use the remote with great finesse and often out of necessity — no friends! (Only joking!) Actually one of the main reasons for their skill with a remote control is that they are used to speaking at big events where the remote is the only viable choice for changing slides on a big stage.

Businesspeople are often not taught the finer distinctions of slide-changing etiquette and so they can make a big mess of their slides. I've seen them moving too quickly through the presentation, apologising and essentially driving their audience mad! In this section, I outline what you need to know so you can do great things for your audience — using a well-crafted message, some beautiful slides and a remote control.

Here some tips for using a remote:

- Know how to use your remote. Become acquainted with the buttons and what they do. Ensure you get to the venue early and practise. Turning up on the day and hoping for the best is not good practice! You are asking for trouble and will probably embarrass yourself. Get there early and rehearse, rehearse, rehearse — no excuses!

- Don't fidget with the remote. Make sure you either put it in your pocket when you don't need it, or rehearse enough times that you know for certain you won't fidget with it. Also try not to fidget with your flip chart pens or any props. Fidgeting means you don't look as prepared, comfortable or confident as you would like.

- Interplay the slides, the space and your message.

Try this method for managing the slides while you present:

- Find the slide you will soon want to show on the screen.

- Use the <blank> button on the remote or the 'B' key on the keyboard to blank out the slides before you start.

- Claim your space and engage your audience.

- Look at them with whites-of-the-eyes contact.

- Deliver your presentation.

- Assume you are presenting with one large screen in the centre of the room (because this is the most common room set-up in business).

- When you come to content that you would like to reinforce on a slide, press the <blank> button on your remote and walk right out of the way of your slides so you are not in the audience's frame of vision. The reason you do this is to ensure that you are not distracting your audience.

- If you have two screens on either side of the room, you can stay in the hot spot, or centre of the room.

- When you are standing out of the way, you can either talk the audience through what they are looking at, or you can remain silent (while the audience reads the slide).

- Enjoy the power of pause and try to avoid breaking your audience's concentration as they read through the points on the screen or absorb your pictorial representation of the message.

- If you would like to talk your audience through your message because the slide needs explaining, make sure you move right out of the way of your screen and use an open palm to indicate to your audience that they should listen to you while still looking at the slides.

If you don't have a remote

If you don't have the use of a remote, you can use the keys of the computer to change your slides. The best way to do this is to find the slide you will soon want to show on the screen and use the 'B' key to blank out the slides before you start. Then follow the instructions in the preceding section, and when you come to content that you would like to reinforce on a slide, walk to the computer and press the 'B' key to reveal the slide that is waiting, and continue following the instructions given earlier.

If someone else operates the slides for you

You may prefer to have someone else change your slides, so you won't be trapped standing next to the computer, and you won't have a mouse or remote in your hand to play with unwittingly. Again, follow the instructions for presenting with slides, and when you come to content that you would like to reinforce on a slide say, 'Next slide please [name]', and move out of the way to the other side of the room. In other words, if the screen is on the right, walk to the left–hand side of the room.

If you are uncomfortable announcing the next slide, simply gesture to the slide operator to indicate you would like the next slide and keep going. If you have plenty of time to rehearse, it's a great idea to work with your slide operator so they can change the slides without any prompting from you.

Michelle says,

'Make time to rehearse the way you will change your slides. Have at least three rehearsals before an important event.'

Using a laser pointer — or not?

I'm not a huge fan of the laser dot. However, I've certainly witnessed many of my amazing, powerful and charismatic clients, particularly in the pharmaceutical industry, use the laser dot with precision and incredible confidence.

I'll admit two more things to you. First, sometimes the laser pointer is the best way to highlight something. And, second, in some cases, if you don't use the red dot your audience might think you're not credible. Some audiences simply expect the use of a laser pointer.

I do think that in an attempt to highlight the most important part of a diagram, graph or picture, many people use that annoying little red laser dot to their detriment. You will probably agree with me that the dot tends to jump around everywhere and make even the most competent presenter look shaky and nervous. Make no mistake: the laser pointer can be a slow and painful way to torture your audience!

So how should you point to something on a slide? This is an important question because the annoying laser dot is not the only unsophisticated thing presenters do when pointing out important points on their slides.

The other tortuous way people indicate what to look at on their slides is that they stand in front of the projector light and reach up on their toes to point to something on the screen. This approach can distract the audience from the message as they check out your shadow on the screen. I'm not sure about you, but I don't know that many people whose nose looks fabulous in profile!

Instead of the laser dot, or walking in front of the projector to point to something on the screen, try colour-coding your slide so you can refer to the different colours from the other side of the room. This way everyone will know where you want them to look.

For example:

- 'Notice that in the last 12 months the figures — *shown in blue* — indicate a significant rise in our share price.'
- 'The areas *shaded yellow* in New South Wales represent our top performing regions, whereas our poorer performers are *coloured blue.*'

This way you help your audience know that they should be listening to you and looking at the screen. Keep in mind that different colours have different meanings — see table 16.1, later in this chapter, for more.

Mike's story

Mike is a subject matter expert in the IT industry. He is frequently asked to fly around the world for organisations that need their IT professionals to hear about Mike's specialisation.

Mike had the opportunity to present in the United States to an audience that numbered in the thousands. When he suggested to the organisers, before the event, that he'd like to have the screen to the side, they were not happy because that was not the way they usually set up their events.

Then he said he'd be happy to submit his slides in advance, but he wanted to be able to change them himself because he wanted to blank out the screen from time to time. The organisers found his suggestion radical and were concerned that if the screen was blank people would not concentrate anymore. Mike eventually convinced the organisers that he knew what he was doing and they let him have it his way.

The audience response was excellent. The organisers said they had never seen someone use slides so convincingly before, and they agreed that blanking the slides at times made a big difference to the audience's focus on the key messages.

You will also be pleased with the results of your next presentation if you follow the straightforward guidelines in this chapter. You will be an engaging presenter who uses visual aids to support your key points. People will enjoy the experience you create for them and will walk out of your room with a heathy pulse. They may even change their behaviour as you desire!

> **TIP**
>
> **Michelle says,**
>
> 'Get what you want from audiences because you connect with them as people and use your slides only to reinforce key points.'

When it comes to presenting with slides — either online or in person — I challenge you to be great. Stand out and be brilliant. Use your slides to ensure that you reinforce your key messages and maximise the chance of changing your audience's behaviour.

Using a flipchart or whiteboard

Mixing up your visual aids when presenting in person in a workplace environment is a great idea. The more ways you can interest your audience and keep them listening, the better.

If you have decided to be brave and draw on a whiteboard or some flipcharts, here are my tips for success:

- When drawing on flipcharts or a whiteboard, make sure you use sentence case. Sentence case is a capital letter at the start of the sentence and lowercase letters after it.

- Use circles to form the basis of round letters like 'a' and 'b'.

- Use precise, vertical lines for letters such as 'f' and 't', and be as neat as possible.

- Remove any distractions from your charts, rub the whiteboard when you have finished with a point, or flip the flip-chart over to reveal a new blank sheet (equivalent to using 'B' on the computer and blanking out your slides).

- Rehearse how you will draw letters, so you know how to fit in any cumbersome words and diagrams.

- Draw with lead pencil on charts beforehand if you need help with the outline and check it can't be seen from the audience's seats. When it's time to draw up the chart during your presentation, you'll simply be tracing over the line — and you'll look like a born artist!

- Different colours have different meanings — follow the guidelines in table 16.1.

Table 16.1 The meaning of different colours for use on whiteboards or flipcharts

Colour	Meaning and use
Dark blue	Colour of authority. Use it for headings and content set in stone.
Red	Makes the word stand out and makes a bold statement.
Green	Creative, organic, expansive. Represents growth and movement — not a good choice for key points.
Black	Factual, strong and absolute. Use it for outlines and as a base drawing colour.
Yellow	Light, energetic. Use it for emphasis or shading, not for words. Always use black around a yellow picture.
Purple	Depth. Used like dark blue to mark out key points. Don't use it as much as dark blue or your headings won't look like headings.
Orange	Use for less significant points. Use sparingly and keep it away from red.
Pink	Vibrant and light. Use as a filler to break up other colours.
Brown	Grounded and earthed. Use as a filler colour to break up other colours.

TRY THIS

After storyboarding your presentation (refer to chapter 4) and completing your Persuasion Blueprint (chapter 5), it's time to design your slides.

1. Using the presentation you have been working on as you read through this book, run through what you are going to say and mark on your script where you think some slides will add extra value for your audience.

2. Create some slides using the guidelines in this chapter, ensuring they remain as simple as possible. Make sure you don't overdo it.

3. Think about whether some flipcharts or whiteboard work might further enhance your message and plan accordingly.

Think about the next presentation you will be making.

1. Do you have the necessary equipment, such as flipcharts, whiteboards (and pens and an eraser) and projector?

2. Schedule a time close to the presentation to check that the bulb in the projector doesn't need changing (a signal appears telling you when the bulb needs changing).

TOP TIPS
for using visual aids

- Slides are for reinforcing your key messages, not for reminding you what to say.

- Slides can cause 'death by PowerPoint' — be careful to use them wisely!

- Ask yourself: is this the best way to visually reinforce this point? Then take the appropriate action depending on your answer.

- Use dark text on a light background, at least 30-point in size in a legible font such as Times New Roman or Verdana.

- Don't use underlining, italics, bold or shadow on your fonts. Only use key words on your slides.

- Change the colour of the font if you need a word to further stand out.

- Replace words with pictures as often as possible.

- Only reproduce the important parts of graphs.

- Colour-code graphs so people see the point of the graph easily from a distance.

- Use beautiful, clever graphics, not overused, tired ones. Ensure your transitions from one slide to the next don't distract.

- Sound clips should add value, not distract from the message.

- Arrive early and set up your room, and keep the lights on.

- Interplay the slides, the space, the message and your personal brand — blanking your slides will help you do this.

- Rehearse with your slides.

- Reduce your use of the laser pointer — it can be distracting for your audience.

- Use flipcharts and whiteboards to add an organic element to your presentation.

- Get what you want from your audience by connecting with them as people, and using your slides and other visual aids to captivate and influence them.

CHAPTER 17

Setting up the room for live presentations

It's true that we want our audience's full attention for as much of our presentation as possible. We know that most people find concentrating on a presenter's message difficult when there are distractions around, so it is critical that you remove all distractions from your personal presentation and your room.

If you have ever been to a presentation where the presenter from the session before left the room in a messy state, you will know how difficult it is to concentrate on what the presenter is saying. I have seen many a meeting room with the previous presenter's drawings still on the whiteboard, handouts and papers still on the tables, and all the old coffee cups and muffin wrappers strewn across the tables — yuck! It's time to listen to the wise words of Apple co-founder Steve Jobs, who said, 'Be a yardstick of quality. Some people aren't used to an environment where excellence is expected'.

The theory of managing distractions in your presentation room is called 'zenning' the space: it is the art of managing people's unconscious responses. Unconscious responses are the responses people have that they don't even know they are having. Interesting, hey?

In this chapter, I take you through setting up the room to your advantage during in-person presentations. For help with your set-up during online presentations, see chapter 19.

The best room set-up

The key to a good room set-up is to respect your audience and remove as many distractions as possible — whether it's your workplace or not.

Pay attention to the following details before you start presenting:

- Remove your security badge for the presentation.

- Remove white fluff from your person and from the floor.

- Wipe the whiteboards clean.

- Remove posters and other paintings and pictures from walls. (Be sure to put them back when you are finished though.)

- Ensure you have the correct number of chairs for the attendees. An empty chair implies that someone couldn't be bothered attending because this presentation isn't worth listening to. If you are presenting to a large audience, I recommend you make up some 'reserved' signs on A4 paper and place these signs on all the back seats of the auditorium. This forces people to sit in all the chairs at the front, including the front row! Only take the reserved signs away from the back chairs when the front row is full. Tricky, hey?

- Ensure the chairs are as comfortable as possible.

- Ensure the temperature of the room is moderate (not too hot or too cold).

- Where possible, ensure catering is top quality.

- If you use flipcharts, once they have been drawn up, remember to hang them up with some removable adhesive or pins on the walls of the presentation room behind you in a symmetrical way to reinforce learning. This is a clever tip, because when your audience members switch off your message from time to time, your message is still embedding for them if they are staring straight at your beautiful flipcharts.

> **TIP**
>
> **Michelle says,**
>
> 'Don't be put off when presenting in someone else's environment. Always manage the space so your audience can focus on you and your message.'

Arriving early and setting up before your audience arrives

You are on show from the moment any audience member lays eyes on you. Don't be caught setting up the technology, fiddling with your equipment, setting up the room or rehearsing your slide sequence when audience members enter the room. Be as prepared as possible so audience members don't feel like they should help you move your equipment around or synchronise your laptop with the data projector. Claim your space and be as prepared, respectful and organised as you can. In other words, make sure you present the right image from the start.

> **TIP**
>
> **Michelle says,**
>
> 'Claim your space and be as prepared, respectful and organised as you can.'

Managing the room set-up for slides

Have you ever been in a meeting or presentation and noticed yourself getting distracted by the messy cords that bunch and weave in full view of you and the rest of the audience?

Not all companies have fancy data projector set-ups that suspend the projector from the ceiling, so when you are the presenter, it's a good idea to check what set-up you will be using. If you are going to present with a projector on a table, remember to bring along your own gaffer tape to your meetings and tape down the cords, or get the venue to tape down the cords for you. That way, you maximise the likelihood that the audience will pay attention to you and your message.

Colin's story

I coached Colin, a director from a large international company, for many weeks before an important presentation he was to give to the organisation's wholesalers. It was a sales pitch designed to get the audience revved up and ready to go out and sell the services of his organisation. Colin had beautiful slides and had rehearsed the presentation many times over. He was destined to be awesome!

After his presentation, Colin called me to give me the update. The first thing he said was, 'I didn't do very well today'. When I asked him why, he said, 'I had to stand behind the lectern because they put my laptop on it and I needed to change my own slides. Next to the lectern was a heavy table that was blocking me from moving into the centre of the stage. I ended up having to stand in the shadows so the audience couldn't see my face.'

Seriously — that's what he said. A director of a business! I asked him the obvious question: 'Why didn't you move the table when you got to the event?'

He replied, 'Marketing put it there and I assumed they needed it for something'.

We can learn a very important lesson from Colin's story. You can see that even for the most senior and experienced presenters, managing what is often known as the ecology, vibe or atmosphere of the room can be difficult. It's sometimes tricky to take charge of the space as if you own it, especially when other people (who may have strong opinions) are involved.

Managing your room and space for your presentation really is worthwhile. You will reduce your nerves if you feel more in control, and also be more likely to achieve your outcomes when people have little to distract them. It is a joy for your audience to witness a presentation when your message and your slides synchronise like clockwork.

Knowing where to stand

I live in Sydney, Australia, and many of my clients are located in high-rise office accommodation that overlooks beautiful Sydney Harbour — with a glorious view of our fabulous Opera House and Harbour Bridge. Many of these clients have also refurbished their offices in the current trend and now have meeting rooms that are completely glass. Glass walls mean that people can see in to your meeting and your audience can see out into the workspace. These kinds of distractions can make it pretty tricky to keep an audience focused — unless you ensure their backs are to all that glass, so they're not looking at the view or out into other workspaces.

If you have a similar situation when you present at meetings, make sure where possible that you seat your audience with their backs to the view. This will be harder for you because you will be facing the glass and the people peering in on their way past. Remember, it's not about you: it's all about your audience — so face the view, connect with the whites of your audience members' eyes, and make it easy for your audience to concentrate.

Predicting the room set-up

Some people ask me what they can do if they have no way of predicting the room set-up they will be working in. I counter this with the following: you can always predict your room set-up. I believe that, as the presenter, you are in control of yourself (the way you dress, move, speak and act), your message (the words you choose to say) *and* your environment (the space you are presenting in). So I recommend you create a diagram that you can send to the conference or meeting organiser suggesting your preferred room set-up. Make sure you provide a diagram rather than a wordy description, so it's easy for the conference organiser to understand. And make sure you send it in plenty of time for the organiser to implement your suggestions.

I do this when I am presenting a keynote speech at conferences and I have never (to date) had an organiser say no. In fact, to my knowledge, when I send that diagram through I'm the only one who has requested anything, so the organisers don't mind doing what I have asked. Why don't you give this a try yourself? Even if they say no, you'll still find out what the room set-up will be like and can make plans accordingly.

TRY THIS

1. Next time you book a meeting room or agree to speak at a conference, check out the room in advance.

2. Design a document that has a picture of your preferred room set-up for use when you present.

3. Where possible, arrange to have your presentation after a break, so you can nip into the space and tidy up a bit before you present.

4. Make sure that you always place your stakeholders' backs to the view, the glass windows or colleagues walking past!

TOP TIPS
for setting up the room

- Take some time to think about the room you will be presenting in.
- Work out where you will stand and where you would like your audience to sit.
- Make any plans you need to, so you ensure your room assists your presentation.
- Manage distractions in the room.
- Tape down your power cords.

CHAPTER 18

Getting positive feedback

In my experience, one of the main reasons many people fear public speaking is that they focus too much on their negative points and their nervousness, rather than on their positive attributes, such as their voice or their personal presentation. It's so common for people to say to me, 'I just don't like being the centre of attention. I don't like all those people looking at me'.

Well, here's what I think. Whoever you are, you are wonderful! Really, you are terrific. You are special and you are exceptional in your own unique way. Remember this important fact and let your positive attributes as a presenter shine through.

Setting up a system in your organisation where you can give feedback and receive it from other people you respect, and who are sensitive to your needs, is a great way of finding out what you are doing well.

Remember the words of bestselling author Ken Blanchard: 'Feedback is the breakfast of champions.' Receiving positive feedback can boost your confidence tenfold. Even feedback on what you need to do differently next time, if given in a kind and respectful way, can be wonderful for your overall confidence.

A feedback model to boost your confidence

The model I recommend for giving and receiving feedback is the four-step feedback model, and it can be used for feedback on your online and offline presenting. It's pretty clear from the name that there are four steps! Table 18.1 explains the four steps.

Table 18.1 The four-step feedback model

Step 1	List all the things you think you did effectively when you presented. In your own opinion, what do you think you did well? Be as specific as possible.
Step 2	List all the things you would like to improve on or do differently next time you present. What would you change if you could deliver the presentation again?
Step 3	Ask your audience or a nominated buddy to give you some feedback on what they believe you might like to improve on or do differently, from their perspective. You can ask clarifying questions at this point, just don't argue or try to justify your actions: this will turn them off wanting to give you their opinion.
Step 4	Ask your audience or nominated buddy to tell you all the things they believe you did effectively. Again, this is from their perspective. You can ask clarifying questions at this point, and, again, don't argue or try to justify your actions, because this will turn them off wanting to give you their opinion.

When you look at the definition of each of the four steps, you can see that the four-step feedback model is an overwhelmingly positive and supportive way to give and receive feedback. I recommend you try it.

Melanie's story

Melanie was a team leader who attended one of my presentation skills programs as a mandatory component in an aspiring leaders program. In other words, she attended because she had to, not because she wanted to be there.

Melanie was a gregarious woman on the outside, but the more I got to know her, the more she alluded to the fact that she was terrified of speaking in public. In fact, Melanie confided in me during one of the breaks that she had had 30 jobs in the past 20 years. Why had she been in so many jobs? Well, she explained that she had done whatever she could to avoid public speaking, including quitting her job!

After learning the four-step feedback model in my program and speaking with her colleagues after one of her presentations, Melanie realised that she had a number of outstanding qualities that made her an engaging speaker. In fact, she was told she was 'an interesting, generous, gentle, sincere, thought-provoking, engaging and likeable presenter'.

She wrote on her course evaluation form:

> Michelle, you have transformed my life! I had no idea I could be good at public speaking. I thought my voice was too high pitched and I didn't feel like I could get my point across in a way that was interesting to people. The group seemed genuinely interested in what I had to say, and they gave me some very honest and positive comments in the four-step feedback session that helped me feel confident and inspired. I am now quite excited about finding some more opportunities to present. Thank you so much.

We learn from Melanie's story that asking the right people for feedback can help your confidence, not hinder it.

TIP

Michelle says,

'Establish a feedback mechanism in your workplace to improve your overall self-confidence.'

It really is important to establish a feedback mechanism in your workplace that works for you and gives you the chance to hear what you could fix up or improve, as well as which aspects of your presentation are effective. I'm sure you'll get a nice surprise!

TIP

Michelle says,

'Don't ask for feedback from people who you know are going to be mean-spirited. You don't need their feedback!'

TRY THIS

1. Explain the four-step feedback model to the people you work with.

2. Organise to have some people (who know the four-step feedback model and whom you respect) become feedback buddies and give you some feedback on your next rehearsal or live presentation.

3. Once you have presented, ask yourself what you did well, as well as what you would like to improve.

4. Find out what your feedback buddies think you might like to improve upon and what you did well.

5. Make a note of the feedback you give yourself and that your buddies give you.

6. Write down your plan to work on the things you'd like to improve.

Another way to get some feedback

In our busy lives, we often don't have time to give feedback to our colleagues, so it's important to find ways to learn about your performance that don't involve others.

I suggest you film yourself, or at least record your voice. I know — we all seem to hate the idea of watching ourselves or the sound of our recorded voice. In my many, many years' experience, watching yourself after the presentation is generally a much more positive experience than you might think. Most of my clients who film themselves tell me they weren't anywhere near as bad as they thought! This gives them increased confidence for the next presentation.

TIP

Michelle says,

'Film yourself — you'll be pleasantly surprised!'

TOP TIPS
for getting positive feedback

- Many people fear public speaking because they focus too much on their negative points and their nervousness, rather than on their positive attributes.

- If you are too self-focused, you are not thinking enough about your audience and how you could serve them.

- Whoever you are, you are wonderful! Remember that and let your positive attributes as a presenter shine through.

- Setting up a positive feedback system (using a model such as the four-step feedback model) can help you learn about what you are doing well.

CHAPTER 19

Delivering your message virtually

COVID-19 lockdowns and the subsequent need for more flexible work practices have resulted in a changing workplace. Most people in business are moving to a hybrid model of working — where they work a few days in the office and some days from home. And most of us now have occasion to present online. We're using platforms such as Zoom, MS Teams, WebEx and a whole lot of other technology to stay in touch remotely.

We've used these virtual platforms mostly because we've had to. As a result our successful use of virtual platforms to present our ideas can still be a bit hit and miss. The other day I had the opportunity to watch someone in a very high-profile executive role commenting on television about the passing of a world-renowned celebrity. And although this person is a very savvy media personality and indeed a professional speaker, she had weirdly positioned her camera so that everybody was looking up her nose while she was talking! And I thought to myself, *What's going on here? Is it not obvious that the audience doesn't want to look up your nose?* I imagine she just didn't think about this.

Sometimes, of course, virtual presenting works brilliantly. One of my clients pitched for a $700 million project. The 27 people in the pitch team had no choice but to embrace virtual presenting, with the whole pitch process taking place on Zoom. I trained them in presentation and pitching skills on Zoom, I coached people individually on Zoom, they pitched everything to their client on Zoom — and guess what? They won the project via Zoom! Without a single face-to-face meeting!

Even when the presenter has the best of intentions, we've all been in online presentations and meetings where the technology just seems to get in the way. Cameras are positioned up noses or on looming foreheads, mute buttons are on or off at the wrong times, or the presenter simply shares their screen and everyone stares at their slides absent-mindedly (or do other work while the presenter is talking). Oh dear!

If presenting, meeting facilitation, on-the-job coaching, or pitching and high-level negotiation skills are critical to your business success, it's essential that you embrace virtual presenting and make it work for you and your audience. In this chapter, I run through the factors to remember when presenting in the virtual world.

My story

In early 2020, my thriving national speaking and training business moved from in person to nothing — overnight. In Australia, we were locked down due to COVID-19 and no face-to-face meetings took place for many, many months. And I have to admit that I panicked. I'd always thought that my presentation skills training had to be delivered live, so I had no experience whatsoever with virtual presenting. As the months ticked by, I realised that virtual would be the only way forward if I wanted to stay in business.

I turned to the guru, the one person in Australia who would ensure that if I did move everything online, I wouldn't lose the mastery that I was so well known for. His name is Warwick Merry CSP, CVP. Warwick is a Certified Speaking Professional — the highest designation for speakers in the world. He has been twice awarded Certified Virtual Presenter (CVP) status. He won the Global Outstanding Intrapreneur Award as well as the Nevin Award (from Professional Speakers Australia) for his work helping speakers and trainers like me to shift to virtual presenting. In 2022, Warwick also won the Breakthrough Speaker Award for his personal flip to online MC work, speaking and presenting. You can probably guess that Warwick loves virtual presenting. He says that you can do things with the technology that you could never do face to face. He says, 'After years of playing with phones and technology, this is what audiences are used to, and this is that they want, so why not give it to them?'

Warwick helped me embrace virtual presenting to the point where many of my clients now choose to book me to deliver my Persuasive Presentation Skills Masterclass and my various keynote speeches online (even though live presenting is once again an option for them). They prefer my delivery on Zoom! Who knew?! Warwick's sage advice is peppered throughout much of this chapter and chapter 20.

TIP

Michelle says,

'Virtual presenting can be just as good as — sometimes even better than — live presenting, as long as you focus on what's important.'

Setting up your visual space

We all know how easy it is to be distracted when we are in an online meeting. So setting up your space properly is critical. I suggest you divide the visual space into five categories:

1. background

2. personal appearance

3. lighting

4. sound

5. technology.

The following sections look at each of these in more detail.

Background

It's both funny and terrible when the audience thinks you're presenting to them from a disco, or they are looking up your nose, or you look like a Muppet with just a head and no body! We can laugh about all these things but, as you know, many people do this when they present online, and it damages their personal brand and credibility.

> **TIP**
>
> **Michelle says,**
>
> 'An unprofessional background can damage your personal brand and credibility.'

The two main things to consider when planning your virtual background are:

1. *You don't want to distract:* You want your audience looking at your face, not captivated by whatever you have positioned in your background. I'm never quite sure why experts, including scientists and journalists on TV, stand with their kitchen in the background of the frame. Distractions are always present if you allow people to see a whole room (especially a kitchen) behind you. One of my clients recently presented to his audience from his young child's bedroom with number charts and animals on the wall behind him. He was pitching an idea to transform the data analytics area. My advice was that his background was not helping him in conveying that message!

2. *You want to maintain your authenticity:* You want your audience to get a sense of who you are and what you stand for. If you are a fun person, don't present against a plain white wall. If you are an authority in your matter or a business

professional, perhaps you need books or certificates on the wall behind you. As an example, I have set up my office with a background of gorgeous flowers and a painting that reflects my personality and sends the right vibe to the audience. I have hung the painting at just the right height for my audience to enjoy it. Truth be told, I have about 10 paintings that are appropriate, and I change them depending on what I'm wearing and who is watching! If I have someone who will love my painting of hot pink flowers, I use that. If, on the other hand, I have an audience who will better appreciate my framed Certified Speaking Professional certificate, then I use that. I'm very careful when I choose a painting that it's not something that will capitate my audience. Rather, it's just a bit of design on a wall to send a joyful, bright, positive vibe.

Here are some other considerations when planning your perfect background.

SET YOUR CAMERA AT EYE HEIGHT

Make sure your camera is at eye height, so people are not looking up your nose or at your forehead. This is especially a trap for new players who are presenting from their laptop or phone — the camera inside the device needs to be at eye height. If you are going to use a portable device for your virtual meetings, pop it up on some books to get that camera at the right height. I've heard of a professional speaker who used the ironing board in their hotel room to position their laptop correctly! These creative solutions are cheap and easy!

CUSTOM BACKGROUNDS

We all know that no-one wants to see your messy house, your brother sitting at the table with you, or your washing all over the lounge room! Thank goodness many of the virtual platforms have an option to blur your background. Another option is to use a custom background.

Keep in mind the following when considering backgrounds:

- Many experts suggest you need to sit with a green screen behind you if you're going to choose a virtual background. This is because, without the green screen, the camera often struggles to process your extremities and you end up with parts of your head or hands missing! You can still use custom backgrounds without a green screen; you just have to decide that you're okay with the odd disconnected image being projected.

- Your corporate marketing department may have created a custom background for all staff to use, with your logo and other graphic elements. These are fine to use as well. Just be careful of corporate backgrounds that have movement in them because they can easily distract people from your message.

- You can also use a custom scene provided at no extra cost by the virtual platform. Perhaps you'd like to position yourself in a coastal scene, or in the rainforest. Again, be careful of movement.

Fransisco's story

My lovely client Fransisco was presenting to his colleagues via Zoom. To liven things up and give people something different to look at, Fransisco had chosen a beautiful snow scene as his background.

After a few minutes of presenting, the group asked him to stop and change his background before he continued — because the animated graphic he had chosen included a lady in a pink coat in the very back of the scene walking backwards and forwards. His audience announced to Fransisco that they simply couldn't listen to what he was saying 'with that lady walking and walking'! It's one thing to liven things up, and quite another to distract or even annoy people with a moving scene.

Handy tip: If you have longer hair and plan to use a virtual background, allow your hair to fall free around your face rather than tying it back. Virtual backgrounds give you a funny alien head if you tie your hair back.

Perhaps you'd even like to present from Hogwarts, Disneyland or the set of *The Simpsons* TV show. Yes! You can buy backgrounds for your virtual platform that, in many cases, will delight your audience.

If you choose this option, select a static image and allow people a moment to absorb the scene before saying anything too important!

TIP

Michelle says,

'Create a library of high-resolution images that are ideal backgrounds because they suit your brand and work-type.'

Above all else, while you must pay attention to your background, remember to not make it *all* about the background. The most important element of your presentation is that you are personally connecting with and serving your audience.

Personal appearance

As the presenter, you may choose to turn off your camera when you're giving your audience a break. So step number one when managing your personal appearance is to take the time to find an appropriate photo of yourself that you can use as your profile photo when you need to turn your camera off. Don't use an old photo of yourself from 20 years ago! And also don't use an image of something that is not your face. I have a client who has a photo of a surfboard resting against a fence for their profile photo and, although it can encourage a bit of chitchat about their hobbies (which can be nice for getting to know people), in general a photo of an object rather than your face says, 'I don't care to build rapport with you'.

Kim's story

My good friend Kim started and finished a contract during COVID-19 lockdowns. That meant she didn't ever go to the office or meet any of her colleagues face to face. Her direct manager chose

(continued)

to use a photograph of a pink flower as her profile photo, and she didn't ever turn her camera on. My friend completed that role and left the organisation never knowing what 'pink flower lady' actually looked like.

Please understand that I am empathetic about the circumstances that may have led 'pink flower lady' to choose not to show her personal environment. People may not want you to see where they live or who they live with for a whole lot of reasons. In addition, many people have difficulties with the internet when they use their camera at all.

The question to ask yourself when making decisions in this area is 'at what cost?' What does choosing to never show your face do for your personal brand as a presenter? Make the decision to use a virtual background or blur your background if you want to keep your home life private. If you're worried about the internet, perhaps go to your local library and log on from there (if they provide adequate speeds). And if you're worried about your personal appearance and happen to be presenting via Zoom, consider using the 'touch up my appearance' option. It can take 10 years off you!

Once you are presenting, you need to take care of the following regarding your personal appearance:

- colours

- grooming

- positioning.

COLOURS

The first thing to be careful of with your appearance is that you don't blend or 'melt' into your background. For example, if your background is corporate blue, don't wear corporate blue. The best colours to wear in the virtual world are bold, bright colours that contrast with your background. Patterns can work — just experiment to make sure the pattern doesn't swirl or cause an optical illusion for your audience.

Do a test in the outfit you have chosen and make sure that, on screen, it complements your hair colour and skin tones, and that you look as healthy as possible. Appearing too pale, tired, sunburnt or unwell negatively affects your credibility.

Handy tip: Regardless of your gender, if you are sunburnt for your virtual event or tend to flush easily, use a green-base foundation cream or powder to take down some of the red on your face.

GROOMING

In the virtual world, people really notice the details of your face, clothes and hands. Therefore, the same rules for grooming yourself for a live presentation apply to your virtual one. I'm surprised at how many people turn up for virtual meetings with wet hair these days. Just as you would never attend a live meeting at work with wet hair, don't do so virtually! Groom your hair, shave, pay attention to your fingernails and choose make-up and clothes that flatter you. Remember — TV presenters of all genders wear make-up when presenting for a reason. Make-up should even out your complexion and help you look your most healthy self! Avoid glitter make-up and shimmer highlighters on virtual screens because they refract the light in unusual ways and can leave you looking pale and drawn with dark circles under your eyes.

POSITIONING

Sit back a bit from your camera rather than positioning yourself too close. Your audience wants to see your shoulders. Many researchers have suggested you use the rule of thirds. This is where you divide your screen into horizontal thirds. Aim for your eyes and nose to be along the top third line, leaving a few centimetres between the top of your head and the top of your screen.

Another trap for new players is to rock forwards and backwards on their seat. This is because, as humans, we have a natural tendency to gesture and many of us have energy in our legs (even though we are sitting down). This energy can cause you to rock backwards and forwards, making your face frequently move way too close to the camera — which is very full-on for your audience! Instead, be sure to sit back a bit. Try to only move your arms, not your whole torso, and definitely don't rock forwards and backwards, towards and away from the camera lens.

Lighting

Good lighting is so important when you're presenting virtually. Always remember that your role is to shift your audience from their current to your desired state, and one of the most important considerations in this endeavour is to make life easy for your audience. You don't want people squinting or losing interest in you because they can't see you as you sit in the dark. One of the main reasons your background might be too dark is that you're relying too much on natural light. All it takes is for the sun to pass behind a cloud and your once beautifully lit face is now completely cast in shadow.

Another reason your virtual environment is too dark could be because you're sitting with your back to the window. This causes the camera to expose for the light and turn you into a silhouette.

The good news with lighting is that you don't need to spend a lot of money on fancy lights to look like a true professional online. Some simple desk lights positioned around you, perhaps a LED set-up behind you for backlight, and the room light will usually do. For some extra professionalism, you could add a ring light near your camera to light your face. You can buy all of these items for less than $20 at your local discount shop or hardware store. Make sure that the lighting flatters you and doesn't create weird shadows on your face.

I recommend you take the time to experiment with what works for you. I personally like to use a ring light because it provides a warm light that flatters my eyes and face. Warwick Merry, who I mention earlier in this chapter, suggests care must be taken if you use a ring light. Make sure it isn't reflecting off your glasses and distracting your audience. I found that positioning the ring light so it shone right into my eyes made me look the best but, unfortunately, also caused me to experience terrible headaches and dizziness. These unpleasant side-effects forced me to find a different way to light my face without making my workplace unhealthy.

Handy tip: A spread of light is better than a torch effect on your face. Warwick Merry's very clever tip if your lights are too bright is to place some baking paper over the light. (It won't burn because it's made to be used in an oven.) Baking paper diffuses the light, stops crazy shadows and makes the light easier on your eyes.

TIP

Michelle says,

'Don't rely on natural light when presenting online. Make use of a simple LED set-up and a carefully positioned ring light so you don't have to shine the lights right into your eyes.'

Sound

Have you ever listened to a podcast where the sound wasn't great? What did you do? Did you struggle through and try to hang on and listen? Or did you switch to something different? People will put up with bad lighting, but they will generally not tolerate bad sound. The microphone in your computer is not satisfactory for a professional, easy-listening experience for your audience. Use an accessory microphone such as a shotgun microphone, a lapel microphone or a quality desk-mounted microphone that plugs into the back of your computer. Investigate which microphone works best for you. At the time of writing, I'm using a Rode NT Mini microphone. It was relatively cheap and it's fantastic.

Handy tip: Borrow a mic from a friend and see if it works before investing yourself.

You want to make sure your microphone projects your voice beautifully, so be careful that your microphone doesn't create an echo. One of the coolest tips I learnt from Warwick Merry was to pad the walls of the room you're presenting in with blankets, hang paintings and throw down a rug and some pillows on the floor — even open cupboard doors — to absorb sound and stop echoes. If you want to be fancy and/ or you're setting up your virtual-presenting studio as a purpose-built room, you can tack some sound absorbing foam to the walls.

Ultimately, when it comes to sound, there's not one way, there's just the right way for you.

TIP

Michelle says,

'Experiment with lighting and sound and choose what works, and then slowly tweak your set-up over time.'

Technology

When setting up my office for the new world of virtual presenting, another great tip I received from Warwick Merry is 'expect the best, plan for the worst'. Make sure you are familiar with your software. Check that everything works well before you are due to begin your meeting or presentation. Do a microphone check. Check that the wi-fi is working. Have your phone nearby and make sure you know how to whip it out and connect to a personal hotspot if the internet fails you. Make sure you've updated to the latest version of the virtual platform you are using. If you haven't run an update in a while, your application could freeze or crash — and what a shame that would be in the middle of your event!

Handy tip: Log on early and make sure everything is working and your platform application is up to date. You don't want to have to download a last-minute system update when the meeting is supposed to start in 2 minutes. Stressful!

A final tip for your set-up

If you're engaging in an important presentation such as a board meeting, pitch, or conference presentation — where the worst-case scenario would be career damaging—please do consider renting a commercial studio. I always ask myself, 'What is this worth?' If I'm worried about glitches with the wi-fi or unstable connections, or I feel the audience will negatively judge my usual office space, I'm quick to book a professional venue that specialises in virtual presenting. Remember—expect the best but plan for the worst!

TRY THIS

In many cases, your audience will be glad about the ease (and time- and cost-saving) of a virtual event. Set yourself a challenge to reread this chapter and implement some improvements in your virtual set-up. Do you need to rethink your background, your lighting or your sound? Is your head positioned in the top third of the screen? Have you updated your software lately? Importantly, enjoy the process and always think about your audience's needs.

A note about hybrid meetings

A hybrid meeting involves a mixture of in-person and remote attendees. Remote attendees join the meeting via their virtual meeting platform, while in-person attendees sit together in a dedicated meeting room. Imagine it's 2.55 pm on a Thursday afternoon and you're about to run your live team meeting. Your manager informs you (with 5 minutes' notice) that four of the 23 people will be logging on from home today. Boom—you have an instant hybrid event to manage!

I'm not a fan of hybrid meetings. As an external person who delivers training and keynote presentations, if the organiser informs me beforehand my audience will be a mix of in-person and online attendees, I'm inclined to ask them to book me for two separate events—one for the online version, the other for the live one, or just one online event and get everyone to log on from their own remote location (even though some people were able to join the live meeting). This does mean the group misses out on everyone being together, but they were missing a lot of connection anyway.

If you must run a hybrid event, here are some aspects to keep in mind:

- Make sure you plan your presentation with everyone in mind. As online presenting guru Warwick Merry emphases, 'inclusion is the magic word'. When you do your five-step analysis (chapter 2), ensure you include the live and virtual people in your analysis.

- Deliver to everyone, not just the people in the live room with you.

- If it's a big audience, you might need two MCs — one who is live and one who is remote. The MC needs to control the energy in the room and entertain people in the breaks.

- Have a big screen in your live meeting room so that everyone can see the various online audience members' faces.

- Ensure your technology has as few glitches as possible — test, test and retest!

- Ensure you use all the interaction tips from the next chapter to ensure your virtual audience is as engaged as your live one.

Handy tip: If you have a few people planning to log on to a virtual meeting from the same computer, try to get them to separate and log on from their own individual device and separate spaces. This way you'll better manage what's happening and better control the outcome.

Ideally, either all attendees are all individually logging in, or everyone is live in the room together. If you've been in a hybrid event yourself, you'll appreciate why I'd rather run two separate events (or one online event with everyone logging in separately). It's generally better for everyone!

TOP TIPS
for setting up your virtual space

- Virtual presenting can be as good as – sometimes even better than – live presenting.

- Areas to focus on are background, personal appearance, light, sound and technology.

- You don't want to distract, and you do want to maintain your authenticity.

- Maintain authenticity and connection by setting your camera at eye height, choosing a background that works for your audience and ensuring you look as healthy as possible.

- Light the space for best results, and ensure your sound is excellent. Always use an accessory microphone.

- Update your virtual platform regularly.

- Consider a commercial studio for really important events.

- If you must run a hybrid event, be sure to present to everyone equally.

CHAPTER 20

Engaging online audiences

In 2020, when we all had to make the obligatory move to virtual meeting and presenting, I was inundated by business journalists seeking the 'secret sauce' on virtual presenting. Their number one question was always, 'What's different when presenting online?' Interestingly my answer to that question remains, 'Not much!' The three phases to a persuasive presentation outlined in this book — analysis, design and delivery — remain the same. You still need to perform the five-step analysis (refer to chapter 2), answer the 4MAT System questions (chapter 3), design your message with storyboarding (chapter 4), and script your presentation using my Persuasion Blueprint (chapter 5). And you still need to deliver with a complete focus on the audience and serve them. As you can see, if you already knew all those things when the move to virtual presenting happened, you'd be pretty nicely set up to do a great job of your virtual presenting.

> **TIP**
>
> **Michelle says,**
>
> 'There's not much difference between live and virtual presenting. You still need to follow the three phases to persuasive presenting to set yourself up for virtual presenting success.'

Moving from live to virtual presenting does create some specific challenges, and these can be grouped into four key areas:

- boundary setting
- eye contact
- slide design and delivery
- interaction.

The good news is that I have proven time and time again that you can make your virtual presenting just as engaging and fascinating as your live meetings, as long as you pay attention to these four areas.

Setting your boundaries for success

No-one is going to tell you engaging in the virtual world is easy. After all, people often log in from unusual locations, they keep their cameras off and sometimes you don't even know if they are actually there. I attended a virtual meeting where the facilitator called on a person in the audience by their name and...silence. Uh-oh! The person had logged on to give the impression to their manager that they were listening but they had then gone off to do something else. Sprung!

To achieve some work–life balance for employees and reduce the very real effects of 'Zoom fatigue', and to reduce the need for high-powered wi-fi when people are working from home, many companies have policies that state employees don't have to have their cameras on, and/or are encouraged to attend virtual meetings while exercising. Most businesspeople I know will admit to logging on to meetings and presentations from their power walk, their car or an equally distracting location such as the doctor's waiting room! My tired (and hungry) husband attended a late-night work meeting last week from our family dinner table so he could get a quick bite to eat at the same time. Oh dear.

Adding to these issues is the feeling that people seem to have completely lost their manners in meetings, perhaps due to the 'remote' feeling we have when we log on. In the past, if someone just walked out of a live meeting without explaining where they were going, most people would have thought that rude or concerning. Yet in the virtual world, people pop in and out with no explanation all the time — they just disappear! Now that virtual presenting is here to stay, it's never been more important to set some rules and boundaries to ensure your meetings and presentations are quick, efficient and productive.

TIP

Michelle says,

'Now that virtual presenting is here to stay, it's never been more important to set some rules to ensure your virtual meetings and presentations are quick, efficient and productive.'

What's the solution? Well, you can see how important the skill of framing is in these circumstances. Chapter 5 covers the process of framing in much more detail, and here's a quick reminder. Framing is the technique you use to set boundaries to control and relax your audience. Pre-framing is all the rules you set prior to the meeting. Many of my clients have had great success by setting some 'this is how we do things around here' rules for their virtual meetings. For example, one of my clients is a large supermarket chain. They have a rule that if you're at the meeting, your camera is on. Another client has a rule that you can only schedule a meeting for a maximum of 50 minutes, so everyone gets a 10-minute break before the next one. When I facilitate my workshops, I set a variety of rules — for example:

- *If you miss one session, you can't re-join.* Attendees need to be there, present and participating (camera on and mute off), for the duration of the workshops.

- *You (and your background) might be screenshotted.* I take a lot of screenshots in my workshops. I warn people about this and suggest they change their background if they are not happy with their current choice.

- *You will get plenty of breaks.* During the meeting, I'm very clear about the number of breaks and when they will happen. I even set rules about how the break should work, such as not having any screen time in a break. The break is to give everyone's eyes and brains a rest, and minimise the chances of Zoom fatigue.

Handy tip: Take regular breaks when presenting online. The current advice is that you shouldn't speak for more than 90 minutes without a 15- to 30-minute break. Remember to also ask your audience to take a proper break. I always suggest my audience go away from their screens and shut their eyes for a few moments to rejuvenate.

You can choose from plenty of rules to make sure everyone gets the best from your presentation — and you get the outcome you're hoping for — in the quickest time possible. If you set rules and ensure you actually follow them, you're setting yourself up for success.

TRY THIS

Think about the working example you have been using through this book. How might your frames change for a virtual presentation as opposed to a live one?

Understanding how eye contact is different online

As you know from chapter 11, the key to connecting with a live audience is to look right into the whites of your audience members' eyes. Unfortunately, when presenting online, your eye contact must be completely different from this. Why? Because if you look at the faces of the people in your meeting, it will look to them as though you have tipped your head forwards and are showing them the crown of your head. You'll also be inclined to flick your eyes between people and even to your own face on the screen — which can make you look like you're following a fly around the screen. Either way, you're not looking at your audience at all and they can tell — it breaks rapport.

Instead of looking at people's faces on your screen, make sure that you look right into the camera. You want the audience members to feel that you are talking directly to them. Looking only at the camera — and not at the live humans with whom you are speaking — is quite a discipline. I've got a little low-tech trick — I have a sticky note with two arrows on it that says 'look here' to force me to remember to look *only* into the camera. I stick it on my computer with the arrows pointing to the camera to remind me that that's where I need to be looking all the time.

TIP

Michelle says,

'As crazy as it sounds, it doesn't matter that you are not actually looking at people when presenting virtually. They need to perceive that you are! You need to be very disciplined to force yourself to look right into that camera the *whole* time.'

Continuing to connect with your audience

As you talk to the camera (not to the faces of your audience), imagine that you're seeing your audience's faces and make sure that you let your face do some talking. Let your smile come out, let your eyes sparkle, let your cheeks move. You want to make sure that your features are still animated while you look into that camera.

Handy tip: If you're worried about losing your authentic personality when you look directly into the camera, imagine you can see the faces of the people you are presenting to inside the camera. That will give your eyes a sparkle and your features a lift. Your audience will perceive that you are pleased to be addressing them.

Anne's story

My friend Anne is a family counsellor. She works with families in crisis. Before the move to online work (due mostly to COVID-19), Anne would meet her clients at her office. Everyone would sit on some comfortable chairs around a table. In this live environment, Anne could read their facial expressions and watch their body language and adapt her behaviour accordingly. Since moving to more frequent online work, Anne (like many of us) has had to move her interactions (in her case, her counselling) to the Zoom platform.

Anne came to me to find out what she should do with her eye contact when facilitating her families in counselling. And, yes, even though it seems wrong in many ways, the advice is to look only into the camera when speaking — not at the faces.

The people in your virtual meeting need to think you are looking at them. They need to think you are connected to them. They need to think you are just talking with them. And the *only* way to do this is to ensure that you only look into the middle of your camera. If you look anywhere else, you'll look as though you are looking down or following a fly!

Using slides in your virtual meeting

Most of the same rules for slide design for live presenting (refer to chapter 16) apply to virtual presenting. Remember that visual aids give you the opportunity to really captivate your audience, reinforce your key messages and embed the points that you want them to remember.

Looking at the differences

The aim of slides in a virtual meeting is to reinforce your point visually, just like in your live meeting. The thing that's different is you really need to think about whether it's better for your audience to be looking at you (as you would in a conversation) or at your screen while you take them through something visual that they really need to see to understand.

Marcus' story

Marcus is my wonderful client, and recently he worked through my Persuasion Blueprint with me in preparation for an online presentation. When he got to Step 7, or the 'how?' section, he realised he needed to take his prospect through seven steps. Marcus initially created a slide with seven bullet points on the left in 12-point font, and an image 'lifted' from Google (and so used illegally, which could get him in a lot of trouble) on the right of the slide. Dreadful! Please don't ever use a slide that looks like this – either virtual or live!

Do you remember that wonderful question from chapter 16 that you should always ask about every slide in your presentation deck? The question is, 'Is this the best way to visually reinforce this point?' When Marcus asked himself this about his very ugly seven bullet point slide, his answer was a resounding 'no'!

What did he do instead? Marcus redesigned the slide. He found a free and perfectly legal image of a winding road (from www.unsplash.com) that he bled to the edges of the slide. He placed each of the seven steps along the road in a different coloured box. In addition, he built/animated the slide so that each step (or coloured box) came up separately when he chose to reveal it. In between each step while he was presenting, he then selected 'stop share' to stop sharing his slides and return to the view where all the participant faces were on the screen. He was then able to talk with his audience (with no slides on the screen) about the point they had just seen.

Marcus was clever because he used the animated slide to reinforce his message, and not at the expense of connecting with his audience and talking with them in a conversational way in between the visual reinforcement.

Marcus received thunderous applause after this presentation, and his audience remembered the seven steps weeks later. The initiative was approved and executed as he had requested. Awesome!

Using slides in tandem with your Persuasion Blueprint when presenting virtually

Some parts of the Persuasion Blueprint are enhanced by slides, whereas at other parts it's better to just connect with your audience and talk with them without any slides up at the time.

Here's how your use of slides connects with the steps in the Persuasion Blueprint:

- *First slide:* I recommend that you always have a Purpose slide as your first slide. (Remember, your purpose is your sexy title that you determine as part of your five-step analysis — covered in detail in chapter 2.)

- *Step 0:* You may also want a slide for your icebreaker. My clever client Meegan from Queensland University of Technology in Brisbane, Australia, stacked nine shocking statistics in her icebreaker in a recent meeting and so she actually had nine slides in her icebreaker — one for each of the statistics she announced, accompanied with nine evocative images that reinforced her point. Using one slide at a time, with one statistic and only one image (which bled to the edges of her screen), was visually captivating and definitely reinforced the shocking information she was delivering. Yes, you read that correctly – nine slides in just the icebreaker! Meegan realised it was more important to shock the crowd with her statistics and the images on the slides (her slides took up the majority of her screen) than to connect with her audience through her face. Therefore, in her icebreaker, she made the slides the hero.

- *Steps 1 to 5:* I don't recommend you have any slides as you go through Steps 1 to 5 of the Persuasion Blueprint. This is because you want to just talk with your audience during these steps and connect. You want these rapport-building steps to do just that, build rapport. Your audience can't feel the rapport when your face is a tiny tile on the side of the screen that they can hardly see.

- *Steps 6 and 7:* You can have as many slides as you like for your *What?* (Step 6) and *How?* (Step 7) sections of your Persuasion Blueprint.

- *Steps 8 to 13:* In the *What if?* and *What else?* sections of your online presentation, you may choose to have a contact details slide and a summary slide. I have also seen some people have great success sharing a slide for their closing statement (Step 13 of the Persuasion Blueprint). You don't need slides for any other parts in these steps. I recommend you bring your view back to all the faces on the screen and just talk with the humans!

Handy tip: Consider using the same image at the end of your presentation as you chose for your icebreaker or purpose slide. Using the same image signifies that this is the end of your meeting or presentation and is called 'closing the loop'.

Presenting with slides

Two main things change when presenting with slides in the virtual world. The first is your use of the 'B' key (which is so helpful in a live presentation) and the second is the way you build your diagrams and graphs. Here's why, and what to do instead:

- *Using the 'B' key:* Using the 'B' key while you're in PowerPoint slide view blanks your screen. Of course, I'm sure you already realise that if you blank your screen while presenting online, people will think the internet has dropped out, or there's a problem! Instead, you simply stop sharing your screen, and take the view back to all the faces on the screen (with no slides up at all). (See Marcus's example earlier in this chapter for an example of how to do this cleverly.)

- *Build your graphs:* Because directing the attention of your virtual audience is so important, it's essential that you build your graphs, diagrams and bullet points, rather than letting them appear all at once. You can even use this for tables with lots of information. In this way, you'll ensure that your audience is only looking at the point you want them to focus on. Just as you'd reclaim your space in the middle of a room or stage when presenting with slides in a live meeting, when presenting virtually you must also reclaim your space in the equivalent middle. To do this, select 'stop share' on your slides and bring the view back to all the faces on the screen.

TIP

Michelle says,

'Stop sharing your slides as often as possible in virtual meetings and presentations. Bring the audience's view back to only faces on the screen and connect, connect, connect!'

Handy tip: You can use the advanced function in your virtual platform to have your slides as your background. This means you don't have to share and stop share because you can continue to look into the camera and your audience can connect with you while simultaneously looking at your slides. If using this feature, you do need to design your slides with the position of your body in mind. For example, if you appear on the left side of the slide, your text or image should appear on the right. Also be aware that you don't cause 'split attention' (refer to chapter 16). At all times, your audience needs to know if they should be looking at you, or your visual aid.

Make sure that you rehearse how to share your slides — and stop sharing — on the virtual platform you are using. People won't notice if everything goes smoothly but they'll really notice if you get it wrong and apologise too much.

Using notes to remember your key points

As mentioned, the Persuasion Blueprint is just as useful when presenting online. One small point of difference when using it online is that I suggest you populate your Persuasion Blueprint template and then print it out. Having your slides and your notes on your screen (even if you have two or three screens) can get very tricky — especially when trying to share your screen and stop sharing and still remember your script. Print your Persuasion Blueprint script in 16-point font (nice and big) and hold it in your hand, or rest it on your desk and refer to it when necessary. Ensure that at all other times you are looking into the camera and you'll be perceived as clear, seamless and confident!

Interacting with your virtual audience

One-way communication, where a presenter stood and talked at their audience while they sat patiently and waited for the presenter to finish, was never cool — and it's certainly not cool in the virtual world, either. Plan in advance to interact with your audience. If you plan it, and even practice it, then you'll remember to do it, and your audience will thank you for it.

My advice is to always remember who your audience is and only do interaction activities for their benefit and to help them listen and understand. Don't get caught up in interaction for the sake of it. It will annoy your adult audience and they will be reluctant to attend your future meetings.

As a general rule, you want engagement every 3 to 5 minutes. That could be through a rhetorical question or through an actual interaction with people where they are typing into the chat function, or using their reaction emojis. At all times, engage, engage, engage!

TIP

Michelle says,

'At all times when online, engage, engage, engage!'

Some ideas for engaging with your audience include using the following:

- simple direct language
- rhetorical questions
- response potential
- questions
- names

- chat functions

- reaction buttons

- breakout rooms

- polls

- performance!

Using simple, direct language

In the virtual space, people are way less patient than they would be in a live meeting, and they need you to get to the point quickly. Never has it been more critical to follow formulas such as the five-step analysis (refer to chapter 2), the 4MAT System (chapter 3) and the Persuasion Blueprint (chapter 5). These winning formulas help you plan your message from your audience's point of view, structure your message so everyone can pay attention, and then deliver in a way that engages everyone and compels them to action. In addition to these winning formulas, be sure to use simple, direct language and plain English to say what you mean. Plain English makes it way easier for your audience to follow you online, especially if your connection is disrupted or you have the odd buffering issue where your screen is freezing.

Using rhetorical questions

Signpost your content with rhetorical questions (that is, questions that you ask and then answer straightaway). When you ask a rhetorical question, you don't give your audience time to respond. It's a clever engagement technique that you can use in any presentation, and especially online.

I recommend you use the questions from the 4MAT System as a guide. For example, *Why is this important? Why are we here today? What are we going to cover? What is the challenge we face? How will we fix this? How will we implement this? What happens if we don't do this? What happens when we do? Is there another way?* Using rhetorical questions like these helps your audience listen more carefully and follow your point.

Using response potential

Another clever engagement trick for all presenting — and, yes, it works brilliantly in a virtual presentation — is to use what is known as 'response potential'. Response potential is where you say something that has a variety of different endings or response possibilities. Using these kinds of statements engages your audience as they start to think what the ending or response could be.

For example, you say, 'And the good news is...', 'The bad news is...', 'Unfortunately...', 'This is important because...' or 'We did this for three main reasons' (and then list the reasons).

TRY THIS

Go to your working presentation and aim to add some rhetorical questions — such as, 'What is our challenge?' Also add some response potential in there — for example, 'The good news is...'

Using questions to get people talking

Aim to ask your audience questions and get them to talk to you and each other in response. Where possible during your online presentations, ask people to have their cameras on and to sign in from a quiet location so they can keep their mute off. If you're going to be facilitating two-way talking, the mute has got to be off. How many times have I had to say to someone in a virtual meeting, 'You're on mute'? And they look at me confused, and so I say it again: 'Fluffy, you're on mute'. Then the group members say, 'Fluffy, you're on mute'. Finally, the person realises and says (inaudibly) 'Oh, I'm on mute! Hang on while I just fix that'. Everyone sighs! Then they have to fuss around and turn it off. Then they repeat themselves. Oh dear, all that fussing, which often feels like it took forever, can be very irritating for people. My concern with this is that if audience members get too irritated they'll log off the call, and then you've lost them.

Handy tip: If people are participating in a noisy space (and so you've requested that they keep their mute on), it's important that you announce you are coming to them (to warn them) and remind them they are on mute. For example, 'Georgia, I'm coming to you next, and you're on mute'. You can then repeat the question while Georgia unmutes, and it's all very streamlined!

If people are in a noisy place (sometimes unavoidable), you may prefer to get them to use the chat for their questions and answers.

Using the sweetest sound (people's names)

If you're aiming to increase interaction, be sure to call people by their name as much as possible. It's really important that everyone in the meeting actually has their name underneath their photo so that you can call them by their actual name and not 'LT74129' (or some other computer-generated name that sits underneath their photograph)! Pre-frame this so people don't waste time in your actual presentation. If people still log in and have not yet changed their name, or they've logged on from someone else's device (perhaps their partner's) so the wrong name is coming up, take the time to digress and fix this immediately, so you can use their name as soon as possible.

Using the chat function

Kinesthetic learners love the chat function on virtual platforms because it gives them something else to do while they are listening! (Refer to chapter 14 for more information on kinesthetic learners.) The chat feature allows your audience to ask questions (which you may prefer if people are in a noisy place and have their mute buttons on), and you can also use it to send instant messages to other audience members in a meeting and send private messages to individual people. As the presenter, you can choose who the participants can chat with and/or to disable chat entirely.

The point is that you should aim to have people participate in your meeting on the virtual platform just the way you would if you were live in a meeting with real people in the room with you. I use the chat function when too many people are in the meeting to go around the room and ask individuals for their answer or feedback. Instead, I ask them to type it into the chat. It's a much quicker way to see what everyone is thinking in one moment. If someone's answer is excellent, I call it out so everyone can hear it. If someone's answer is wrong or needs work, I re-teach the point so that everyone is on the right page.

I have found that enabling group chat makes everyone feel part of the meeting and they focus well. Just be sure to use your framing (refer to chapter 5) and set up the 'values' around what's nice (and what's not) so people know how to behave to each other. I have found that audience members tend to be even kinder and more generous to each other in the chat than they might usually be. They use the chat to boost people's confidence and add their personal thoughts to what I'm saying, which makes it better for everyone.

Handy tip: Be very firm with people about how to use the chat feature, or you'll have people going out of scope in the chat and distracting themselves needlessly with nonsense that annoys everyone.

TRY THIS

Think about your working example and plan to add some use of the chat function in your next meeting or presentation. What firm rules will you need to set to make sure everyone sticks to the point? Be sure to set the rules at Step 5 of your Persuasion Blueprint.

Using reaction buttons

Have you ever hosted an online meeting or presentation where everyone in the audience had their camera off and no-one spoke? Argh! It's not fun presenting to no-one! These days, many organisations work with speakers like me to upskill their people virtually via webinar-style events. In many cases, organisations tell their staff if they don't attend, they don't get the recording. So many people log on, but don't hang around — they just want the recording!

Under these circumstances, it's tricky to know who is actually there and who is just logged on so they get the recording sent later! In the early days of virtual presenting, I found myself saying, 'Is anyone there?' On one occasion, no-one replied (even though 120 people were registered for the event), and I realised I was just presenting for the recording. Very demotivating indeed! In situations where you know most of your audience will have their cameras off (or just for fun and to boost engagement anyway), emphasise how essential it is for everyone to use the non-verbal feedback buttons. This gives *every* participant a way to engage and participate, regardless of their noisy background or washing in the background.

As with everything online, be clear with your boundary setting. Perhaps you want people using all the emojis as they feel the mood take them, or perhaps you want people to use the 'hands up' before they interrupt with a question. Whatever your frames, be clear about them. I have found people to be very responsive with those emojis — they see being able to use them as having permission to have fun and participate to stay engaged. Just keep it under control and remember you're there for a reason — no interaction should ever replace you achieving your persuasive objectives.

Using breakout rooms effectively

Breakout rooms give your audience a moment to discuss something or work together in smaller groups. They are best used to brainstorm ideas, practise something, and/or decide something. While you can join breakouts at your discretion, unlike putting people into subgroups in a live meeting, you can't see what's going on in all the rooms simultaneously. For this reason, it's super important that you explain clearly what you want people to do, demonstrate it yourself and then explain again what the activity is. Otherwise, you may find people go to the breakout room and discuss whatever they want — and potentially topics unrelated to your meeting outcome.

TIP

Michelle says,

'In most virtual platforms, you can pop in and out of the various breakout rooms you have set up. Make use of this function to ensure everyone is on track. You can achieve good results from using breakout rooms when you manage the process properly.'

Make sure you control the controllables when using breakout rooms. Keep your breakout rooms to no more than eight people (two to four people is an ideal number) and bring everyone back to the main group after a maximum of 10 minutes. When I use breakout rooms, I allocate no longer than 5 minutes at a time so I can keep control of what everyone's doing with the time. If the breakout goes for too long, you may find that people go off track and you waste time — or, worse, they get bored and leave the meeting. When you call everyone back, the remaining people let you know, 'Oh, Fred had to leave'. Oh dear!

Handy tip: If you're going to ask for feedback after the breakout, perhaps use a tool such as the virtual whiteboard for participants to take notes on during the breakout session.

Jane's story

Jane facilitates global meetings regularly in her business. When she asks participants to go into breakout rooms, she explains clearly so people know exactly what she's asking them to talk about. Then she gives some examples of the sort of things they might include in their discussion. Then she explains the activity for a third time before opening the rooms for people to join.

Jane then pops in and out of the breakout rooms to help where needed — and also to check everyone is doing what she asked.

She's known as a top-class virtual facilitator across her business.

Using polls

People seem to have a bit of love/hate relationship with polls in online meetings. Some people hate them. Others love them. The polling feature for meetings allows you to create single-choice or multiple-choice polling questions for your meetings. You can launch the poll during your presentation and gather the responses from your audience in real time or you can also download a report of polling after the meeting.

If you can run a poll well, then it's another way to have your audience engage and interact. Some of my clients have used polls very successfully when doing team-building events. You can even take advantage of someone else's hard work and Google 'top funny questions to ask via polls' to get you started. As is the case in any presentation, activity for the sake of activity is annoying to adults. Plan your interaction with polls wisely and only do them to stimulate thought or relevant conversation that moves people to your desired state.

TRY THIS

Think about your working example and plan to add some reactions and a breakout room in your next meeting. What is the best way to set out how you want the reactions used? How will you facilitate a breakout to maximise engagement and meaningful participation?

Using performance!

When you are presenting online, the only energy (most of the time) is the energy coming from you, the presenter. For this reason, it's wise to listen to the sage advice of Warwick Merry, the guru of online presenting, who says, 'Be yourself amplified when presenting online'. That means, be yourself, just give yourself an energy boost so that people get a lift from your vibe. You need to be animated on the screen without going over the top.

You can make sure your energy is a bit higher in two key ways: gestures and facial expressions.

Let's look at these in more detail.

USING GESTURES IN VIRTUAL PRESENTATIONS

In chapter 13, I provide a lot of detail about gesturing, and some of the rules for live gestures do apply online. For example, you should still do the gesture with confidence (as though you mean to do it), and you should be aware of the past, present and future positions when indicating a direction with your hands. The one main thing that changes when using gestures online is where you place your gesture in the space.

In a live meeting, bringing your hands up and ensuring you have air under your armpits when you gesture is going to be really powerful for your audience. If you're emphasising three things in a live meeting, you'd bring your arm right up with air under your armpits while you ticked them off (palm to the front). In the virtual world, that's ridiculous. It looks silly. You don't want to put your arm right out there in space. Instead, (even when you are standing to present virtually) you should place your hand nearer your face so your audience can see your whole hand in the frame. For example, if you're highlighting five things, you'd put your hand near your face with your palm to the front and you'd use your fingers to indicate the numbers as you run through them — one, two, three, four and five. Yes, weirdly, your gesture needs to be right next to your face inside the frame of your camera.

If you're saying something's exciting in a live meeting, you'd put your arms right up in front of your body like you're in a charismatic church! The contrast in a virtual meeting is that, if something's important, you still need to place your hands out, but they'd need to be right up near your face. You'd say, 'This is really important'. And your hands would go up on either side of your cheeks (with your thumbs nearly touching either side of your face).

This applies for all gestures — they need to be quite close to your face when you're presenting virtually, so they fit neatly within the camera frame.

TIP

Michelle says,

'Gestures need to be quite close to your face when you're presenting virtually.'

FACIAL EXPRESSIONS

Remember, your mood is contagious. If you look enthusiastic and excited, you'll likely encourage your audience to feel the same! Make sure you let you face do the talking. Smile, laugh, frown and grimace (as required). Let all your authentic emotions out and you'll find your audience stays engaged with you throughout your virtual presentations.

TOP TIPS

for engaging online audiences

- You still need to follow the three phases of persuasive presenting: analysis, design and delivery.

- Set boundaries before and during your virtual meeting to ensure people know the rules.

- Look right into the camera and imagine you are speaking to real people.

- Design your slides with your virtual environment in mind.

- Always ask of every slide in your deck, 'Is this the best way to visually reinforce my point?'

- Select 'stop share' as often as possible.

- At all times, engage, engage, engage!

- Make sure that you plan and prepare what you're going to say and say it in the fewest words possible, using simple, clear English.

- Make sure that you interact with your audience. Use rhetorical questions and response potential, ask them questions, call them by their name, and use the chat, reaction and breakout room functions. Try a poll if you think you can do it well — and perform!

- Gesture right up near your face and remember past, present and future positions.

- Remember your mood is contagious — be yourself amplified!

AND NOW IT'S UP TO YOU

Congratulations! The end of this book marks the end of one of the exciting stepping stones in your journey to persuasive presenting. In many ways, it also signifies the beginning of the rest of your journey. How exciting!

By reading this book, you have demonstrated your commitment, desire, and motivation to improve your ability to present your ideas at work more persuasively and impressively. Now it's time to seize as many opportunities as possible to present! Rise up and be who you were born to be. Step up and make the most of opportunities that arise for you. You no longer have any reason to delegate the presentation to someone else, or to present without engaging, inspiring and compelling your audience to action. Please let go now of any old habits that have caused you to be a nervous, or egocentric, self-focused presenter in the past.

I encourage you to take even further ownership of your new wisdom, so your learning journey is as productive as possible and you always present with confidence, clarity and charisma!

Here are some suggestions for continuing your learning:

- Find as many opportunities to present as possible.

- Integrate your learning into as many different aspects of your life as possible, such as at work and home, and in your sporting clubs, hobby groups, emails, phone calls, meetings and formal presentations (online or in person).

- Use your new skills every day in your life and conversations, particularly the pacing and leading pattern. It's how to get more of what you want.

- Keep this book handy and refer to it where necessary.

- Teach others what you now know. Colleagues, friends, and family need these skills too. And if you have children, teaching them is a great place to start! Imagine the power of knowing everything in this book from childhood!

And if you're keen to access some more knowledge from me, you can do so via the following:

- joining me at one of my Persuasive Presentation Skills Masterclasses

- downloading the free resources that have been specifically designed to help you

- subscribing to my monthly ezine, also called *How to Present*, and packed full of techniques and tips for results-focused presenting

- reading my comprehensive blog, which is filled with tips for presenting and persuading in business

You can access more information on all of these options by visiting my website at www.michellebowden.com.au.

If you'd like to delve further into the area of persuasion, please check out my other book *How to Persuade: The skills you need to get what you want* (also published by Wiley).

Remember — when you implement any or all of the suggestions outlined in this book, you will continue to improve your ability to achieve results through your presentations.

Most importantly, please do contact me with your stories of success, and to tell me all about how you achieved exciting results through improving your presentation skills! I would love to know you and hear from you. Connect with me via my website or on LinkedIn (www.linkedin.com/in/michellebowdenenterprises) — and be sure to ask me your questions and update me on your successes so I can see how you are going!

Happy presenting!

Michelle Bowden

PRESENTER CHECKLIST

I believe everyone can be an exceptional presenter. It's just a matter of knowing what to do, and doing it! So I have created this handy checklist that you can go through to evaluate your ability as a presenter. Give it a try — it will help you work out what you need to improve (and take it from me, all these things are so easy to improve). It will also show you what you are already doing well — and there are probably more positives than you realise!

Phase 1: Analysis

☐ Do you know how to work out what you're trying to achieve?

☐ Have you completed a five-step analysis on this presentation?

☐ Can you think about your presentation from your audience's point of view?

☐ Do you know what the venue or room is like?

☐ Have you arranged parking?

☐ Do you know the agenda? Are you speaking before or after anyone else?

☐ Are you happy with the time of day you have been scheduled? If not, have you done what you can to change this? What will the other speakers be talking about? What is their presentation style?

☐ Do you need to ask for a certain type of room set-up?

☐ Have you chosen the perfect background for your virtual presentation?

☐ Is your lighting and sound online working for your audience?

☐ Should you be booking an external venue for your virtual meeting to ensure reduced wi-fi glitches?

☐ Do you need to take any supplies yourself, such as flipchart paper, pens, participant handouts or writing implements?

Phase 2: Design

☐ Do you know how to structure a presentation with your audience's needs in mind?

☐ Can you design your presentation in a minimal amount of time?

☐ Do you deliver your opening in a way that builds rapport and motivates your audience?

☐ Do you prepare for and manage objections?

☐ Did you remember to explain the boundaries for the presentation (agenda, timings, questions, cameras, mute, phones)?

☐ Do you deliver compelling facts, figures and research?

☐ Do you plan to tell stories that link to your content and help bring your data to life?

☐ Do you use a variety of presentation aids, such as a whiteboard, slides, video, handouts, breakout rooms, chat, polls and props?

☐ Can you present with limited use of speaker's notes?

☐ Do you rehearse?

☐ Do you eat well and rest yourself before presenting?

☐ Do you remember to steer away from caffeine and alcohol so your throat isn't too dry?

☐ Do you warm up your body, voice and mind before presenting?

☐ Do you send through a checklist to your venue so they set the room up as you require?

☐ Do you have the right cords and connections to ensure your technology works?

Phase 3: Delivery

☐ Have you tested your lapel microphone?

☐ Is the lighting right?

☐ Have you removed the empty chairs or put reserved signs on the back rows or tables so the audience fills up the front row?

☐ Can you see everyone in your audience from the stage?

☐ Is your clothing smart and appropriate?

☐ Did you groom your hair and nails?

☐ Do you smell great?

☐ Are you planning to enter the stage from the audience's left (their past — otherwise known as stage right)?

☐ Have you remembered you should greet the MC on arrival on the stage?

☐ Do you stand tall with a straight back?

☐ Do you allow your natural facial expressions to show?

☐ Do you look at people?

☐ In virtual presentations, do you look right into the camera?

☐ Do you let your hands move freely when you speak?

☐ Are you using rehearsed gestures and are they either big and expansive in live meetings or within the frame in virtual presentations?

☐ Do you move around in the space?

☐ In a virtual presentations, are you ensuring you don't rock forwards and backwards in your chair?

☐ Do you allow your voice to exhibit a variety of pitch, speed and volume?

☐ Do you sound the same presenting as you do when you speak normally?

☐ Do you speak clearly?

☐ Do you minimise rambling?

☐ Are you able to stay on track with your message?

☐ Are you able to avoid filler words such as 'um', 'ah', 'like'?

☐ Do you engage your audience?

☐ Have you built questions, chat, breakouts and other interesting engagement ideas into your virtual presentations?

☐ Do you tell stories?

☐ Do you use metaphor, analogy, case studies and examples?

☐ Have you incorporated linguistic devices such as alliteration, tricolon, epistrophe, conduplicatio, anaphora and rhetorical questions to ensure your messages are even more memorable for your audience?

☐ Are you able to present with slides as an aid instead of letting the slides take over your presentation?

- [ ] Do you know where the critical 'B' key is on your computer?!
- [ ] In virtual presentations, have you planned to share and stop share where appropriate?
- [ ] Do you summarise key points towards the end?
- [ ] Do you remember to call your audience to action?
- [ ] Can you manage a Q&A session effectively?
- [ ] Do you know how to manage difficult audience members?
- [ ] Do you stick to the time allocated to you?
- [ ] Is there anything else you do well?
- [ ] And what else?
- [ ] And what else?

INDEX

Printed and bound by CPI Group (UK) Ltd, Croydon, CR0 4YY
01/11/2022
03158958-0001